RESEARCH IN ACCOUNTING REGULATION

Volume 13 • 1999

RESEARCH IN ACCOUNTING REGULATION

Editor: GARY JOHN PREVITS
Weatherhead School of Management
Department of Accountancy
Case Western Reserve University

Associate Editor: THOMAS R. ROBINSON
School of Business Administration
University of Miami, Coral Gables

Assistant Editor: NANDANI CHANDAR
School of Management
Rutgers University

VOLUME 13 • 1999

JAI PRESS INC.
Stamford, Connecticut

100 Prospect Street
Stamford, Connecticut 06901

ISBN: 0-7623-0520-7
ISSN: 1052-0457

Transferred to digital printing 2005

CONTENTS

PART IV. BOOK REVIEWS

LIST OF CONTRIBUTORS

Robert James Bricker	Weatherhead School of Management Case Western Reserve University
Karen L. Brown	School of Business Administration Penn State, Harrisburg
Richard E. Brown	Department of Accounting Kent State University
F. Greg Burton	School of Accountancy University of Nebraska, Lincoln
Jeffrey R. Casterella	Department of Accounting and Finance University of Auckland
Anthony J. Cataldo, II	Department of Accountancy Western Michigan University
Roman M. Fatkhiyev	Weatherhead School of Management Case Western Reserve University
Timothy J. Fogarty	Weatherhead School of Management Case Western Reserve University
Janet S. Greenlee	Department of Accounting University of Dayton
Kyle M. Hannaford	Weatherhead School of Management Case Western Reserve University
Keith Hawkins	Centre for Socio-Legal Studies Oxford University
William Hillison	Department of Accounting Florida State University
Oscar Holzmann	Department of Accounting University of Miami
Gregory J. Jonas	Arthur Andersen, LLP Chicago, Illinois

Joseph Legoria	School of Accountancy Mississippi State University
Barry L. Lewis	Department of Accounting and Information Systems University of Colorado
Alan T. Lord	Department of Accounting and MIS Bowling Green State University
Dwight M. Owsen	University of Portsmouth United Kingdom
Carl Pacini	School of Accountancy Georgia Southern University
John A. Pendley	Department of Accounting and Information Systems University of Alabama in Huntsville
Obeua S. Persons	Department of Accounting Rider University
Jenice Prather-Kinsey	School of Accountancy University of Missouri
Gary John Previts	Weatherhead School of Management Case Western Reserve University
Jack C. Robertson	Department of Accounting The University of Texas
George D. Sanders	Accounting Department Western Washington University
Daniel T. Simon	Department of Accountancy University of Notre Dame
David Sinason	Department of Accountancy Northern Illinois University
Kumar Sivakumar	School of Accountancy Georgia State University
Mark H. Taylor	School of Accounting University of South Carolina

Paul L. Walker	McIntire School of Commerce University of Virginia
Stephen J. Young	Arthur Andersen, LLP Chicago, Illinois

INVITED REFEREES

Elizabeth Almer
University of Miami, Coral Gables

Lee Blazey
The Accountants Coalition

Dale Buckmaster
University of Delaware

Barbara Clemenson
The City Mission of Cleveland

Edward N. Coffman
Virginia Commonwealth University

Ray Dever
PricewaterhouseCoopers, LLP

Dale Flesher
University of Mississippi

Ross Fuerman
Suffolk University

Jimmy W. Martin
University of Montevallo

Judy O'Dell
Beucler, Kelly & Irwin, LTD

Terry O'Keefe
University of Oregon

David Pearson
Ernst & Young, LLP

Paul Rosenfield
Valley Stream, New York

Nancy Suttenfield
Case Western Reserve University

Daniel Tinkelman
Pace University

Ara Volkan
State University of West Georgia

PART I

MAIN PAPERS

INDUSTRY AND AUDITOR EFFECTS IN THE TIMING OF ADOPTION OF MANDATED ACCOUNTING STANDARDS

A STUDY OF SFAS NO. 87

Kumar Sivakumar

ABSTRACT

This paper studies the timing of adoption of Financial Accounting Standards Board's Statement of Financial Accounting Standards No. 87, "Employers' Accounting for Pensions." The study extends existing research on the timing of adoption of mandated accounting standards by combining economic variables, which have been the primary focus of accounting researchers, with institutional variables, specifically the effects of competitors and auditors. An empirical analysis of the timing decisions of 657 firms from 1985 to 1988 shows that firms with a positive income effect on their reported income and large firms adopt early, and firms with a high debt-equity ratio delay adoption. The results also reveal that as the proportion of firms within an industry that have adopted the standard increases, the probability that other firms in the industry will adopt the standard also increases. The findings also indicate that clients of large auditors appear to adopt early,

Research in Accounting Regulation, Volume 13, pages 3-20.

ISBN: 0-7623-0520-7

especially if they have a positive income effect. Taken together, these results suggest that institutional and economic factors influence the decision of timing of adoption of mandated accounting standards.

INTRODUCTION AND BACKGROUND

The adoption of mandated accounting standards by business organizations is an issue that is of considerable relevance to accounting and institutional researchers. It has become topical for accounting researchers because the Financial Accounting Standards Board (FASB) has instituted a multi-year window for firms to implement a number of its accounting standards (Langer and Lev 1993; Amir and Ziv 1997a, 1997b). Firms have to implement the standard within the pre-specified time window but have the ability to choose any adoption date within the time window. Hence, a key concern for accounting researchers is to understand the factors that affect compliance costs and the choice of the adoption date.

Mandated accounting standards are important to institutional researchers for two reasons. To begin with, conformity to mandated accounting standards legitimates organizations and enables them to raise capital from financial markets (Meyer and Rowan 1977; Zald 1984). Moreover, all firms face a common coercive constraint in the form of a deadline, but also enjoy some discretion in choosing the time of adoption. Thus, mandated accounting standards are a useful setting to examine the extent to which adoption decisions are driven by the institutional effects of competitors and auditors, and the interests of managers, especially their earnings management motives.

Economic factors that affect the timing of adoption of accounting standards have been the primary focus of various studies of adoption of mandated standards. Accounting researchers trace the adoption of mandated accounting standards to earnings management motives, the desire to share good news and to mask bad news, and compliance costs, especially the costs of renegotiating agreements with lenders and suppliers (Ayres 1986; Sami and Welsh 1992; Langer and Lev 1993; Amir and Livnat 1996). More recently, Amir and Ziv (1997a, 1997b) have studied the adoption decisions of firms and the economic consequences of alternative adoption rules for new accounting standards. Ali and Kumar (1994) studied the interactive effects of political sensitivity, exposure to revenues from regulated activities and debt, and compensation contracts in the decisions of firms to adopt SFAS 87. However, accounting researchers have not analyzed the effects of prior adopters in a firm's industry and the role of auditors on the timing of the adoption of mandated accounting standards. Prior adopters of accounting standards generate templates for negotiating contracts with suppliers and lenders, leak information about the industry to external monitors, and make it difficult for non-adopters to explain their conduct. Auditing firms, like other centrally located entities such as consulting organizations, promote the diffusion of new rules and norms across business organizations (Mezias 1990). This paper is partly motivated by these gaps in the accounting literature.

Additionally, this paper is also motivated by gaps in the institutional literature. Institutional theory asserts that the adoption of new rules occurs because of coercion by powerful organizations, mimetic pressure from competitors, and normative pressures from trade associations, consulting firms, auditors, and professional societies (DiMaggio and Powell 1983; Meyer and Scott 1983). However, institutional researchers have paid little attention to the adoption of mandated accounting rules. Only one study by Mezias (1990) looked at the choice of alternative accounting methods. Moreover, institutional theory has been criticized for understating the significance of managerial interests and choices (DiMaggio 1988, 1991; Oliver 1991).

In the context of mandated accounting standards, all firms face common coercive pressure from the FASB in the form of a deadline, but can choose the adoption date within the window of time available to them. This paper looks at the mimetic and normative pressures of other firms in the industry and auditors, against the backdrop of this common coercive constraint. Mandated accounting standards are a natural setting to study the effects of competitors and auditors, and analyze whether poorly performing firms are more vulnerable to these effects. In turn, such analyses can allow institutional researchers to understand how the interests of adopters in conjunction with institutional processes drive the adoption of new rules (Scott 1994).

I explore these issues by studying the adoption of a mandated accounting rule pertaining to pensions—Statement of Financial Accounting Standard (SFAS) No. 87. While SFAS 87 was issued in 1984 and the adoption period was from 1985 to 1989; it still is relevant to empirically examine the adoption timing in that setting. Firms had very little discretion in the timing of the adoption of almost all standards issued by the FASB in the 1970s.[1] However, the board appears to have extended the adoption window for its standards issued in the 1980s so that they are not effective at a uniform date immediately following their issuance (see Langer and Lev 1993). Alleviating firms' implementation costs appears to be FASB's justification for extending the adoption window (FASB 1985, par. 259–260). The institutional mimetic effects of other firms in the same industry and auditor effects assume importance in a longer adoption window. Therefore an analysis of this long-window adoption period is of relevance to any new standard that FASB may be considering with a similar extended window for adoption. Finally, accounting researchers have documented the economic effects of the adoption of the pension standard; therefore, this provides a suitable environment to study the incremental effects of industry and auditor effects in the timing of the adoption of mandated accounting standards.

An empirical analysis of the timing decisions of 657 firms from 1985 to 1988 shows that firms with a positive income effect on their reported income and large firms adopt early, and firms with a high debt–equity ratio delay adoption. The results reveal that as the proportion of firms within an industry that have adopted the standard increases, the probability that the other firms in the industry will adopt the standard also increases. The findings also indicate that clients of large auditors appear to adopt early, especially if they have a positive income effect. Taken together, these results suggest that institutional and economic factors influence the date of adoption of mandated accounting standards.

HYPOTHESES

Economic Determinants of the Timing of Adoption of SFAS No. 87

Prior accounting studies that looked at the timing of adoption of FAS No. 87 have focused primarily on economic determinants. Langer and Lev (1993, 517) classified these economic determinants into two categories: (1) compliance costs, and (2) investor perception motives. They find that only one proxy, increased reported earnings, consistently discriminates between early and late adopters. They also report that company size and the number of outstanding loans were associated with the adoption timing decision in some cases. I include these variables to control for the economic determinants of the timing of the adoption decision in our analysis.

Institutional determinants and SFAS No. 87

A rapidly growing body of research demonstrates the significance of interorganizational effects on the diffusion of social arrangements; indeed as DiMaggio (1991, 32) notes, "the successful application of institutional models to the adoption of structural elements...has become a growth industry." However, these inter-organizational effects have been largely ignored in the accounting literature when considering adoption timing decisions of organizations.

Institutional researchers suggest that mimetic pressure from competitors induces organizations to adopt new practices (DiMaggio and Powell 1983). Network theorists hold that firms seek to conform to their competitors even in the absence of direct contact (Galaskiewicz and Burt 1991). The larger the number of competitors who have adopted a social practice, the more likely a blueprint is to be codified, and the social practice is likely to be adopted at a higher rate (see Fligstein 1985; Haveman 1993). Also, when a sizable proportion of peer organizations adopts a standard, compliance costs for closely located prospective adopters also decline (Arthur 1989). In the case of accounting standards such as SFAS No. 87, adoption by peers in the industry also promotes the development of templates to renegotiate agreements with lenders and suppliers (Langer and Lev 1993), and thereby reduces compliance costs for prospective adopters. Therefore:

H1. Organizations facing a high proportion of adopters in their industry will adopt SFAS No. 87 earlier than others.

Similarly, prior adopters who share the same auditor as the focal organization can also reduce compliance costs and speed up adoption. As the number of prior adopters of an accounting standard who use the same auditor as a prospective adopter increases, auditor expertise is likely to grow, blueprints of implementation are likely to be created, and prospective adopters are likely to face fewer compliance costs. Therefore:

H2. Organizations facing a high proportion of prior adopters who share the same auditor will adopt SFAS No. 87 earlier than others.

However, individual auditors may not be as consequential as categories of auditors: indeed, like other industries, the auditing industry is also stratified by size and standing into big and small groups (Simunic 1980).[2] Although it is unclear whether auditors influence clients or clients shape the stances of big auditors (Williams, Frazier, and McKee 1993), clients of large firms are likely to implement accounting rules earlier than others for two reasons. First, large auditing firms have greater resources to swiftly implement new accounting rules; and second, on average, their clients are likely to be larger than those of smaller auditors are and hence, have a higher propensity to adopt accounting rules earlier. Therefore:

H3. Clients of large auditors will adopt SFAS No. 87 earlier than others.

Trombley (1989) found that the positions taken by auditors in their reactions to proposed FASB standards influence the subsequent adoption decisions of their clients in the software industry. Thus, clients of large auditors who express support for a standard in their responses to FASB proposals may be likely to adopt the standard sooner than clients of auditors who opposed the standard or were neutral in their responses. However, as Williams, Frazier, and McKee (1993) observe, client preferences may be influencing auditor positions and not vice versa. One way to reconcile these findings is to view the relationship between big auditors and their clients as one characterized by mutual self-selection and the exercise of mutual influence rather than a one-way influence process in which auditor positions determine client decisions. Therefore:

H4. Clients of large auditors who supported SFAS No. 87 in the proposal stage will adopt it earlier than others.

To summarize our hypotheses regarding auditor effects, hypotheses 2, 3, and 4 pertain to different facets of these effects. H2 concerns the effect of individual auditors, H3 pertains to differences between the large and small audit firms, and H4 relates to differences within the category of large audit firms based on their reactions to the exposure draft given by FASB prior to the issuance of SFAS No. 87.

Interaction of Institutional and Economic Determinants

The impact of these institutional pressures is likely to be modified by economic considerations, especially the earnings management motives of managers. Ceteris paribus, mimetic pressure from peer organizations is likely to hasten adoption by organizations with a positive income effect. Corporate managers may also be seen as contestants in a market for reputations where speedy disclosure of good financial news to institutional investors and financial analysts enhances personal and organizational fortunes. Being fast to the market with good news is doubly important because no news may be viewed by the market as bad news (Watts and Zimmerman 1986). In this context, the adoption of an accounting rule by peer organizations in the same industry creates a "leakage" of information and thereby, may jeopardize the standing of organizations if they lag with good news. Hence, as organizations in the industry adopt an accounting rule, managers of positive income effect organizations have every incentive to rush to adopt the new accounting rule and disseminate the good news of their financial performance to financial analysts and institutional investors. In short, mimetic pressure goads managers of positive income effect organizations to swiftly adopt the accounting rule and disclose the good news about their coffers. Therefore:

H5. Organizations that have a positive income effect from implementing SFAS No. 87 and face a high proportion of adopters in their industry will adopt SFAS No. 87 earlier than others.

Similarly, a symbiotic relationship is likely to exist between large auditors and organizations securing a positive income effect from implementing SFAS No. 87. As mentioned earlier, large auditors have larger resources than smaller auditors do, and organizations with a positive income effect from adopting an accounting rule have independent incentives to adopt it anyway. Thus, auditors and managers influence each other and as a result, normative pressure and managerial interests generate convergent effects on the timing of adoption.

H6. Organizations with a positive income effect from implementing SFAS No. 87 who are also clients of a large auditor will adopt SFAS No. 87 earlier than others.

Table 1. Description of Variables

Variable	*Description*	*Operationalization*	*Purpose*
CLOCK	Time-trend variable	A value of 1 for 1985, 2 for 1986 and so on.	Control: Time trend
INTCOV	Interest Coverage	Income divided by interest expense.	Control: Economic determinant
GROWTH	Growth in earnings	Annual change in reported earnings divided by earnings in year t-1.	Control: Economic determinant
SIZE	Firm Size	Size measured as log of annual sales.	Control: Economic determinant
DERATIO	Debt-Equity ratio	Ratio of book values of total liabilities to common equity	Control: Economic determinant
INCGAIND	Income Gain Dummy	An indicator variable with a value of 1 for firms that reported a positive income effect from adopting SFAS No. 87, 0 otherwise.	Control: Economic determinant
CINDPROP	Proportion of adopters within same industry	Cumulative proportion of organizations that had adopted SFAS No. 87 in the two-digit SIC code of the focal firm.	Hypothesis 1
CAUDPROP	Proportion of adopters with same auditors	Cumulative proportion of organizations that had adopted SFAS No. 87 with the same auditor as the focal firm.	Hypothesis 2
BIGAUD	Client of large audit firms	An indicator variable with a value of I if the firm had a large auditor, 0 otherwise	Hypothesis 3
BIGAUDPRO	Client of large audit firms who supported SFAS 87 proposal	An indicator variable with a value of 1 if the firm had a BIGAUD who had expressed support for the proposed pension standard, 0 otherwise.	Hypothesis 4

RESULTS

I use event history methodology to model the adoption of SFAS No. 87 and to test my hypotheses (see appendix). The analysis is done on a sample of 657 manufacturing and trading firms. The details of sample selection, description, data, and methodology are discussed in the appendix. Table 1 presents the variables used in this study. The control variable *CLOCK* is a time-trend variable that controls for the effect of time, i.e., for the inevitability of implementation as the adoption period runs out. *INTCOV*, *GROWTH*, *SIZE*, *DERATIO*, and *INCGAIND* are control variables for economic determinants of adoption as documented in prior studies. The other variables are used to test my various hypotheses.

Table 2. Maximum Likelihood Estimates of Logit Model Main Effects

Spells:	1655		
Events:	657		
Df:	9		
Model χ^2:	899.47		
Significance level:	<.001		
Variable	*Parameter Estimate*	*Standard Error*	*p-value*[a]
Intercept	−6.6048	0.6367	<.001
Clock	1.8197	0.4794	<.001
Intcov	−0.0189	0.0148	.100
Growth	−0.0047	0.0275	.432
Incgaind	0.2727	0.1530	.037
Size	0.2358	0.0425	<.001
Deratio	−0.1990	0.1178	.046
Cindprop	1.4916	0.5074	.002
Caudprop	0.3581	1.0150	.362
Bigaud	0.7206	0.1427	<.001

Notes: [a]One-tailed significance levels.
See table 1 for description of variables

Table 2 presents the main effects of the primary independent variables and control variables using the event history methodology. Of the control variables, *Clock* has a significant and positive effect, while *Growth* is insignificant. The significant and positive effect of *Incgaind* supports the results in Langer and Lev (1993) and suggests that organizations reporting a positive income effect were more prone to adopt SFAS No. 87 early.[3] The coefficient for *Size* is also positive and significant, suggesting that larger firms adopted SFAS No. 87 earlier than smaller firms. Similarly, the effects of debt-equity ratio are significant and negative, showing that firms with large debt in their capital structure adopted SFAS No. 87 later than others.

The impact of *Cindprop* is significant and positive, thereby showing that mimetic pressure exerted by the adoption of the standard by other firms in the same industry promoted the early adoption of SFAS No. 87 (H1). *Caudprop* is not significant, rejecting a similar effect by other firms with the same auditor adopting the standard (H2). The *Bigaud* variable is significant and positive and in accord with the hypothesis (H3) that clients of large auditors were more likely to adopt SFAS No. 87 earlier than others.

Table 3 reports the results of tests incorporating H4 and the interactions proposed in H5 and H6. H4 hypothesizes that clients of large auditors who supported SFAS No. 87 in the proposal stage will adopt the standard earlier than others. H5 hypothesizes that firms with a positive income effect from adopting SFAS No. 87 and with a high proportion of adopters in their industry will adopt the standard

Table 3. Maximum Likelihood Estimates of Logit Model With Interaction Effects

Spells:	1655
Events:	657
Df:	12
Model χ^2:	905.20
Significance level:	<.001

Variable	*Parameter Estimate*	*Standard Error*	*p-value*[a]
Intercept	-6.6351	0.6517	<.001
Clock	1.8681	0.4818	<.001
Intcov	−0.0171	0.0149	.125
Growth	−0.0046	0.0276	.434
Incgaind	−0.1636	0.3418	.316
Size	0.2460	0.0430	<.001
Deratio	−0.1822	0.1185	.062
Cindprop	1.3465	0.5659	.009
Caudprop	0.2985	1.0145	.384
Bigaud	0.5417	0.2282	.009
Cindprop X Incgaind	0.2604	0.5077	.304
Bigaud X Incgaind	0.5589	0.2885	.026
Bigaudpro	−0.2183	0.1999	.137

Notes: [a]One-tailed significance levels.
See table 1 for description of variables

earlier than others. H6 hypothesizes a similar interaction effect between positive income effect of adoption of the standard and clients of large auditors.

The effects of all other previous variables remain unaltered except for the *Incgaind* dummy, which now becomes insignificant. However, the interaction of *Incgaind* with *Bigaud* assumes significance.[4] There is no support for H4, as seen by the insignificant coefficient for *BigaudPRO.* There is no support for the hypothesis (H5) that mimetic pressure from other adopters in the industry increases adoptions by positive income-effect organizations: the interaction term for *Cindprop* x *Incgaind* is insignificant. Thus, the results show that the impact of mimetic pressure from other firms adopting the standard in the industry was uniform for all organizations and unmodified by managerial interests. A similar interaction effect between positive income and large auditor (H5) is supported because the coefficient for the interaction term *Bigaud* x *Incgaind* is significant.

Large organizations were significantly more prone to adopt SFAS No. 87 early, while organizations with a high debt–equity ratio were likely to postpone adopting the standard. The results also are consistent with other adopters within the same industry promoting early adoption by a firm. A similar effect is found for firms with large auditors. These firms were more likely to adopt SFAS No. 87

early. Although there was no significant interaction between a positive income effect and the proportion of adopters in an industry, organizations with a positive income effect who were also clients of large auditors tended to adopt SFAS No. 87 earlier than others.[5]

DISCUSSION

This research was motivated by the dearth of attention given to prior adopters and auditors in accounting research, and to the adoption of mandated accounting standards in institutional research. The results obtained from this study speak to both accounting researchers and institutional theorists.

One implication of the study for accounting researchers is that mimetic effects from other firms in the same industry adopting the standard lead to the rapid adoption of mandated accounting rules. I suggest that this may be due to a reduction in compliance costs. Accounting researchers have largely emphasized economic determinants of compliance costs such as debt-equity ratios, size, the number of outstanding debts, and interest coverage ratios (see Ayres 1986; Langer and Lev 1993; Trombley 1989) but have omitted the examination of interorganizational determinants. This study found that adoption by peer organizations in the same industry significantly increased the early adoption of SFAS No. 87 even after controlling for the effects of positive income effect, size, debt–equity ratio, growth, and interest coverage ratio. This finding suggests that newly mandated accounting standards need to be viewed as administrative innovations that diffuse in a social field. Research on the diffusion of administrative innovations suggests that implementation costs depend not only on adopter characteristics, but also on characteristics of the innovation itself (Roger 1983; Burt 1987). An important characteristic of any innovation is the number of prior adopters, because prior adopters of innovations generate templates for negotiating contracts with suppliers and lenders. Moreover, if other firms in an industry have adopted a mandated accounting standard, non-adopters may incur a cost from not adopting the standard.

The results also shed light on auditor effects on the choice of the adoption date. One implication is that large auditors, as a category, influence the adoption decision, compared to individual audit firms. The results show that the number of prior adopters using the same auditor as a focal firm did not have any significant effect on the adoption of the standard. However, affiliation with a large auditor significantly increased the early adoption of SFAS No. 87. Subsequent analyses revealed that there were no significant differences within the large auditor category based on their comment letters to the exposure draft issued by FASB on pension standards.

The findings also enlarge institutional research. A crucial limitation of neo-institutional research on adoption is that it potentially overstates the significance of institutional pressures because it seldom controls for the effects of managerial interests (DiMaggio 1988). This study shows that managerial interests significantly influence the adoption of accounting rules even when organizations are compelled to adopt an accounting rule. Organizations with a positive income effect adopted early; this is consistent with corporate managers wanting to build a favorable reputation. Large sized organizations also adopted SFAS No. 87 significantly earlier than others. Moreover, organizations with substantial debt–equity ratios significantly delayed adoption, thereby suggesting that the costs of rescheduling agreements with lenders have an effect on the timing of adoption. The delayed adoption by these high-debt firms also might have resulted from the additional disclosures regarding pension liabilities that were required by SFAS No. 87. These findings suggest that organizations are not naive and unaware actors who respond passively to FASB rules; but are self-interested actors who exercise discretion and purposefully time the adoption of accounting rules within the window opened by regulators.

The findings also contribute to accounting and institutional research by illuminating the interactions between earnings management motives and institutional processes. The hypothesis that mimetic pressure would ratchet up pressure on positive income effect organizations was not supported. This result indicates that the effect of mimetic pressures on the propensity of organizations to adopt accounting rules does not vary according to the interests of managers, but is uniform across organizations. By contrast, the prediction that the effect of large auditors would be significantly higher for a positive income effect was supported. This finding suggests a symbiotic relationship between large auditors and positive income effect organizations wherein auditors and managers, in a sense, use each other to mutual advantage and exert convergent rather than contradictory effects on the propensity of organizations to adopt innovations.

The limitations of this study point to some directions for future research. One limitation is that this study focused on the adoption of accounting rules by for-profit, publicly traded firms that were seeking to mobilize resources from strangers. It is possible that a different set of variables or operationalizations may underlie the adoption of accounting rules by non-profit organizations or for-profit organizations that are privately held (such as family businesses) and do not trade securities in financial markets.

Another limitation of this study is that it studied the adoption of accounting rules in a stylized context in which all organizations compulsorily had to adopt the rule in question, but enjoyed the latitude to choose the date of adoption in the window of time made available to them by regulators. An advantage of this design is the clarification of the effects of managerial interests, and mimetic and normative pressures when organizations are exposed to homogeneous coercive pressure. However, in other settings where organizations have the freedom to adopt or not to adopt, the interplay of managerial interests and institutional pressures may be very different, because managers can choose to defy, avoid, coopt, or even actively oppose institutional actors (Oliver 1991). Future research is needed to shed light on the institutional antecedents of voluntary adoption and to delineate the boundary conditions of these strategic responses.

ACKNOWLEDGMENTS

Financial support of this research was provided by the University Research Committee of Emory University. An earlier version of this paper was co-authored with Hayagreeva Rao. I am indebted to him for his various contributions in the development and completion of this project. I am also grateful to Kirsten Ely, Mary Ann Glynn, Gary Previts (Editor), Greg Waymire, and two anonymous referees for their helpful comments.

APPENDIX

Sample

The sample of SFAS No. 87 adopters was selected from a search of the *NAARS* database of *LEXIS/NEXIS*. I obtained a list of 822 organizations with annual reports from 1985 to 1988 with footnote disclosures relating to the adoption of the pension standard. I eliminated organizations that were not included in the *Compustat* and *CRSP* databases and whose securities were not publicly traded on the

Table A1. Timing of Adoption of SFAS No. 87

		Adoption Effect[b]		
Year of Adoption[a]	*Number of Firms*	*No Effect*	*Income Increasing*	*Income Decreasing*
1985	40	13 (32.5%)	26 (65.0%)	1 (2.5%)
1986	278	103 (37.0%)	172 (61.9%)	3 (1.1%)
1987	297	171 (57.6%)	109 (36.7%)	17 (5.7%)
1988	42	27 (64.3%)	11 (26.2%)	4 (9.5%)
Total	657	314 (47.8%)	318 (48.4%)	25 (3.8%)

Notes: [a]The year of adoption is the fiscal year (as reported by the firm in its annual report in the NAARS database) in which the firm adopted SFAS No. 87 for its domestic pension plans.

[b]The adoption effect is the reported effect on the income of the firm in the year of adoption. Adoption has an income increasing (decreasing) effect when it increases (decreases) reported income or decreases (increases) reported losses. The study uses a 'No effect' classification, when the firm reports that the adoption does not have a material effect on reported income or does not state any effect in its disclosure.

New York and American stock exchanges, in order to be able to collect meaningful organization-level data, and to conform to prior studies of the adoption of SFAS No. 87 (Langer and Lev 1993). Following Langer and Lev (1993), I also deleted organizations from my sample that belonged to financial services (banks, insurance companies, etc., with SIC code greater than 6000) because their financial structure, pension obligations, and balance sheets differ substantially from manufacturing and trading organizations. The final sample consists of 657 manufacturing and trading organizations over the period 1985–1988.

I take the year of adoption of the pension standard as the fiscal year of the annual report in the NAARS database in which the organization discloses that it has adopted SFAS No. 87 for its domestic pension plans.[6] Table A1 presents the timing and income effect of the adoption of SFAS No. 87 for the firms in my sample.

Measures and Methods

Control Variables

Since all organizations in our sample had to adopt SFAS No. 87 by 1988, a time trend variable called *Clock* was computed to account for the fact that the rate of adoption increased with time. The variable *Clock* has a value of 1 for 1985, 2 for 1986 and so on. To control for the income effect of the adoption of SFAS No. 87, an indicator variable, *Incgaind*, was created and set to 1 for organizations that reported a positive income effect from adopting SFAS No. 87. The size of the organization (*Size*) was defined as the natural logarithm of sales; it was updated annually and was used to control for the size of the firm. The debt–equity ratio (*DERatio*) and interest–coverage ratio (*Intcov*) were used as proxies for contracting costs and updated annually for organizations. *DERatio* was defined as the ratio of the bookvalues of total liabilities to common equity. *Intcov* was defined as income divided by interest expense. Income growth before adoption was also used as a control because managers of organizations with high income growth before the changeover to the new accounting rule are less likely to accelerate the adoption of an accounting rule to increase reported income than others (Ayres 1986). A variable called *Growth* was created and updated annually.[7] *Growth* measures the annual change in reported earnings.[8]

Test Variables

The cumulative proportion of organizations that had adopted SFAS No. 87 in the two-digit SIC code[9] (*Cindprop*) to which a focal organization belonged was computed to measure mimetic pressure (H1). The cumulative proportion is defined as:

$$CINDPROP_{i,t} = \frac{\sum_{T=1985}^{t-1} NUMADOPT_{i,T}}{TOTFIRMS_i}$$

where $NUMADOPT_{i,T}$ is the number of organizations in our sample from industry i adopting the pension standard in year T, and $TOTFIRMS_i$ is the total number of organizations in industry i in our sample, excluding the focal firm.

The cumulative proportion of other organizations that had adopted SFAS No. 87 using the same auditor as the prospective adopter (*Caudprop*) was computed similarly (H2). The cumulative proportion is defined as:

$$CAUDPROP_{j,t} = \frac{\sum_{T=1985}^{t-1} NUMADOPT_{j,T}}{TOTFIRMS_j}$$

where $NUMADOPT_{j,T}$ is the number of organizations in our sample with the same auditor as the focal firm adopting the pension standard in year t and $TOTFIRMS_j$ is the total number of organizations with the same auditor j in our sample, excluding the focal firm.

Indicator variables were created to test hypotheses 3 and 4. *Bigaud* had a value of 1 for organizations that were clients of Arthur Young, Coopers and Lybrand, Price Waterhouse, Arthur Anderson, Ernst and Whinney, Deloitte, Haskins and Sells, Touche Ross, and Peat Marwick, and Main. Also, a dummy variable called *BigaudPRO* was set up with a value of 1 for firms that had a *Bigaud* who had expressed support for the proposed pension standard (H4). This data was collected from comment letters of these audit firms sent to FASB in response to its exposure draft.

Table A2 provides descriptive statistics and correlations for the continuous variables: *Size*, *DERatio*, *Growth*, and *Intcov*. Since both *DERatio* and *Intcov* measure the level of debt in the financial structure of firms, the two variables are highly correlated (–0.4354, p-value = < 0.001.) Larger firms have higher annual changes in reported income as indicated by the significant correlation between log of sales and *Growth* (0.1930, p-value = < 0.001.)

Unlike other studies of SFAS No. 87 that divided firms into early and late categories (Sami and Welsh 1992; Langer and Lev 1993) and used early adoption as the dependent variable, I follow organizations from the time they are at "risk" of adoption, that is the start of the adoption window, and observe them until the time of adoption. In other words, I use event history techniques to model the adoption of SFAS No. 87 by organizations in our sample during the 1985–1988 period. An

Table A2. Descriptive Statistics and Correlations

	Mean (Std. Deviation)	Correlations (p-values)			
		SIZE	INTCOV	DERATION	GROWTH
1. SIZE	6.4377 (1.6998)	1.0000	−0.0474 (0.0539)	−0.0720 (0.0034)	0.1930 (0.0001)
2. INTCOV	3.5394 (5.2828)		1.0000	−0.4354 (0.0001)	0.0791 (0.0013)
3. DERATIO	0.7584 (0.6674)			1.0000	−0.0444 (0.0711)
4. GROWTH	0.2873 (3.0053)				1.0000

Note: See table 1 for description of variables.

event history is a record of an organization that provides details about its characteristics (Tuma and Hannan 1984). Event history analysis has discrete time and continuous time specifications: the former is used when events occur at discrete intervals, as in elections or when the time has been measured grossly, and the latter is used when time has been measured finely enough to be exact and continuous. Since organizations adopt accounting rules within their financial year, I use discrete time event history analysis (Allison 1984). I split the event history of all sample organizations into one-year records or spells, and code all spells except the year of adoption as right censored. This procedure allows me to use time varying covariates, that is, the values of the various independent variables were updated annually.

The event of interest was the adoption of SFAS No. 87 and the dependent variable was the discrete hazard rate, $P(t)$, which is the probability than an event will occur at a particular time to a particular organization, given that the particular organization has the potential to adopt at that time. I chose the logit transformation and used logistic regression to estimate the effects of explanatory variables. The model is expressed as follows:

$$\log(P(t)/[1\text{-}P(t)] = a + \Sigma b_i x_i + \Sigma c_j x_j(t)$$

where b_i is the set of coefficients for explanatory variables, x_i, that do not change over time, and c_j is the set of coefficients for explanatory variables $x_j(t)$ that do change with time, and a is a constant.

NOTES

1. The standards for leases (FAS No. 13) and for oil and gas producers (FAS No. 19) are two notable exceptions. While FAS No. 13 was effective for new leases on January 1, 1977, the retroactive application to existing leases was deferred to 1981. SEC subsequently overruled this extension and required retroactive application in 1978. FAS No. 19, issued in 1977, had an adoption window until 1979, but was effectively vetoed by the SEC before it became effective.

2. The BIG 8 firms made up the large audit firms during the adoption window for the pension standard. I refer to these BIG 8 firms as "large" audit firms in this paper.

3. In models not reported here, I tried different measures of the magnitude of the income effect (reported income effect, reported effect as a percentage of total reported income, and log of reported income effect). None of these magnitude effects was significant. I interpret the significance of the indicator variable, and lack of significance for any continuous specification of magnitude of the income effect, as suggesting that the overall effect on income is relevant in the adoption decision for SFAS No. 87, i.e., whether it is income-increasing or decreasing, rather than the magnitude of the increase or decrease.

4. The significance for the interaction of *BIGAUD* and *INCGAIND* comes at the loss of the previous result on the *INCGAIND* control variable. However, *BIGAUD* continues to be significant at less than 0.01 level. The significance of the interaction could be due to the interaction explaining some propensity of firms to adopt early, or could be due to the significance of *INCGAIND* being shifted to the interaction term.

5. Since some of the industries have very few firms, I replicated these tests excluding industries with fewer than five companies in my sample (SIC codes 14, 16, 17, 31, 42, 47, and 51). These results are not qualitatively different from the results for the whole sample. In additional unreported analyses, I explored some alternative explanations for the results by looking at the interaction of *Bigaud* with *Size* and *DERatio* and the interaction of *DERatio* and *Incgaind*. None of these interaction variables was significant.

6. I have a four-year adoption window because I use the fiscal year of adoption as the year of adoption in my analysis. However, firms had three fiscal years in which to adopt the standard. To verify that the use of a four-year window is not driving my results, I replicated my analyses on a sub-sample of 458 firms that had fiscal years ending in December, using an adoption window of three years for these firms. The models are significant at p-values less than .01. The income gain interaction effects are less significant and the debt–equity ratio is significant at the .05 level. The industry effect (*CINDPROP*), size and clock are significant at the .01 level.

7. Since these variables had some extreme observations, I constrained the value of these outliers to be equal to the 95th percentile values of their respective distributions.

8. In models that are not reported here, I introduced other controls for media visibility (number of mentions in the Dow Jones retrieval system for the focal organization using search terms "earnings, income, profit or loss") to capture the number of reports relating to earnings, two measures of insider control (percentage of insider ownership and proportion of inside directors to total directors), and number of debts outstanding. These variables had insignificant effects.

9. Other studies have also used the two-digit SIC code to capture the mimetic pressure exerted by peers (Fligstein 1985).

REFERENCES

Allison, P. 1984. *Event-History Analysis*. Beverly Hills, CA: Sage.

Ali, A., and K.R. Kumar. 1994. The magnitudes of financial statement effects and accounting choice: The case of the adoption of SFAS 87. *Journal of Accounting and Economics* 18: 89–114.

Amir, E., and J. Livnat. 1996. Multiperiod analysis of early adoption motives: The case of SFAS 106. *The Accounting Review* 71: 505–519.

Amir, E., and A. Ziv. 1997a. Economic Consequences of Alternative Adoption Rules for New Accounting Standards, *Contemporary Accounting Research* 14(3): 543–568.

Amir, E., and A. Ziv. 1997b. Recognition, disclosure, or delay: Timing the adoption of SFAS No. 106. *Journal of Accounting Research*. 35: 61–81.

Arthur, W.B. 1989. Competing technologies and lock-in by historical events: The dynamics of allocation under increasing returns. *Economic Journal* 99: 116–131.

Ayres, F. 1986. Characteristics of firms electing early adoption of SFAS No. 52. *Journal of Accounting and Economics* 8: 143–158.

Burt, R. 1987. Social contagion and innovation: Cohesion versus structural equivalence, *American Journal of Sociology* 92: 1287–1335.

DiMaggio, P., and W.W. Powell. 1983. The iron cage revisited: Institutional isomorphism and collective rationality in organizational fields. *American Sociological Review* 48: 147–160.

DiMaggio, P. 1988. Interest and agency in institutional theory. In *Institutional Patterns and Organizations: Culture and Environment*, ed. L.G. Zucker, 3–21. Cambridge, MA: Ballinger.

DiMaggio, P. 1991. Introduction. In *The New Institutionalism in Organizational Analysis*, eds. W.W. Powell and P. DiMaggio, 1–40. Chicago: University of Chicago Press.

Financial Accounting and Standards Board (FASB). 1985. *Statement of Financial Accounting Standards No. 87: Employers' Accounting for Pensions*. Stamford, CT: FASB.

Fligstein, N. 1985. The spread of the multi-divisional form among large firms; 1919–1979. *American Sociological Review* 50: 377–391.

Galaskiewicz, J., and R.S. Burt. 1991. Interorganizational contagion in corporate philanthropy. *Administrative Science Quarterly* 36: 88–105.

Haveman, H. 1993. Follow the leader: Mimetic isomorphism and entry into new markets. *Administrative Science Quarterly* 38: 593–627.

Langer, R., and B. Lev. 1993. The FASB's policy of extended adoption for new standards: An examination of SFAS No. 87. *Accounting Review* 68: 515–533.

Meyer, J.W., and B. Rowan. 1977. Institutionalized organizations: Formal structures as myth and ceremony. *American Journal of Sociology* 83: 340–363.

Meyer, J.W., and W.R. Scott. 1983. Centralization and the legitimacy problems of local government. In *Organizational Environments: Rituals and Rationality*, eds. J.W. Meyer and W.R. Scott. Beverly Hills, CA: Sage.

Mezias, S. 1990. An institutional model of organizational practice: Financial reporting at the fortune 200. *Administrative Science Quarterly* 35: 431–457.

Oliver, C. 1991. Strategic responses to institutional processes. *Academy of Management Review* 16: 145–179.

Roger, E.M. 1983. *The Diffusion of Innovations*. New York: Free Press.

Sami, H., and M.J. Welsh. 1992. Characteristics of early and late adopters of pension accounting standard SFAS No. 87. *Contemporary Accounting Research* 9(1): 212–236.

Scott, W.R. 1994. Institutional analysis: Variance and process theory approaches. In *Institutional Environments and Organizations: Structural Complexity and Individualism*, eds. W.R. Scott, John W. Meyer, et al. San Francisco: Sage.

Simunic, C. 1980. The pricing of audit services: Theory and evidence. *Journal of Accounting Research* 18(1): 161–190.

Trombley, M. 1989. Accounting method choice in the software industry: Characteristics of firms electing early adoption of SFAS 86. *The Accounting Review* 64: 529–538.

Tuma, N., and M T. Hannan. 1984. *Social Dynamics. Models and Methods*. New York: Academic Press.

Watts R., and J. Zimmerman. 1986. *Positive Accounting Theory*. Englewood Cliffs, NJ: Prentice-Hall.

Williams, P.F., K.B. Frazier, and A.J. McKee, Jr. 1993. A comment on "Accounting method choice in the software industry," *Accounting Review* 65(4): 946–954.

Zald M.N. 1984. The sociology of enterprise, accounting, and budget rules: Implications for organization theory. *Accounting, Organizations, and Society* 11: 327–340.

THE EFFECTS OF SELECTED ENGAGEMENT CHARACTERISTICS ON AUDITORS' JUDGMENTS

Alan T. Lord

ABSTRACT

Prior research has reported the effects of client (or engagement) characteristics on auditors' *perceived* judgments (Shockley 1981; Knapp 1985; Gul 1989; Lindsay 1989), but has not investigated the effects of client characteristics on *actual* judgments made by auditors. This study investigates the effects of four of these characteristics on auditors' judgments about financial reporting alternatives. Experienced audit managers (CPAs) employed by an international public accounting firm examined a set of 16 cases that were created by combining an auditor–client conflict scenario about an audit opinion with all possible sets of "strong" and "weak" treatment levels for each of four client characteristics. The conflict scenario for this study was designed so that uncertainty existed about accepting the client's position, and

Research in Accounting Regulation, Volume 13, pages 21-41.

ISBN: 0-7623-0520-7

provided an optimal opportunity to test whether engagement characteristics influence auditors' judgments.

The results of this research document judgments that may be undesirable, despite a fairly transparent manipulation of the treatment levels of the engagement characteristics. The client's historical financial condition (which had the most significant effect), an auditor's competitive environment, and a client's relative revenue contribution to an auditor's firm were each found to have a statistically significant effect upon auditors' judgments about financial reporting alternatives. In contrast, the auditor's provision of non-attest services to a client was not a significant factor in the judgment process.

There are conditions commonly related to audit engagements that (normatively) should not influence an auditor's judgment process or resulting decision behavior related to financial recording or reporting issues. These conditions have been referred to as client (or engagement) characteristics. However, there is research evidence that some of these factors may influence auditor decision behavior. The work of Farmer, Rittenberg, and Trompeter (1987) provided evidence that two factors—the potential loss of a client and the potential threat of lawsuits—significantly affect auditors' judgments regarding how an accounting transaction should be recorded. The current study extends the investigation of such factors by investigating four client characteristics that research suggests also may be influential in the judgment process and decision behavior of auditors regarding financial reporting issues. These characteristics are (1) the auditor's competitive environment, (2) the provision of non-attest services, (3) the relative revenue contribution of the audit client, and (4) the client's historical financial condition.

DEVELOPMENT OF RESEARCH HYPOTHESES

The Auditor's Competitive Environment

The market for audit clients is competitive and the cost of replacing lost audit clients can be high. As a result, auditors operating in a highly competitive situation for a specific client have an incentive to opportunistically acquiesce to client demands. This incentive occurs because clients can implicitly or explicitly present a real threat of termination, which would impose incremental costs on an auditor (DeAngelo 1981).

The Commission on Auditors' Responsibilities (the Cohen Commission) (1978) expressed concern that excessive competition in the public accounting profession was causing substandard audits as a result of time and budget pressures. Mautz asserted that if a compromise of accounting principles as a result of competition were to occur, it probably would be an "unintended and often unrecognized result of trying to meet the needs of clients in the face of competition from other firms. The ever present knowledge that there are other firms of equal prestige and status that just might see the results of a transaction differently is a specter difficult to shake from the minds of any who make audit decisions" (Mautz 1972, 91).

Research reported by Farmer, Rittenberg, and Trompeter (1987) expressed concerns that competitive pressures may cause auditors to subtly or unknowingly compromise their judgment on accounting issues. In addition, studies by Shockley (1981) and Knapp (1985) have also suggested that increased competition among auditors is associated with compromises in auditor judgments.

Hypothesis 1 addresses whether auditors are more likely to accept management's position regarding a financial reporting issue when there is aggressive competition for the client.

H1. Auditors will be more likely to accept management's position regarding a financial reporting issue when there is aggressive competition for audit clients, as opposed to no aggressive competition.[1]

The Provision of Non-Attest Services

CPAs offer clients a wide range of services beyond those required for the attest (audit) function, and most large CPA firms are structured to offer these services from several different departments or divisions. The effects of the provision of these services upon the perceived and actual judgments of CPAs have received significant attention in Congressional hearings, public speeches, and published literature. Carmichael and Swieringa (1968) stated that the effects of these services on actual and perceived judgments of auditors must be investigated differently. Their conclusion was that the provision of non-attest services was not a priori a hazard to an auditor's integrity, but that it was a potentially dangerous hazard to maintaining objectivity. They recommended opinion surveys to determine the perceived decisions and attitudes of auditors and experimental research to investigate the effects that non-attest services might have upon the "unintentional" or "subconsciously motivated facet" of auditor objectivity.

Much of the behavioral research in accounting has indicated that the provision of non-attest services adversely affects the perceived decisions of auditors (Shockley 1981; Knapp 1985). Conversely, the public accounting profession has pointed to the fact that there has been no evidence produced which demonstrates an instance where the provision of these services has *actually* impaired the decisions of auditors (Cohen Commission 1978; Armstrong and Vincent 1988). To obtain evidence about the influence that the amount of the provision of non-attest services has on auditors' actual decisions, this study is designed to address auditors' judgments rather than the perceptions of others about these judgments.

Non-attest services provided by international accounting firms often are classified in one of two service categories: management consulting services or tax services. Examples of management consulting service include executive recruiting, actuarial services, computer system design and application, human resource consulting, and feasibility studies. Tax services include not only corporate tax return preparation, but also corporate tax planning and tax return preparation for executives.

Although some research studies have defined non-attest services as only management advisory services (e.g., Pany and Reckers 1984), others have taken a more comprehensive approach and combined tax services with management advisory services (e.g., Reckers and Stagliano 1981; Pany and Reckers 1983; Scheiner and Kiger 1982; Scheiner 1984). Because the effect of providing any particular non-attest service is not the focus of this study, the hypothesis is phrased generally as non-attest services, because it is more comprehensive than management advisory services, and thus encompasses all non-audit services. The operationalization of this independent variable refers to non-attest services while specifying both management advisory services and tax services. Hypothesis 2 addresses whether auditors are more likely to accept management's position regarding a financial reporting issue when a high level of non-attest services of the audit firm is provided consistently.

H2. Auditors will be more likely to accept management's position regarding a financial reporting issue when the audit firm consistently provides a significant number of non-attest services to the client, as opposed to providing a minimal number of non-attest services.

The Relative Revenue Contribution of the Audit Client

The Cohen Commission (1978) examined the implications of audit firm size upon auditor independence. It expressed concern that independence would be more difficult to maintain in audit firms that had a few large clients supplying a large portion of the firm's total revenues. DeAngelo (1981) provided an analytical argument to investigate this concern. She concluded that the larger the audit firm, the lower the likelihood that the firm will grant concessions to audit clients. The support for this argument centers around the potential losses an audit firm would suffer due to diminished reputation effects if the audit firm were to be caught "cheating" (e.g., by inappropriately conceding to a client position).

The large public accounting firms have responded to the Cohen Commission's concern by pointing out that no single client represents a significant portion of the firms' revenues and by arguing that the size of a single client would not affect the judgments or decision behavior of their auditors. However, when DeAngelo's argument is applied to an individual auditor, the importance of a large client can increase. She suggests that an auditor will be more likely to concede to client demands when the client represents a large percentage of the total audit fees for which the auditor is responsible.

Even if individual audit engagement partners are representing the entire firm, the decisions these partners make have an effect upon their *personal* professional careers (Shank 1978). If an audit partner makes inappropriate decisions that cause the direct loss of several significant clients, it is likely that the partner's professional career will be affected negatively. Although large firms, in general, may be less likely to grant concessions to audit clients, as noted in DeAngelo (1981), Alchian and Demsetz (1972) suggest that the increased number of partners in the large firms provides a greater incentive for an individual partner to shirk responsibilities. To investigate the effect of client size on the judgments of auditors in large firms, it would seem more appropriate to frame the relative size of an audit client in comparison to the local office in which the engagement partner operates than the total revenues of a firm.[2]

Hypothesis 3 addresses whether auditors are more likely to accept management's position regarding a financial reporting issue when the client is a large client versus a moderate size client.

H3. Auditors will be more likely to accept management's position regarding a financial reporting issue when the client represents a significant portion of the revenues for their office, as opposed to a moderate portion of the revenues for their office.

The Client's Historical Financial Condition

Few, if any, scenarios could be developed that normatively would suggest that an auditor's competitive environment, an auditor's provision of non-attest services to an audit client, or the relative revenue contribution of an audit client to an auditor should influence the judgment process related to a financial recording or reporting issue. Each of these three engagement characteristics is clearly a non-accounting issue that may affect auditor's judgments.

The recent historical financial condition of a client is a relevant factor to consider for judgments in the planning phases of most audits, and perhaps in the evidence evaluation stages of an audit. It is a particularly relevant factor in the determination of an auditor's preliminary judgments about materiality (AICPA 1992, paragraph 312.14) in the evaluation of the inherent and business risks a client exhibits. Although not all auditors agree that business risk should be considered in planning an audit, a factor affecting the business risk associated with a client is the probability that a client will have financial difficulty after the audit report is issued (Arens and Loebbecke 1991, 258). Walo (1995) reported that her experimental results indicated that the financial condition of a client significantly affects auditors' judgments regarding audit scope.

The determination of materiality levels and a materiality level's relationship to an audit risk or audit scope determination, as well as adjustments to these determinations because of business risk considerations, are features of audit planning. These determinations and adjustments have limited relevance in evaluating results of the evidence gathered in the audit process (Arens and Loebbecke 1991, 265).

When audit evidence collection procedures have been completed, the historical financial strength of a client could have relevance to the determination of the materiality of a transaction during the evidence evaluation process. However, once the effect on the financial statements of an item has been determined to equal or exceed the primary materiality level, the "auditor must insist that management adjust the financial statements if a qualified opinion is to be avoided" (Leslie 1985, 9). The audit process then proceeds from the evidence-gathering and evaluation stages to the determination of proper financial reporting and disclosure treatments. At this point in the judgment process, the financial health of a client enterprise would no longer be relevant in terms of an accounting disclosure treatment.

For example, suppose an auditor had two client firms within the same industry and the only substantial difference between the two firms was their historical financial strength. Let's assume as well that the two clients entered into independent contractual arrangements with a common third party, and that the results of these arrangements were unequivocally material to the financial position of each of the client firms. After the audits have been planned and the audit evidence has been gathered and evaluated, decisions must be made about the proper reporting treatments for these contracts for each of the client firms. If the contracts with the third party were identical, and the effects on the financial statements of both clients were material, it would seem that the financial reporting treatment for the contracts should be the same. The historical financial strength of the client would not appear to be a relevant factor in determining the reporting treatment.

However, the business risks associated with each client are not identical and can not be substantially changed as a result of audit procedures. Clients that have been in excellent financial health probably still will be perceived as being less likely to become a business failure in the near future than clients that recently have been having financial difficulties. Because most audit failures (or lawsuits against public accountants (St. Pierre and Anderson 1984)) are determined only after a client business reversal or failure, the risk of a discovered audit failure (if one were to exist) would be lower for financially strong clients. Additionally, the risk of a "baseless" federal securities fraud claim against an audit firm is higher when auditing a client with weaker recent financial performance (Arthur Andersen & Co., Coopers & Lybrand, Deloitte & Touche, Ernst & Young, KPMG Peat Marwick, and Price Waterhouse 1992). As a result, the business risk to an audit firm would probably be viewed by an auditor as being lower when the decision relates to the financial report of a financially strong client (Gul 1989).

Deis and Giroux (1992) suggested that a client with a strong recent financial history can, through threats of auditor replacement, exert more pressure on an auditor than a client with a weaker recent financial history. Therefore an auditor might be more concerned about the potential loss of a financially strong client than the loss of a financially weak client. Research by Hackenbrack and Nelson (1996) presented evidence that auditors are more likely to accept reporting decisions that are favored by specific incentives faced by auditors (such as a more likely retention of a client). They specifically examined the influence of business risk upon auditors' judgments and determined that, under their experimental conditions, changes in the business risk of an engagement could influence the likelihood of an auditor accepting a particular reporting decision desired by a client. Thus, in an auditor-client conflict situation over a material reporting issue, it is hypothesized that an auditor will be more willing to accept a client's position if the client has exhibited a strong recent financial position.

Hypothesis 4 addresses whether auditors are more likely to accept management's position regarding a financial reporting issue when the client has had a good recent financial history.

H4. Auditors will be more likely to accept management's position regarding a financial reporting issue when the client exhibits a good, as opposed to a poor, recent financial history.

RESEARCH DESIGN AND METHODOLOGY

Subject Selection and Research Setting

Although audit partners typically have the ultimate decision responsibility for their clients, this research used 16 experienced audit managers as surrogates for these partners. These managers were each within a few years of expected promotion to partnership, and each had participated in negotiations and decisions related to major audit engagements. The subjects, who were from several geographically dispersed U.S. offices, were attending a U.S. national training "school" presented by their firm.[3] They had a mean age of 32, with a range from 30 to 39, and their public accounting experience ranged from nine to 12 years with a mean of 10.1 years.

Subject Accountability Pressure

Decisions made for an audit firm in a significant auditor-client conflict situation typically will be made by audit partners who will be held accountable for their judgments. The experience level of the subjects in this research indicates that they were appropriate surrogates for audit partners since as very senior managers their experience should provide judgment processes similar to those of audit partners. By utilizing these senior managers as subjects, an experimental design was developed to influence the subjects to face accountability pressure for their judgments. This created a judgment environment that was more representative of actual practice than the environment created by the typical anonymity guarantee offered by researchers.

The case description repeatedly stated that the subjects were answering as engagement partners and that they were expected to respond in a manner consistent with their expectation of audit partner judgments, given their professional experience and impression of the judgments of their firm partners. Although no experiment can perfectly replicate the judgments that subjects would make in their professional practice, the incentives in this research were designed to motivate the subjects to record judgments that were their best estimates of what the partners in their firm would like the judgments to be.

The accountability pressure was induced when a prepared introduction to the exercise was delivered by a very influential and well-known senior partner in the international headquarters office of the firm. To reduce the probability that the managers would discover that they were in a research experiment the experimental materials had the firm's logo on the cover, and the experiment was referred to as an exercise by the firm's partner.[4]

The oral introduction provided by the partner clearly implied that the managers' judgments for the exercise would be individually evaluated by senior partners of the firm, and that the exercise was an important project developed by the firm to better understand judgments made by current and future audit partners. The introduction did not state specifically who would be evaluating the subjects' judgments, but the implication was that some unknown individuals in the firms' international headquarters would evaluate the responses. Thus, the subjects could not have known, with certainty, what the preferences of this unknown group of individuals might be for each of the hypothetical audit situations presented. The partner implied that the judgments in this experiment would be considered a reflection of the subjects' judgment process in audit situations.

The auditors were required to record their name and employee number on the materials and were told that all of their colleagues in the school were also completing the exercise. Since the subjects were under the impression that the same evaluative information would be available from all auditors, and personal identifying information was required on everyone's materials, the intended inference was that the results of their judgments might indirectly affect future promotion considerations.

The operationalization of the pressure treatment was accomplished by *temporarily* deceiving the subjects. The subjects were initially informed that they were participating in a firm exercise and were not informed that they were participating in a research project until all experimental materials had been completed and they were debriefed. The experiment was conducted with the full support of the subjects' firm and the firm participated in the development of the instrument used in the experiment. The deception in the experiment's design was implemented through the oral introduction provided by the senior partner of the subjects' firm. It would have been a relatively simple matter to provide the subjects' responses to the participating senior partners in the audit firm. However, this researcher and the senior audit partners determined that it was critical that the subjects be protected from any potential negative reviews resulting from participation in this research. Thus, the researcher controlled all completed materials and the firm did not receive any information to link any subjects with their responses.[5]

The General Scenario

The potential for engagement characteristics to influence auditors' judgments is greatest when negotiations are undertaken to resolve a disagreement between client management and an auditor over some aspect of the attest function. This is particularly true when the conflict involves a material reporting issue about which there is no guidance provided by the pronouncements of the profession, and about which auditors may not agree concerning the appropriate accounting procedures and/or interpretations (Magee and Tseng 1990). When generally accepted accounting principles would lead to a specific reporting treatment, there would be no incentives for an auditor to adopt a client's disconforming reporting treatment, and "the client's [threats of] 'opinion shopping' will be ineffective" (Magee and Tseng 1990, 317). The scenario for this study was designed as an auditor-client conflict situation where uncertainty existed about accepting the client's position. Therefore, it provided an optimal opportunity to test whether engagement characteristics influence auditors' judgments.

Each audit situation was based upon a general scenario involving a conflict between an auditor and an SEC registrant client over the proper reporting treatment of a new, unique set of contracts. This situation, which was developed in cooperation with executives in the international headquarters office of the participating firm, was selected because it was determined to be a realistic event that could occur on an audit engagement. In the scenario, the client and the auditor are in unequivocal agreement that the difference between the treatment methods definitely would have a material effect upon the current year's financial statements. Variations in the situations were obtained by manipulating "strong" and "weak" treatment levels of each of the four client engagement characteristics previously discussed.

Independent Variables

Audit partners and experienced managers are often involved concurrently with several clients, and each engagement is likely to have different levels of the four characteristics examined in this research. To increase the external validity of the

ENGAGEMENT CHARACTERISTIC	TREATMENT LEVELS	
	Strong	Weak
Auditor's Competitive Environment	Aggressive Competition For Audit Client	No Aggressive Competition For Audit Client
Provision of Non-attest Services (NAS)	Client Consistently Utilized NAS Services	Client Seldom Utilized NAS Services
Relative Revenue Contribution of the Audit Client	Significant Portion of Revenues for Office and Partner	Moderate Portion of Revenues for Office and Partner
Client's Financial Condition	Overall Financial Condition is Good	Overall Financial Condition is Poor

Figure 1. Treatment Levels of Engagement Characteristic Independent Variables

results of this research, each auditor was presented with multiple client cases, each of which contained a different complete set of treatment levels for the independent variables. To do this, the experiment utilized a full-factorial within-subjects (repeated-measures) design that presented each of the 16 possible combinations of the independent variable treatment levels.[6,7] Figure 1 summarizes the treatment levels of the engagement characteristics that were the independent variables in this study.

To establish that the independent variables would effectively communicate to the subjects the differences in treatment levels, the experimental instrument was pretested extensively. The pretest procedures initially included discussions with audit partners from four international firms that did not provide the subjects for the experiment. In addition, senior auditor partners and managers from the international headquarters office of the participating firm (other than those that participated in the development of the materials) completed the experimental materials. After completion of the materials, the author conducted discussions with these executives to determine the appropriateness of the general scenario and the effectiveness of the wording of the independent variables. No substantial changes were made to the general scenario or the wording of the independent variables as a result of these discussions.

Competition

Sack and Tangreti (1987) stated that the competitive pressures facing auditors are now greater than ever since "the simple fact of increased client turnover as a result of the merger-and-acquisition boom increases the pressure for client retention and new-client acquisition" (Sack and Tangreti 1987, 99–100). This study used a corporate acquisition situation to present an environment within which an auditor is faced with two distinct levels of competition for a client. The "aggressive competition" treatment level was created by having the client acquire 100 percent of a company that was previously audited by a strong competitor of the subjects' audit firm. Although the subjects' audit firm retained the engagement, the competitor audit firm still provides services to the client and maintains unusually strong relationships with the client's senior management. In the alternative treatment level, the acquired company previously was audited by the subjects' firm and other audit firms in the area are not providing aggressive competition for the client.

Non-Attest Services

Scheiner and Kiger (1982) examined more than 400 proxy statements and reported that only about 11 percent of them indicated that the company received non-attest services in excess of 50 percent of the audit fees. Pany and Reckers (1988) noted that three-year average percentages of non-attest fees to audit fees in excess of 60 percent would be very rare in practice. The "high" level for the provision of non-attest services suggested that the client consistently utilized the audit firm's tax services and that the audit firm had conducted several consulting projects over the last five years. The fees from these non-attest services averaged approximately 40 percent of each year's annual audit revenues. In the alternative treatment level, the client seldom utilized the consulting and tax services offered by the audit firm.

Relative Revenue Contribution

The appropriate base from which to compare the relative size of an audit client within this study is not the total revenues of a firm, but the revenues of the local office in which the engagement partner operates. Shank (1978) suggested that a client's revenue contribution should be compared to the revenues for which the individual engagement partner is responsible. The development of the treatment levels for this engagement characteristic considered both of these reference points. The "strong" level suggested that the client contributed a significant portion of the office revenues and that it was one of the three largest fee-generating clients in the office on an annual basis. Furthermore, the subjects were informed that the client was by far the largest engagement they serviced. In the alternative treatment level, the client was a small public corporation that accounted for a moderate portion of revenues for the office. More than half the clients in the office generated more annual fees and the subjects were told that they were responsible for several considerably larger clients.

Historical Financial Condition

The experiment's scenario in this research was a critical determinant of the ability to examine a client's historical financial condition as a factor affecting auditors' judgments regarding a financial reporting and disclosure issue. The stationary scenario in this research unequivocally explained that the difference between the client's desired method and the auditor's suggested alternative would have a material effect upon the financial statements.[8] The stationary scenario also specified that the rest of the audit had been completed and there were no other accounting or disclosure issues that had not been resolved.

Facts regarding a client's historical financial condition, when considered by auditors at the particular stage of the audit described in this research, have been presented to be conceptually not relevant in terms of an accounting disclosure treatment. To test the effect of this factor, wording similar to that developed by Knapp (1985) was utilized. The "good" financial condition treatment described a client with liquidity and profitability ratios favorable to industry averages, and growing sales and net income levels over the past five years. The "poor" financial condition treatment described a client with deteriorating liquidity, profitability, sales, and income positions over the past five years. However, it specifically was stated that the client's viability as a going concern was not currently an issue.

Dependent Variables

Subjects' judgments consisted of two measurement items. This was to reduce potential measurement error and reliability difficulties arising from the use of a single item measurement for subjects' decisions in hypothetical situations (Nunnally 1978). The estimated dependent variable used for each case ranged from zero to nine, and was computed by averaging each subject's responses to the following measurement items:

1. What is the likelihood that the client's proposed treatment and disclosures would be permitted by yourself?
2. If the client insisted on their proposed treatment and disclosures, what is the likelihood that an unqualified (clean) opinion would be issued if the decision was made by your decision alone?

These two questions were designed to be two different measurements of each subject's likelihood to issue an unqualified opinion. For the discussion in this paper, I refer to the variable created by averaging these two items as the mean estimate of auditor likelihood to issue an unqualified opinion. The internal-consistency reliability of these measurement items was determined to be high, as evidenced by Cronbach's coefficient alpha equaling .968. Pearson's correlation coefficients

Table 1. Engagement Characteristic Marginal Means, Standard Deviations, and Significance Test Results

Engagement Characteristic	*Treatment Level*	*Mean*	*Standard Deviation*	*Wilks' Lamda*	*SS and MS*	*F*	*p*
Competition	Aggressive	3.52	2.10	.752	1.3	4.95	.0419
	Minimal	3.37	1.98				
Non-attest	Consistently	3.49	2.11	.887	0.5	1.91	.1874
Services	Seldom	3.40	1.97				
Client	Significant	3.54	2.14	.749	2.3	5.04	.0403
Revenue	Moderate	3.35	1.94				
Contribution							
Financial	Good	4.13	2.05	.399	118.9	22.51	.0003
Condition	Poor	2.76	1.80				

Note: The numerator degree of freedom was 1 and the denominator degrees of freedom were 15. The multivariate analysis of variance did not indicate any significant interactions ($p < .10$) between any of the engagement characteristics.

were also computed for item 1 and item 2 (.939), item 1 and the average of both items (.985), and item 2 and the average of both items (.984).[9]

RESULTS AND DISCUSSION

Overall Analysis Results

This section presents the principal empirical findings of the multivariate analysis of variance (MANOVA) executed for the experiment. The marginal means and standard deviations for the independent variable main effects and a summary of the significance test results are presented in Table 1.[10] There is no established and developed theory that would predict interactions between the investigated engagement characteristics. The MANOVA did, however, test for all possible interaction effects and found none that were significant at $p < .10$.

H1. The results presented in Table 1 indicate that the data provided statistically significant support ($p < .05$) for hypothesis 1. When auditors face uncertainty in an auditor-client conflict, the amount of competition for audit clients appears to influence their judgments.

H2. The description of non-attest services in this study was designed to be all-inclusive and to encompass services provided through several different departments or divisions of a major CPA firm. Also, the difference between the treatment levels of this independent variable was established to maximize the potential effects. Nevertheless, the results indicate that the level of non-attest services did not affect auditors' likelihood of issuing unqualified opinions at a statistically significant level and hypothesis 2 was therefore rejected.[11]

H3. The audit client's size was compared to the size of the auditor's office and to the portion of revenues for which the auditor was responsible. The findings of the overall analysis support ($p < .05$) the acceptance of hypothesis 3 that the effect of a client's revenue contribution did affect the judgments of auditors.

H4. Table 1 indicates very strong support for the acceptance of hypothesis 4 ($p < .001$). The results indicate that under the conditions present in this experiment, financial statement reporting preferences of clients with a strong recent financial condition are more likely to be accepted by auditors than identical preferences of clients with a poor recent financial condition.

Individual Analysis Results

To better understand the effects of these engagement characteristics upon the subjects' judgments, an individual ANOVA model was computed for each auditor. The omega-squared statistic was computed to assess the proportion of variance accounted for by each variable's main effect (Kirk 1982). Because no significant interactions were identified by the overall analysis, only the proportion of the variance accounted for (omega squared) by each significant main effect for each subject was estimated. The insignificant interactions were used to estimate the error term.[12]

Table 2 illustrates which independent variables were significant ($p < .10$) in the individual judgment models, and the proportion of the variance accounted for by each significant variable. The frequency of significant effects in the individual

Table 2. Auditors' Judgment Models From ANOVA

Effect	*1*	*2*	*3*	*4*	*5*	*6*	*7*	*8*	*9*	*10*	*11*	*12*	*13*	*14*	*15*	*16*	*Average*
C	—	—	—	—	—	—	05	—	—	—	—	—	—	—	—	—	.31
N	—	—	—	—	—	—	05	—	—	—	—	—	—	—	—	—	.31
R	—	—	—	—	07	—	08	—	—	13	—	—	—	—	04	—	2.00
F	78	80	—	100	73	100	67	—	—	13	46	100	93	63	74	64	59.44
Total	78	80	—	100	80	100	85	—	—	26	46	100	93	63	78	64	62.06

Note: Note: *C* = Competition; *N* = Non-attest Services; *R* = Client Revenue Contribution; *F* = Financial Condition.

The table contains omega square values (in percentages) for all independent variables that were significant in an individual's ANOVA at $p < .10$. All interactions were used to estimate the error term, and thus interactions are not estimable.

subjects' models and the direction of the impact of these effects are indications of judgment consensus among the subjects (Schultz and Gustavson 1978; Knapp 1985). The direction of the differences of the means for all significant effects in the individual models was consistent with the hypothesized directions. As indicated (Table 2), the model on average explained 62 percent of the variance in the individual auditors' judgments. The variance explained for each auditor ranged from zero (no factors significant) for three subjects to 100 percent for two subjects.

Discussion

This research was not designed to determine *why* any of the engagement characteristics affected auditors' judgments. Nevertheless, an analysis of the results suggests possible reasons for these effects.

Auditors appear to be more cautious in accepting management's proposed accounting treatments for financially weak clients than for financially strong clients. The results presented in Table 2 indicate that the financial condition factor was significant in 80 percent of the individual models and that there was unequivocal consensus in the factor's directional influence. To measure the auditors' self-insight into their judgments, a post-experiment questionnaire asked the subjects which factor in the cases was of the most significance in their judgment process.[13] The questionnaires indicated that the financial condition of the client was the factor of most influence. These results indicate a level of consistency in the auditors' judgments and contribute to the validity of the results (Schultz and Gustavson 1978).

The financial condition of a client is probably an important issue to consider when determining the acquisition or retention of a particular client. It is likely to be a valid consideration when determining the audit risk model for a client, determining materiality levels, evaluating the internal controls of a client, determining the audit scope and procedures necessary to issue a financial report, evaluating evidence collected during the audit, and determining the materiality of specific transactions. *However*, this factor is not as conceptually relevant during the final stages of an audit when financial reporting and disclosure-related judgments are being made about acknowledged material reporting issues. This author could locate no regulatory or other authoritative literature that suggests that an auditor's opinion regarding the accounting reporting and disclosure treatment of identical situations, which would be material to a client's financial statements, should differ because of the historical financial strength of the client.

What these results may represent is an indication of business risk management by the auditors. The largest accounting firms have acknowledged that the pressures of what they perceive to be a liability crisis have caused accountants to practice "risk reduction" (Arthur Andersen & Co. et al. 1992, 5). Based on comments made in public and private settings by partners in "Big Five" firms, the last decade has seen an increase in the review procedures conducted by the firms before they accept new clients. These comments have indicated that these review procedures have increasingly focused on the effect that a new client may have upon the risk associated with an audit firm's audit client portfolio. Audit firms are today more likely than they were several years ago to decline to service potential audit clients that are in high-risk industries or that individually may represent a higher risk of a client business failure than the audit firm's or office's overall client portfolio. Existing clients are also being evaluated regarding some audit firms' interest in continuing to perform audit services. These are valid and reasonable business responses to the litigious environment in which audit firms operate.

However, there is a significant difference between an auditor deciding not to provide services to a client that might increase the audit firm's business risk and an auditor providing differing audit opinions for identical transactions for two different clients. The possibility that these practices might cause identical transactions to be recorded differently in client financial statements as a result of auditor's perceived business risk may deserve further investigation by practitioners, researchers, standard setters, and regulatory bodies.

With respect to the auditors' competitive environment and the client revenue contribution engagement characteristics, the empirical results are less conclusive. The results of the overall analysis indicate that these factors both appear to affect the decision behavior of auditors when they are faced with uncertainty in an auditor-client conflict situation. However, unlike the client's historical financial condition factor, the pretest interviews with auditors from several different firms and the results of the post-experiment questionnaire suggested that almost all of the auditors thought that these factors should not influence decision behavior. In this study, these factors were found to be significant only at the $p < .05$ level and the differences between the means of the treatment levels were much smaller than the difference between the financial condition means. The individual analysis results indicate much less consensus among the auditors as to the importance of these factors as compared to the financial condition factor. Knapp (1985) reported similar empirical results for two of the factors considered in his research. In this study, as in his, the most defensible conclusion is that these two factors each slightly increases the apparent likelihood of a conflict being resolved in favor of the client (Knapp 1985, 208). It may be that these two factors affect an auditor's objectivity, without the auditor realizing that an effect has occurred.

The influence of the competition factor would support the suggestions by Mautz (1972) that any effect of competition on an auditor's opinion is "unintended and often unrecognized," and by Farmer, Rittenberg, and Trompeter (1987) that competitive pressures affect, at least subtly, auditors' decision behavior. In addition, the Cohen Commission expressed concerns related to the amount of competition in the public accounting profession. The results of this research indicate that the concerns of the Cohen Commission may be valid. Furthermore, they provide justification for the concerns of the Securities and Exchange Commission regarding "opinion shopping" by clients.

An unintended and unrecognized bias of an auditor's objectivity also may be related to a client's contribution to the revenues of an auditor's local office. The Cohen Commission also expressed concern that small audit firms may face greater problems maintaining independence because a few large clients supply a large portion of the firm's total revenues. These results not only suggest the legitimacy of this concern, but also expand that concern to the office level of large CPA firms. Auditors, when faced with uncertainty in an auditor-client conflict, may alter their decision behavior in very large firms due to consideration of client size related to decentralized or personal benchmarks. By identifying such biases, mechanisms to adjust out such biases can be developed, or further justified if they are already in place (e.g., the concurring partner's review).

The influence that the provision of non-attest services has upon auditors' decision behavior has been widely discussed by regulators, academics, and practitioners. This study indicates that although some users may perceive the performance of non-attest services by auditors to be incompatible with the attest function, the actual judgments of auditors were not affected by the level of these services. This conclusion is contrary to many of the theoretical positions advanced in the academic and professional literature. However, it does support the work of Corless and Parker (1987) and Parker, Corless, and Tucker (1988), which concluded that non-attest services did not affect auditors' judgments related to the evaluation of internal control.

The results of this research may also deserve consideration by the practice community. During the development of this research project the author had numerous discussions with senior partners in the participating firm about their expectations regarding the research results. Their initial expectations were that the engagement characteristics that are the focus of this research would have little if any effect upon the judgments of the participants. Although their expectations were accurate for the non-attest services characteristic, and perhaps for the competitive environment and client revenue contribution characteristics, their expectations were not supported regarding the effect that a client's financial condition might have upon auditors' judgments. The increased emphasis many firms are placing upon considering the risk profile of potential and existing clients may be having unexpected effects upon the judgments of the firm's partners. If so, the effects of business risk considerations upon auditors' judgments deserve more research and understanding.

LIMITATIONS TO THE RESEARCH

As with all experiment-based auditing research, several limitations of this study should be noted. First, all the subjects were from the same international firm, and hence the ability to generalize the results should be explored in future research. In particular, the engagement characteristics investigated in this study may have very different effects upon auditors from small, local firms.[14] The partners in local firms operate in a very different professional environment. They often have a greater familiarity with the day-to-day operations of many of their clients than do audit partners servicing multinational organizations. In addition, the partners in local firms may be responsible for a more diversified professional practice because they may be providing tax and consulting services to clients. This would be in contrast to audit senior managers or partners in large firms that are responsible for a more specialized audit practice. Second, experienced managers were used as surrogates for audit partners, and the judgments of partners may differ from the experienced managers. Third, the small number of subjects may have affected the statistical results: however, the presence of the significant results even with the small sample size suggests the effects to be very substantial (Wallace 1991). The statistical tests conducted in a study with a small sample size (such as this research) will have less statistical power than in tests with larger sample sizes. Thus, other things being equal, when the results indicate a rejection of the null hypothesis, there is stronger evidence against the null in studies with smaller sample sizes than in studies with larger sample sizes and larger statistical power (Lindsay 1993). Fourth, it is possible that the pressure created in the experiment did not accurately replicate the pressures and/or incentives that exist in audits. But, the pressure *did* appear to have an effect on the auditors' judgments, and auditors *do* face accountability pressure on audit engagements (Lord 1992). Fifth, it is possible that the within-subjects design may have been responsible for judgments that would differ from actual practice or from a between-subjects design. However, the selection of a within-subjects design had advantages over a between-subjects design. In particular, all factors could be simultaneously presented to each of the subjects and individual judgment models could be computed for each subject. Sixth, the experiment concentrated on personal judgments, and the subjects were not able to confer with other individuals. Decisions in auditor-client conflict situations often are made in consultation with other partners in the firm, and the consultations may influence or change an individual's decision behavior. Indeed, regulation supporting concurring partner reviews may be directed toward the types of biases explored herein, and may effectively offset the effects evidenced. Further research is necessary to determine whether the effects seen in this study are mitigated by these reviews, or whether they are simply repeated.

ACKNOWLEDGMENTS

I would like to thank the Deloitte & Touche Foundation for providing funding for this research. This paper has benefited from the suggestions made by Linda Bamber, Dave

Campbell, Al Michenzi, Larry Parker, Lee Parker, Gary Previts, Wanda Wallace, and participants in workshops at the University of Alabama. The support of an anonymous international CPA firm is appreciated.

The data and all experimental materials used in this study can be acquired upon request from the author. The ownership rights to this data and experimental materials are maintained by the author and the use of this data or experimental materials in subsequent research projects or published works requires specific written authorization from the author.

NOTES

1. All hypotheses within the paper are formulated in the alternate rather than null condition.

2. In a related study, Pany and Reckers (1980) used this approach when they examined the influence that the size of the client (in relation to office revenues) would have on shareholders' perceptions.

3. The anonymity of the international CPA firm that provided the subjects will be protected by referring to it as "the firm."

4. The design of this study and all research materials completed by the participants were approved in advance by the Institutional Review Board for the Protection of Human Subjects at the author's institution.

5. More comprehensive discussions of the use of deception in behavioral research in auditing are contained in Lord (1992), Dopuch (1992), and Gibbins (1992).

6. More comprehensive discussions of the advantages of within-subjects designs, particularly when the treatments occur simultaneously in the actual decision environment, can be found in Greenwald (1976), Harsha and Knapp (1990), and Schepanski, Tubbs, and Grimlund (1992).

7. The ordering of the cases presented to the subjects, and the ordering of the factors within each case were randomized to prevent any order effects from affecting the statistical results.

8. The case was pre-tested extensively; including detailed debriefing sessions and follow-up interviews with subjects. All subjects in the pre-tests and the actual experiment reported that they understood that the accounting issue in question would result in a material effect upon the financial statements.

9. In addition to the dependent variable computed as the average of the two items, item 1 and item 2 were used individually as dependent variables in separate statistical analyses. These two analyses yield results similar to those presented in the paper and are not discussed further.

10. Because each of the factors examined in this study had two treatment levels, the numerator degree of freedom of the MANOVA was one. A repeated measure design that has a numerator degree of freedom of one in a MANOVA could also be analyzed as a series of ANOVA models. The F statistics and related p values under these separate models would be identical to the results presented in Table 2. The more general MANOVA analysis was used for the paper for a more efficient presentation of the results.

11. An alternative explanation for the lack of significance for this factor could be that the two treatment levels were not perceived to be meaningfully different by the subjects. However, a statistical analysis of data provided by an independent group of subjects that responded to identical material under an anonymity guarantee indicated that this factor was significant ($p < .05$). This additional test significantly reduces the probability that the instrument is responsible for the lack of significant results for this factor.

12. This analysis follows the approach used by Lindsay (1990) and Schultz and Gustavson (1978) to determine individual ANOVA models for their subjects.

13. This approach is similar to one used by Schultz and Gustavson (1978).

14. Lord (1998) presents related research into the effects of these engagement characteristics on the judgments of partners in local CPA firms.

REFERENCES

Alchian, A., and H. Demsetz. 1972. Production, information costs, and economic organization. *American Economic Review* (December): 777–795.

American Institute of Certified Public Accountants. 1992. *Codification of Statements on Auditing Standards*. New York: AICPA.

Arens, A.A., and J.K. Loebbecke. 1991. *Auditing: An Integrated Approach*, 5th ed. Englewood Cliffs, NJ: Prentice Hall.

Armstrong, M.B., and J.I. Vincent. 1988. Public accounting: A profession at a crossroads. *Accounting Horizons* 2(March): 94–98.

Arthur Andersen & Co., Coopers & Lybrand, Deloitte & Touche, Ernst & Young, KPMG Peat Marwick, and Price Waterhouse. 1992. The liability crisis in the United States: Impact on the accounting profession. *Journal of Accountancy* 174(November): 19–23.

Carmichael, D.R., and R.J. Swieringa. 1968. The compatibility of auditing independence and management services: An identification of issues. *The Accounting Review* 43(October): 697–705.

Commission on Auditors' Responsibilities. 1978. *Report, Conclusions, and Recommendations*. New York: The Commission on Auditors' Responsibilities.

Corless, J.C., and L.M. Parker. 1987. The impact of MAS on auditor independence: An experiment. *Accounting Horizons* 1(September): 25–29.

DeAngelo, L.E. 1981. Auditor size and audit quality. *Journal of Accounting and Economics* 3: 183–199.

Deis, Jr., D.R., and G.A. Giroux. 1992. Determinants of audit quality in the public sector. *The Accounting Review* 67(July): 462–279.

Dopuch, N. 1992. Another perspective on the use of deception in auditing experiments. *Auditing: A Journal of Practice and Theory* 11(Fall) 109–112.

Farmer, T.A., L.E. Rittenberg, and G.M. Trompeter. 1987. An investigation of the impact of economic and organizational factors on auditor independence. *Auditing: A Journal of Practice and Theory* 7(Fall): 1–14.

Gibbins, M. 1992. Deception: A tricky issue for behavioral research in accounting and auditing. *Auditing: A Journal of Practice and Theory* 11(Fall): 113–126.

Greenwald, A.G. 1976. Within-subjects designs: To use or not to use? *Psychological Bulletin* 83(2): 314–320.

Gul, F.A. 1989. Bankers' perceptions of factors affecting auditor independence. *Accounting, Auditing, and Accountability Journal* 2(3): 40–51.

Hackenbrack, K., and M.W. Nelson. 1996. Auditors' incentives and their application of financial accounting standards. *The Accounting Review* 71(2): 43–59.

Harsha, P.D., and M.C. Knapp. 1990. The use of within- and between-subjects experimental designs in behavioral accounting research: A methodological note. *Behavioral Research in Accounting* 2: 50–62.

Kirk, R.E. 1982.*Experimental Design: Procedures for the Behavioral Sciences*, 2nd ed. Monterey, CA: Brooks/Cole.

Knapp, M.C. 1985. Audit conflict: An empirical study of the perceived ability of auditors to resist management pressure. *The Accounting Review* 60(April): 202–211.

Leslie, D.A. 1985. *Materiality: The Concept and Its Application to Auditing*. Toronto, ON, Canada: The Canadian Institute of Chartered Accountants.

Lindsay, D. 1989. Financial statement users' perceptions of factors affecting the ability of auditors to resist client pressure in a conflict situation. *Accounting and Finance* 29(November): 1–18.

Lindsay, D. 1990. An investigation of the impact of contextual factors on canadian bankers perceptions of auditors' ability to resist management pressure. *Advances in International Accounting* 3: 71–85.

Lindsay, R.M. 1993. Incorporating statistical power into the test of significance procedure: A methodological and empirical inquiry. *Behavioral Research in Accounting* 5: 211–236.

Lord, A.T. 1992. Pressure: A methodological consideration for behavioral research in auditing. *Auditing: A Journal of Practice and Theory* 11(Fall): 89–108.

Lord, A.T. 1998. The effects of selected engagement characteristics on the judgments of partners in local CPA firms. Working paper, Bowling Green State University.

Magee, R.P., and M. Tseng. 1990. Audit pricing and independence. *The Accounting Review* 65(April): 315–336.

Mautz, R.K. 1972. Toward a philosophy of auditing. In *Auditing Looks Ahead: Proceedings of the 1972 Touche Ross/University of Kansas Symposium on Auditing Problems*, ed. H.F. Stettler, 85–99. KS: University of Kansas Printing Service.

Nunnally, J.C. 1978. *Psychometric Theory*, 2nd ed. New York: McGraw-Hill.

Pany, K., and P.M.J. Reckers. 1980. The effects of gifts, discounts, and client size on perceived auditor independence. *The Accounting Review* 55(January): 50–61.

Pany, K., and P.M.J. Reckers. 1983. Auditor independence and nonaudit services. *Journal of Accounting and Public Policy* 2: 43–62.

Pany, K., and P.M.J. Reckers. 1984. Non-audit services and auditor independence: A continuing problem. *Auditing: A Journal of Practice & Theory* 3(Spring): 89–97.

Pany, K., and P.M.J. Reckers. 1988. MAS, auditing, and your orientation. *The CPA Journal* 58(February): 70–72.

Parker, L.M., J.C. Corless, and M.J. Tucker. 1988. Audit firm size and internal control assessment: An experiment. *Research in Accounting Regulation* 2: 155–166.

Reckers, P.M.J., and A.J. Stagliano. 1981. Non-audit services and perceived independence: Some new evidence. *Auditing: A Journal of Practice and Theory* 1(Summer): 23–37.

Sack, R.J., and R. Tangreti. 1987. ESM: Implications for the profession. *Journal of Accountancy* 163(April) 94–100.

Scheiner, J.H. 1984. An empirical assessment of the impact of SEC nonaudit service disclosure requirements on independent auditors and their clients. *Journal of Accounting Research* 22(Autumn): 789–797.

Scheiner, J.H., and J.E. Kiger. 1982. An empirical investigation of auditor involvement in non-audit services. *Journal of Accounting Research* 20(Autumn): 482–496.

Schepanski, A., R.M. Tubbs, and R.A. Grimlund. 1992. Issues of concern regarding within- and between-subjects designs in behavioral accounting research. *Journal of accounting Literature* 11: 121–150.

Schultz, J.J., and S.G. Gustavson. 1978. Actuaries' perceptions of variables affecting the independent auditor's legal liability. *The Accounting Review* 53(July): 626–641.

Shank, J.K. 1978. Independence: Accusations in search of an issue. In *"The Accounting Establishment" in Perspective*, ed. S. Davidson, 51–64. Chicago, IL: Arthur Young and Company.

Shockley, R.A. 1981. Perceptions of auditors' independence: An empirical analysis. *The Accounting Review* 56(October): 785–800.

St. Pierre, K., and J.A. Anderson. 1984. An analysis of the factors associated with lawsuits against public accountants. *The Accounting Review* 59(April): 242–263.

Wallace, W.A. 1991. *Accounting Research Methods: Do the Facts Speak for Themselves*? Homewood, IL: Irwin.

Walo, J.C. 1995. The effects of client characteristics on audit scope. *Auditing: A Journal of Practice and Theory* 14(Spring): 115–124.

PRELIMINARY SUPPORT FOR THE FASB'S REVISED SEGMENT REPORTING REQUIREMENT

Jenice Prather-Kinsey

ABSTRACT

The debate continues about the usefulness of the geographic segment disclosures required by accounting regulatory bodies, including the Financial Accounting Standards Board (FASB), the International Accounting Standards Board (IASB) and the Accounting Standards Board (AcSB) of the Canadian Institute of Chartered Accountants (CICA). The AcSB, FASB and IASC revised their accounting regulation regarding segment reporting in 1997 from an external to an internal perspective. Specifically, the FASB went from an external to a "management approach" but continued to use the ten percent materiality threshold in its newly revised segment reporting requirement: Statement of Financial Accounting Standard (SFAS) 131. Extant accounting literature and financial analyses support that geographic disaggregations that are reported using the ten percent materiality threshold are not useful to market participants in assessing the varying risks and returns of an enterprise. This article addresses the usefulness of geographic segment reporting from an external perspective using the ten percent materiality threshold in explaining cross-bor-

Research in Accounting Regulation, Volume 13, pages 43-53.

ISBN: 0-7623-0520-7

der listing activities of multinational corporations (MNCs). The empirical results show that SFAS 14 disclosures provide significant explanatory power about firms' cross-border listing activities. These results may partially explain why the ten percent materiality threshold is consistent between the internal approach, SFAS No 14, and the "management approach," SFAS No. 131, of the FASB's geographic segment reporting regulations.

INTRODUCTION

Debates on the usefulness of geographic segment disclosure requirements of accounting regulatory bodies, including the Financial Accounting Standards Board (FASB), the International Accounting Standards Board (IASB) and the Accounting Standards Board (AcSB) of the Canadian Institute of Chartered Accountants (CICA) are continuous. Initially, Statement of Financial Accounting Standard (SFAS) 14 (FASB 1976) required disclosure of geographic segments based on criteria external to the firm and a ten percent materiality threshold. Analysts, including the Association for Investment Management and Research (AIMR) which represents professional analysts worldwide, complained that the materiality threshold should be less than the promulgated ten percent (AIMR 1993). For example, Caterpillar did not disclose significant Brazilian sales that constituted five percent of their operations, because it did not meet the ten percent materiality threshold. Analysts believe that these Brazilian sales are material information needed in assessing the amount, timing, and uncertainty of the future cash flows of Caterpillar. Salter, Swanson, Achleitner, de Lembre, and Khanna (1996) propose a materiality threshold of between two and four percent for useful segment reporting. Analysts also complain that because management is allowed to use their judgement in developing geographic segments, segment results are ambiguous and misleading (see Herrmann and Thomas 1997 and Bavishi and Wyman 1980).

When the FASB issued the revised segment reporting regulation, SFAS 131, they continued to use the ten percent materiality threshold. This study provides some implications about the usefulness of the ten percent materiality threshold and the usefulness of SFAS 14 geographic segment disclosures based on empirical results. Logistic regression tests indicate that in addition to three control variables (i.e., disclosure level, size, and relative equity), SFAS 14 geographic segment disclosures are significant in explaining cross-border listings on the London Stock Exchange (LSE) or on the U.S. stock exchanges.[1] That is, public segment information, SFAS 14 geographic segment disclosures rather than private information,[2] a country's exporting level, explains multinationals'[3] (MNCs') cross-border listing activity. The following section will describe the contents and history of geographic segment reporting from SFAS 14 to 131. Next, empirical results on the usefulness of SFAS 14 geographic segment disclosures are presented. Finally, a deductively derived conclusion is presented describing why the FASB adopted the "management approach" and ten percent materiality threshold in SFAS 131.

SFAS 14 AND 131

SFAS 14 requires disclosure of geographic segment information by public business enterprises. Businesses are required to present sales, operating profits, and identifiable assets of each foreign geographic segment that has unaffiliated customer revenues or identifiable assets greater than or equal to ten percent of consolidated revenues or consolidated assets, respectively. Geographic regions reported are based on management's judgement relative to differences in international business environments, economic environments, and proximity (FASB 1976). This notion of segment reporting is referred to as *the external approach.* Management looks at factors external to the firm in developing reported geographic segments.

The FASB revisited SFAS 14 after considerable criticisms of its contents by analysts and academia. The FASB was criticized by analysts, creditors, and investors who believe that management abuses the flexibility allowed in SFAS 14 in defining geographic segments (see Herrmann and Thomas 1997 and Bavishi and Wyman 1980). Hays and Lundholm (1996) demonstrate, through analytical models, that management can trade off the benefit of informing market participants about firm value and the cost of aiding the competitor under SFAS 14 regulations. Firms may disaggregate segments with results similar to permanent earnings and hide segments with dissimilar to permanent results within disaggregated segments. This can be done given the discretion that management is allowed in reporting about geographic segments. The AICPA's Special Committee on Financial Reporting stated that two of the problems associated with SFAS 14 are the materiality threshold of ten percent and the flexibility given management in developing disaggregated regions. Academic results also point to these shortcomings of SFAS 14.

Prior studies have found country-based geographic segment reporting to be more useful in assessing risk than regional disclosures reported using SFAS 14 guidelines. Doupnik and Rolfe (1989) state that an MNC may report a geographic area in "Europe/Mideast/Africa," but for example, the country risk of Lybia is far different from that of West Germany. Doupnik and Rolfe (1989) conducted an experiment with 54 Master of International Business Students during their last semester of study. The subjects were presented with differing levels of geographic segment disaggregations. They found that the country-based segments resulted in more relevant risk assessments than global- and continent-level disaggregations. Hussain (1997) found that segment disclosures based on segments finer than region are associated with greater financial analysts' forecast accuracy.

Balakrishnan, Harris, and Sen (1990) took SFAS 14 reported geographic segment disclosures and further segmented them by country to develop segments that would be useful in predicting earnings. These studies imply that the ten percent materiality threshold does not provide the fineness needed to produce segment information useful in assessing firm risk or predicting earnings.

The FASB and AcSB published the research report "Reporting Disaggregated Information," in March 1993. An invitation to comment was published by the boards in May 1993, and 29 comment letters were received. In 1995 the Boards received another 80 comment letters on their publication, "Tentative Conclusions on Financial Reporting for Segments." The FASB and the AcSB in January 1996 issued an Exposure Draft "Reporting Disaggregated Information about a Business Enterprise." The FASB and AcSB received 295 comment letters about the Exposure Draft. A field study of the Exposure Draft was conducted during March 1996 and a public meeting to discuss the proposal was held in Norwalk, Connecticut in October 1996. With the participation of the AcSB and the IASC, the FASB issued SFAS 131 "Disclosures about Segments of an Enterprise and Related Information" in June 1997. Two of the most discussed issues during the FASB's deliberations were the discretion and flexibility allowed management in defining segments and the ten percent materiality threshold.

In SFAS 131, the FASB decided to minimize the flexibility allowed management in defining reportable segments by promulgating the "management approach." Financial reporting periods beginning after December 15, 1997 are required to define segments based on the segments used by the "chief operating decision maker" in making allocations of resources to segments and in assessing the performance of segments. The "management approach" is believed to be more objective in developing reportable segments than the external approach.

Academicians may believe that SFAS 14 geographic segment disclosures are not useful in explaining MNC's cross-border listing activities. Saudagaran and Biddle (1995) and Biddle and Saudagaran (1989) use two identical logit models to explain MNCs' cross-border listing behavior. Saudagaran and Biddle's 1995 (Biddle and Saudagaran 1989) study includes listings at 1992 (1991) year-end of 459 (207) internationally traded MNCs. They find that financial disclosure level and size of exports to a foreign country explain MNCs' cross-border listing behavior. One might speculate that private information—level of exports to a foreign country—might have been used to explain cross-border listing activity because geographic segment disclosures are not perceived as useful information. This research extends prior studies by substituting country export level with SFAS 14 geographic segment sales level to explain why and where MNCs engage in cross-border listing.

The results of this study provide implications for why the ten percent rule of SFAS 14 permeates in SFAS 131. Some argue that SFAS 131's ten percent materiality threshold is inadequate. The External Relations Committee of the International Accounting Section of the American Accounting Association (Salter et al. 1996) proposes that SFAS 131 should have required a two to four percent materiality threshold. The FASB argues that a finer than ten percent materiality threshold can result in misleading segment reporting, especially when smaller thresholds result in more than ten reported geographic segments. The FASB (1997) states that the ten percent materiality threshold is objectively applied and that users and preparers of financial reports understand it. This study shows that the ten percent materiality threshold provides information that is useful in explaining MNCs' cross-border listing activity. For those who support the two to four percent materiality threshold, the FASB (1997) does allow for reporting on finer than ten percent disaggregations if the finer segment is deemed material by management. However, the FASB suggests a limit of ten geographic segments.

EMPIRICAL STUDY

The question addressed in this empirical analysis is whether geographic segment sales disclosures are useful in explaining why and where MNCs choose to cross-border list. Before testing this research question, control variables are developed based on results of prior studies. This study replicates that of Saudagaran and Biddle (1995) and Biddle and Saudagaran (1989) because the control variables; disclosure level, size, and relative equity value outstanding, are included in this study too. However, in this study an additional variable is used, geographic segment sales instead of a country's level of exports to a foreign country. This study also uses a more current database, 1991 through 1994.

Logistic regression is used to explain MNC's cross-border listing behavior. The dependent variable is the MNC's decision to cross-border list or not to cross-border list. The independent variables are disclosure level, size, relative equity, and geographic segment sales location and level.

Disclosure Level

Empirical evidence finds that companies are reluctant to list on the NYSE, AMEX, and NASDAQ stock exchanges because they require geographic region and line of business disclosures that are not required by their home country's stock exchange. Reporting segment information could result in a competitive disadvantage to the reporting MNC (Nagarajan and Sridhar 1996; Biddle and Saudagaran 1991). The U.S. stock exchanges require a greater frequency of financial reporting (semi-annually and/or quarterly) and initial listing requirements and auditing practices are also more extensive in the U.S. than abroad (see Frost and Lang 1996; Biddle and Saudagaran 1991). Disclosure requirements are so extensive in the U.S. that no German firms listed on the NYSE until October 1993 and no Korean or Finland companies listed until 1994. Further, Biddle and Saudagaran (1989) found a disclosure level index to be significant when a foreign stock exchange's disclosure requirements were more extensive than those of an MNC's home country stock exchange. Because the U.S. stock exchanges and LSE have such extensive disclosure requirements, disclosure level is included in the logistic regression model to determine whether cross-border listing choice is influenced by disclosure level.

Size

Larger companies are more likely to list abroad (Saudagaran 1988). More recently, companies have grown through international sales and international mergers and acquisitions. Smaller companies may transact most of their business domestically and therefore have almost no motivation for listing abroad. To control for cross-border listing decisions related to the size of an MNC, the log of total sales is used in the logistic regression model.

Relative Equity

Empirical evidence confirms that when MNCs find that their home market does not provide enough capital to finance their equity needs, they cross-border list into larger capital markets (Sofianos 1995; Biddle and Saudagaran 1991). Baker (1992) found that managers listed abroad to expand their investor base and thus increase the demand for their stock. The foreign listing also minimizes the cost of capital, because foreign markets are sometimes willing to provide a less expensive source of funds. Further, issuing large dollar values of equity shares abroad would not dilute the larger international financial markets as it would the smaller local financial markets (Alexander, Eun, and Janakiramanan 1988). To control for cross-border listing decisions related to the size of the local equity markets, the total equity value of an MNC's equity capital relative to the size of the local financial market's equity capital is used to measure relative equity.

SFAS 14 Geographic Sales

The relative size of geographic segment sales may explain an MNC's decision to cross-border list. In addition, the location of geographic segment sales may explain where an MNC is more likely to cross-border list. Biddle and Saudagaran (1989) hypothesize that domestic exports of an MNC's industry and home country to a foreign country might explain an MNC's cross-border listing behavior. They use a country-based variable—level of the MNC's home country exports—as a proxy for a firm's exports going to a specific country. Perhaps they did not use geographic segment sales because they believed this information was misleading or was not useful in explaining cross-border listing activity. They find that private information—country-based exports—is significant in explaining cross-border listing behavior. In this study, a company-specific variable,

Table 1. Geographic Logistic Models for Years 1991–1994

$$EXCH_i = \beta_0 - \beta_1\, DISLEV_i + \beta_2\, SIZE_i + \beta_3\, RELEQU_i + \beta_4\, (D_iGS_i) \qquad (1)$$

	Stock Exchanges			
	London		*United States*	
Coefficients (Wald Chi-Square)				
Intercept	−4.152**	(0.008)	−0.845	(0.082)
Disclosure Level	0.134**	(0.714)	−1.988**	(0.000)
Log of Total Sales	0.080	(0.373)	−0.029	(0.403)
Relative Equity	46.913**	(0.000)	29.655**	(0.001)
Geographic Sales	4.115**	(0.000)	1.832**	(0.000)
Pseudo R^2 (Somers' D)	69.0%		66.2%	
Fraction of Concordant Pairs	84.3%		82.9%	
Tied Pairs	0.5%		0.4%	

Notes: * = $p < .05$

** = $p < .01$

EXCH = Dependent variable; 1 if listing is on the London or a U.S. stock exchange; 0 otherwise.

DISLEV = If the stock exchange is located in the U.S. and an MNC's country of incorporation is the United States or Canada then disclosure level (DISLEV) = 0; 1 otherwise.
If exchange is London stock exchange and country of incorporation is United States, Canada,
or the European Union,[7] then disclosure level (DISLEV) = 0; 1 otherwise.

SIZE = The log of total sales, revenue, or turnover of firm *i* at year end.

RELEQU = MNC *i*'s total equity value outstanding/total equity value of domestic stock exchange.

D = Dummy interaction variable, 1 if geographic segment description is the London or U.S.; 0 otherwise.

GS_i = Geographic segment sales of firm *i*/total sales of firm *i*.

geographic segment sales, is used to explain not only the decision to cross-border list, but also where the MNC is likely to cross-border list.

Geographic segment sales are also a proxy for the significance of a foreign market to an MNC's operations. That is, the greater the degree of foreign operations in a country, the more likely the MNC will cross-border list in that country (Mittoo 1992). An MNC may recognize a foreign country as an important market for their product or service by listing there (Baker 1992). Listing in that country may improve relations between an MNC and the foreign community and government, and may mitigate negative nationalistic reactions to wholly owned foreign subsidiaries. Further, foreign listings can enhance marketing efforts with broadened product visibility to investors and consumers in the host country (Baker 1992). Geographic sales is used as a proxy for the importance of a foreign country in making cross-border listing decisions.

Table 2. Full Logistic Model for Years 1991–1994

$$EXCH_i = \beta_0 - \beta_1\, DISLEV_i + \beta_2\, SIZE_i + \beta_3\, RELEQU_i \qquad (2)$$

	U.S. and London Cross-border-listers
Coefficients (Wald Chi-Square)	
Intercept	−0.123
	(0.691)
Disclosure	−0.557**
Level (DISLEV)	(0.001)
Log of Total	−0.026
Sales (SIZE)	0.283
Relative	52.799**
Equity (RELEQU)	(0.001)
Pseudo R^2 (Somers' D)	.322%
Fraction of Concordant Pairs	65.1%
Tied Pairs	2.0%

Notes: * = $p < .05$
** = $p < .01$
EXCH = Dependent variable; 1 if cross border-listing is on any foreign stock exchange; 0 otherwise.
DISLEV = If an MNC's country of incorporation is the United States or Canada then disclosure level (DISLEV) = 0; 1 otherwise.
SIZE = The log of total sales, revenue, or turnover of firm *i* at year end.
RELEQU = MNC *i*'s total equity value outstanding/total equity value of domestic stock exchange.

Worldscope and *Standard and Poor's Compustat Business Information File* are used to develop the sample of companies listing on the LSE or one of the U.S. stock exchanges. Equity market values are taken from *Emerging Stock Markets Factbook 1994* (International Finance Corporation 1994). The sample is 2,386 observations domiciled in 25 different countries. Two logistic regression models are used. The full model includes all MNCs that list on a U.S. stock exchange or on the LSE during 1991–1994. There are two geographic logistic regression models: one including MNCs listed on the LSE, and another of MNCs listed on a U.S. stock exchange.[4]

FINDINGS

The logistic regression results are somewhat similar to the findings of Saudagaran (1988), Biddle and Saudagaran (1989), and Saudagaran and Biddle (1995). The extensiveness of disclosure requirements of a foreign stock exchange and the relative equity value of an MNC explain why MNCs do or do not cross-border list on a foreign stock exchange. The logistic geographic models for LSE and U.S. stock exchange observations are displayed in Table 1. These models show that disclosure level requirements, relative equity value, and geographic segment sales explain why and where an MNC cross-border lists.[5] The LSE and U.S. stock exchange models are accurate 84% and 83% of the time, respectively. This represents an improvement when comparing the geographic logistic regression models with the full logistic regression model that does not include geographic segment sales as an explanatory variable (see Table 2). The full logistic model that excludes geographic segment sales only explains 65 percent of the variability in MNCs' decisions about whether to list on a foreign stock exchange.[6]

The geographic logistic regression models explain that the lower the level of extensiveness of the disclosure requirements of the foreign stock exchange, and the greater the MNC's relative equity, the more likely the MNC is to cross-border list. These results are similar to those of Saudagaran (1988), Biddle and Saudagaran (1989), and Saudagaran and Biddle's (1995) private variable, MNCs' home country level of exports. In addition, as the level of geographic sales in a foreign country increases, the more likely the MNC is to invest in the geographic region of the foreign sales.

This study's extension of past accounting research on cross-border listing choice is the inclusion of geographic segment sales in the logistic regression model that explains an MNCs cross-border listing decision. SFAS 14 geographic disclosures, based on the ten percent materiality threshold, significantly explain why and where an MNC is likely to cross-border list. These results may explain why the FASB maintained its ten percent materiality threshold in SFAS 131. In other words, an MNC may consider cross-border listing on a foreign stock exchange after they have significant sales that exceed the ten percent materiality threshold, in a foreign country.

CONCLUSIONS

The objective of this study is to describe and explain the FASB's geographic segment regulations from SFAS 14 to SFAS 131. The FASB listened to arguments against SFAS 14 (FASB 1976) for almost 20 years before promulgating a revised statement, SFAS 131, in 1997. Two major arguments against SFAS 14 are the discretion management is allowed in developing reportable segments, and the ten percent materiality threshold. Analysts, academics, and market participants want a segment regulation whereby reported segments are determined objectively. The FASB responded in 1998 with SFAS 131, which required the "management approach." In the "management approach," MNCs have to report segments using the same sub-units that the "chief operating decision maker" uses in making resource allocations to segments and in assessing segment performance internally. The FASB, however, did not require a materiality threshold of less than ten percent. Empirical analysis using geographic segment disclosures finds that the ten percent materiality segments reported under SFAS 14 results in information which is useful in explaining MNCs' cross-border listing activity. These results imply that the extensiveness of disclosure requirements of the foreign stock exchange relative to the home country stock exchange, the size of MNCs' equity value outstanding relative to the size of its home market, and geographic segment sales reported under SFAS 14 are significant in explaining the likelihood of an MNC to cross-border list.

ACKNOWLEDGMENTS

The author appreciates programming assistance from Chris Penning and comments from John Howe, Brad Jordan, Grace Pownall, and participants at the University of Alabama and University of Missouri Research Colloquiums.

NOTES

1. U.S. stock exchanges are the American Stock Exchange (AMEX), NASDAQ, and the New York Stock Exchange (NYSE).
2. Private information is any data not disclosed in a firm's annual financial reports.
3. A multinational corporation is one that lists some or all of its equity securities outside of its home country stock exchange.
4. I do not use one full model for the geographic regressions, because some companies list on a U.S. exchange and on LSE and would therefore bias the regression results towards MNCs listing on both exchanges and against those listing on only one of the exchanges.
5. The geographic logistic model for both the U.S. and LSE cross-border listers is also developed for each year: 1991, 1992, 1993, and 1994. The annual geographic segment model's qualitative results are no different from the combined four-year results.
6. There was concern that because the full logistic model contained repeated measures that the results might be biased. For example, a company may be included for each of the four years, 1991–1994. The annual model's qualitative results were identical to the combined years' model results.
7. The European Union countries include Belgium, Denmark, France, Germany, Greece, Ireland, Italy, Luxembourg, Netherlands, Portugal, Spain, and the United Kingdom.

REFERENCES

Alexander, G., C. Eun, and S. Janakiramanan. 1988. International listing and stock returns: Some empirical evidence. *Journal of Financial and Quantitative Analysis* (June): 135–151.

Association for Investment Management and Research, Financial Reporting Policy Committee (AIMR). 1993. *Financial Reporting in the 1990s and Beyond: A Position Paper of the Association for Investment Management and* Research. Prepared by P.H. Kunston. Charlottesville, VA: AIMR.

Baker, H.K. 1992. Why U.S. companies list on the London, Frankfurt and Tokyo stock exchanges. *The Journal of International Securities Markets* (Autumn): 219–227.

Balakrishnan, R., T.S. Harris, and P.K. Sen. 1990. The predictive ability of geographic segment disclosures. *Journal of Accounting Research* (Autumn): 305–325.

Bavishi, V.B., and H.E. Wyman. 1980. Foreign operations disclosures by U.S.-based multinational corporations: Are they adequate? *The International Journal of Accounting Education and Research* (Fall): 153–168.

Biddle, G.C., and S.M. Saudagaran. 1989. The effects of financial disclosure levels on firms' choices among alternative foreign stock exchange listings. *Journal of International Financial Management and Accounting* 1(1): 55–87.

Biddle, G.C., and S.M. Saudagaran. 1991. Foreign stock listings: Benefits, costs, and the accounting policy dilemma. *Accounting Horizons* (September): 69–80.

Doupnik, T.S., and R.J. Rolfe. 1989. The relevance of level of aggregation of geographic area data in the assessment of foreign investment risk. *Advances in Accounting* (7): 51–65.

Financial Accounting Standards Board (FASB). 1976. *Statement of Financial Accounting Standards No. 14 Financial Reporting for Segments of a Business Enterprise*. Stamford, CT: FASB.

Financial Accounting Standards Board (FASB). 1997. *Statement of Financial Accounting Standards No. 131 Disclosures about Segments of an Enterprise and Related Information*. Stamford, CT: FASB.

Frost, C.A., and M.H. Lang. 1996. Foreign companies and U.S. securities markets: Financial reporting policy issues and suggestions for research. *Accounting Horizons* (March): 95–109.

Hayes, R.M., and R. Lundholm. 1996. Segment reporting to the capital market in the presence of a competitor. *Journal of Accounting Research* (Autumn): 261–279.

Herrmann, D., and W.B. Thomas. 1997. Reporting disaggregated information: A critique based on Concepts Statement No. 2. *Accounting Horizons* (September): 35–44.

Hussain, S. 1997. The impact of segment definition on the accuracy of analysts' earnings forecasts. *Accounting and Business Research*: 145–165.

International Finance Corporation. 1994. *Emerging Stock Markets Factbook 1994*. Washington, DC: International Finance Corporation.

Mittoo, U.R. 1992. Managerial perceptions of the net benefits of foreign listing: Canadian evidence. *Journal of International Financial Management and Accounting* (4): 40–62.

Nagarajan, N.J., and S.S. Sridhar. 1996. Corporate responses to segment disclosure requirements. *Journal of Accounting and Economics* 21(3): 253–275.

Saudagaran, S. 1988. An empirical study of selected factors influencing the decision to list on foreign stock exchanges. *Journal of International Business Studies* (Spring): 101–127.

Saudagaran, S.M., and G.C. Biddle. 1995. Foreign listing location: a study of MNCs and stock exchanges in eight countries. *Journal of International Business Studies* (Spring): 319–341.

Salter, S.B., E.P. Swanson, A. Achleitner, E. de Lembre, and B.S. Khanna. 1996. Reporting financial information by segment: A comment of the American Accounting Association on the IASC draft statement of principles. *Accounting Horizons* (March): 118–123.

Sofianos, G. 1995. Foreign access to the U.S. capital markets: The NYSE's view. Working paper, KPMG Peat Marwick and AAA International Accounting Research Conference, March 24, Montvale, NJ.

CERTIFIED PUBLIC ACCOUNTANTS' SELF-REGULATION IN SOCIO-LEGAL PERSPECTIVE

Jack C. Robertson and Keith Hawkins

ABSTRACT

The regulation of Certified Public Accountants' (CPA) activities has been described by CPAs for CPAs in numerous sources, generally in the spirit of praising and promoting CPAs' efforts to keep their own house in order. Except for periodic Congressional critiques of CPAs' practices, very few efforts to evaluate CPA self-regulation in a more critical spirit have been made. However, the field of socio-legal studies, which explores the institutions, practices, and professions of law from a social-scientific standpoint, contains an emerging literature—indeed a set of generic theoretical ideas—of regulatory law enforcement, which can be recruited to help us look more closely at CPAs' regulatory practices. Most of this socio-legal literature deals with the theory and practice of social regulation and was developed from the established literature on police activities. As a result, socio-legal scholars have not, to any

Research in Accounting Regulation, Volume 13, pages 55-80.

ISBN: 0-7623-0520-7

significant extent, turned their theoretical attention toward self-regulation as a form of social control, nor to the enforcement of standards in the learned professions.

Quite recently, the accounting profession embarked on an extensive visioning project—looking to the prospects for accountancy in a rapidly changing business world. The *CPA Vision—2011 and Beyond* report paints a challenging futuristic picture for CPAs. The picture combines the business of accounting practice (especially public practice) with the forces of professionalism. A judicious combination of business and professionalism deserves continual debate and discussion, and we bring to bear the socio-legal perspective to point out the need for attention to traditional self-regulation institutions and processes.

The socio-legal theoretical perspective applied herein introduces some of the language and concepts of law and social science and applies them to CPA self-regulation. The main thesis is that effective self-regulation depends upon (1) designing an effective system, (2) establishing the system in institutions and processes and providing sufficient resources, and (3) operating the system to the satisfaction of both the regulated persons and outside observers. Hence, our general hypothesis is that CPA self-regulation meets these criteria, and now we seek observational evidence to negate the hypothesis. Our analysis shows some little-acknowledged deficiencies in the ways CPAs conduct their self-regulation, and we suggest that CPA self-regulation can benefit from certain changes.

This paper studies the control of U.S. Certified Public Accountants' (CPA) activities from the distinctive standpoint of socio-legal scholarship. The socio-legal perspective analyzes the institutions, practices, and professions of law with the tools of social science, thereby exploring the workings and the role of law in society. The field of socio-legal studies contains a very large and diverse literature. Overviews of the field are available in Lempert and Sanders (1986), Lipson and Wheeler (1986), and Tamanaha (1997). A segment of the literature deals with regulatory theory, mostly from the perspectives of political science and economics (Mitnick 1980; Ogus 1994). However, socio-legal scholars have paid relatively little attention to regulation practiced in private by professional organizations and their associated state professional regulatory agencies. This paper is an entry in this particular gap.

While the socio-legal perspective is the focus herein, another point of view related to control of the accounting profession as a whole is a motivation for this paper. It is the market-for-services view found in the AICPA's CPA Vision Process (Thomas 1998). According to Thomas (1998, 23): "CPAs decided to embrace change and used the CPA Vision Process as the mechanism for creating a future in which they would be in a good position to turn the challenges of the new business world into opportunities." Basically, the CPA Vision Process produced a look into the future of the accounting *business*.

At the same time, the vision acknowledges *professionalism* in accountancy by asserting that the future is based on CPAs' time-honored traditions of integrity and competence; that the public interest will be served with greater breadth and depth of CPA expertise; and that the combination of old values with new competencies will enjoy a virtually unbeatable competitive advantage (Thomas 1998, 24; AICPA 1998, 4). The *CPA Vision—2011 and Beyond* report displays eight forces impacting the profession, but none of them specifically names professionalism (AICPA 1998, 5). The report lists ten leadership perspectives (AICPA 1998, 7), and they all seem to be related to the business (market) for accounting services.

The five CPA Vision core values include Integrity and Objectivity. Integrity ranks third behind the core values of Continuing Education (which enhances business and personal growth) and Competence (which enables more specialized services and more business). The fourth core value is Attune to Broad Business Issues (which brings CPAs in tune with the overall realities of the business environment), and the fifth is Objectivity (which presumes CPAs can deal with information free of distortion, personal bias, or conflicts of interest; and will create opportunities to cross-sell and expand) (AICPA 1998, 13, 15–16). The implications for the entire profession emphasize opportunity, respect, rewards, aggressive marketing, and cultural adaptation (AICPA 1998, 21).

The CPA Vision clearly acknowledges CPAs' historic role as protectors of the public interest, and asserts: "The profession will not abandon this fundamental element as we move into the 21st century" (AICPA 1998, 25). Nevertheless, the conflict between accountancy as a *business* and accountancy as a *profession* persists. If the rank order of the core values is a reliable indicator, the business of accounting seems to be uppermost in CPAs' strategic thinking.

This conflict is not new. Zeff discussed it years ago (Zeff 1987). Now, motivated by the latent conflict between the basic business orientation of the CPA Vision and traditional views of professionalism, this paper concentrates on the socio-legal forms of regulatory control that may be applied to professions. (While other aspects of regulation such as courts and government are important, space does not permit their integration herein.) We intend to prompt debate and discussion of the role of CPA self-regulation in the spirit of emphasizing the desire to maintain CPAs' fundamental commitment to the pubic interest in the face of powerful business pressures.

The present analysis has two purposes: (1) to describe and analyze CPA self-regulatory institutions and processes from a socio-legal perspective, drawing analogies to other forms of law enforcement, and (2) to identify some apparent weaknesses in CPA self-regulation. Our approach is one of constructive criticism, pointing out difficulties and potential shortcomings in CPA self-regulation. (Praise of CPAs' efforts can be found in other sources.) The analysis begins with an introduction to the legal context of the regulation of professions, followed by a general discussion of enforcement in regulatory systems. This foundation supports a treatment of compliance and sanctioning features of CPA self-regulation. Some observations and conclusions end the paper.

Though the analysis is primarily concerned with self-regulation in the United States at the national and state levels, we also incorporate some comparative insights on British regulatory experience (one author's special expertise). A strong tradition of self-regulation exists in Britain, probably with cultural origins (Vogel 1986), and the British experience can lend perspective to the U.S. scene. The British cultural features include a well-developed sense of trust in officialdom and a corresponding tendency to defer to those in authority. Britain enjoys widespread reliance on voluntary agreement that may have its roots in a state with a non-codified constitution, coupled with a resilient network of informal control and communication among the elite which "has operated in lieu of formal written rules and statutory powers" (Baggott 1989, 443). Accordingly, the research findings and knowledge that lend an empirical foundation to this paper are partly drawn from socio-legal research in England (e.g., Hawkins 1984) and the United States and from one author's practical experience in self-regulatory enforcement at the national and state levels in the United States.

Self-regulation purports to be the primary instrument for control of Certified Public Accountants.[1] The analysis of regulatory social control is a central part of socio-legal scholarship, and when it is applied to CPA self-regulation, this literature can contribute to understanding the underlying processes by introducing ideas and analytical perspectives that would not otherwise be available to accountants.

This is not to suggest that the accounting literature has no socio-legal character. Indeed, some views of law in action in the social context of CPA self-regulation do indeed appear in the accounting literature (Burns and Haga 1977; Campbell and Parker 1992; Carey 1947; Loeb 1983, 1984; Mautz 1983, 1984; Tidrick 1992; Parker 1994; Ponemon 1992; Thomas 1983; Zeff 1987), but this literature was produced by ethically concerned accountants for other ethically concerned accountants. Fogarty (1996) took a different approach and examined the peer review element of self-regulation using the framework of institutional theory. Nevertheless, while the extant literature borrows heavily from moral philosophy, ethics, political science, and knowledge of enforcement practices, it does not draw direct connections with the broad fields of criminology, law, or socio-legal scholarship in general.

REGULATION AND PROFESSIONAL SELF-REGULATION

Law is an important and ubiquitous presence (Friedman 1977, 2). It cohabits with other normative or law-like systems in society, sometimes overlapping, sometimes conflicting with them. Nonetheless, legal rules are major forces that help organize society in various ways and exert pressure on people to behave in accordance with accepted norms (Schauer 1991, 1–15). People, organizations, and nations order their everyday activities in response to law, often to comply with rules and regulations addressing an immense variety of behaviors, but also from time to time to violate them, either by outright noncompliance, or by avoiding compliance with the apparent spirit or intent of the law.

The concept of regulation is used in a number of ways. The literature of public administration recognizes that governments institute various forms of regulatory control in the public interest. Perhaps the most familiar form of regulation is by way of so-called "command-and-control" techniques (Daintith 1989; Graham 1994). This approach (also known as "direct regulation") eschews economic controls in the form of taxes or subsidies. Instead, the criminal law apparatus of the state is used to enforce public policy. In some cases, however, governments prefer to pursue public aims by essentially private means and adopt forms of "self-regulation." Here we encounter "the delegation of public policy tasks to private actors in an institutionalized form" (Graham 1994, 190).

In socio-legal terminology, "regulation" is a term of multiple meanings. As a *state*, it refers to the existence of a regulatory statute or a legal order promulgated under the authority of a statute. As a *process*, it refers to the functions of an administrative agency and a set of social interactions between the regulators and the regulated (Ogus 1994, 1; Breyer 1982). Socio-legal scholars have so far largely been concerned with matters of process, in particular for understanding the nature and workings of command-and-control regulation, of which we have many examples in modern societies—securities market regulation, food and drug administration, health and safety, pollution control, and more (Wilson 1980). Most types of regulation in the United Kingdom and the United States are forms of direct regulation (i.e., "command-and-control") and are coercive in nature, since failure to comply may lead to the imposition of punishment. The criminal sanction is applied for breaking a rule, violating a standard, or engaging in unlicensed activity.

However, direct regulation by command-and-control methods is becoming increasingly controversial (Baldwin 1997), and other forms of regulatory control find increasing support. One of these is self-regulation, which is often seen as the antithesis of direct regulation. Self-regulation has been defined as "an institutional arrangement whereby an organization regulates the standards of behavior of its members" (Baggott 1989, 436). This self-regulation may enable members to maintain and retain certain standards for their own mutual benefit, to secure public support or approval, or to avoid direct regulation by the state (Baggott 1989, 436). It is found in various forms, the least directive being voluntary self-regulation (Rees 1988, 9–12). Self-regulation tends to be found where cooperation in the implementation of governmental policies is essential, and where those who are regulated have a monopoly of technical expertise. Government itself may well have an interest in saving resources and not assuming a direct regulatory role over certain kinds of occupational groups. Following a careful review of the issues,

Baggott (1989) concluded that self-regulatory systems become ineffective when they are insulated from external pressures and become dominated by private interests.

The formal case for self-regulation was set out in the case of financial regulation by Davison (1987a, 1987b, as quoted by Baggott 1989): it is said to permit more effective regulation because it can enforce the spirit, rather than the letter, of the law; it can be quicker to adapt to problems; and it is cheaper because those who are regulated bear its costs. However, self-regulation, like direct regulation, is also controversial and is a matter that concerns many social policy analysts because it suggests a withdrawal of the direct regulatory role of the state (representing the "public interest"). Hence, questions about public control and accountability inevitably arise. These concerns are all the more acute because of a general suspicion that the control exerted in a self-regulatory system may be minimal, and directed towards protecting the best interests of those subject to control by under-regulation and under-enforcement. Clearly, professions have a strong self-interest in regulating their own activities and avoiding direct regulation by the state, as well as in winning public approval and being in a position to maintain certain standards of behavior of their members for their own benefit (Baggott 1989).

Professional self-regulation in the United States differs from statutory regulation primarily because it arises from what we call private professional law enacted by a profession's board or council (e.g., AICPA Council) and not from an enabling statute enacted by a legislature.[2] On the other hand, statutory regulation and professional self-regulation are similar in form—an administrative body with policies and procedures, personnel assigned to monitor and inspect, and the authority to police improper activity by imposing sanctions.

However, instead of thinking about self-regulation as the antithesis of direct regulation, it may be more helpful to think of a continuum of degrees in the formality of regulatory control, on which informal self-regulation and direct governmental regulation stand at opposing ends (an example is set out by Baggott 1989, 437). A mixed form is often adopted in which the preferred, less formal regulatory arrangements are backed up by more formal powers. In the United States, the National Association of Security Dealers is an example of a formalized professional self-regulatory organization, and it is backed up by the statutory authority of the U.S. securities acts. The government–private interaction is also evident in the U.S. Securities and Exchange Commission's (SEC) reviews of the AICPA Public Oversight Board's peer review supervision (Wallace 1989). Also, most state boards of accountancy conduct ethics enforcement and peer review programs in parallel or in cooperation with state societies of CPAs. In the United Kingdom, self-regulation of financial services takes place within a complex statutory framework (Black 1997).

The ostensible primary mission of both the statutory regulatory agencies and the professional self-regulatory bodies is to obtain compliance with objectives stated or implied in law or in policy. Self-regulatory bodies possess the weapon of sanction—presumably designed to deter violations. Their ability to conduct investigations which may lead to sanctions, such as expulsion from AICPA and state society membership, has an obvious analogy with enforcement of criminal law that leads to the imposition of a penalty. The statutory regulation by the state boards of accountancy operates in similar fashion.

CPA SELF-REGULATION

We employ the term "private professional law" to refer to rules and regulations relating to professional behavior that are not enacted or enforced in a constitutional political and judicial forum. This paper contemplates the "law" enacted by accountants for the purpose of regulating accountants. For CPAs, the body of private professional law includes continuing education requirements, peer review systems, and the rules of conduct. Other professionals work within this type of self-regulatory approach. Examples in the United States include attorneys and their state bar associations, physicians and their medical societies, and brokers and their National Association of Securities Dealers (NASD). Similar self-regulatory systems exist in Britain.

While anchored by definition in the realm of private law, CPA self-regulatory rule-making and enforcement activities are a microcosm of the creation and enforcement of public law. To illustrate: When the American Institute of CPAs (AICPA) enacts private professional law (e.g., education requirements, peer review requirements, rules of conduct), approval must be obtained from the AICPA Board of Directors (executive) and AICPA Council (representative legislature), and then be submitted to the members (citizens) for a vote to approve or reject. The AICPA and the state societies of CPAs conduct monitoring activities similar to statutory regulatory agencies (monitoring continuing education, supervising peer reviews), and they conduct enforcement activities (enforcing the rules of conduct) in the manner of judicial systems. The statutory regulators in the state boards of accountancy conduct similar activities, particularly in terms of requirements for professional qualification, continuing education, peer review programs, and ethics enforcement. Wallace and Campbell (1988) described the early stages of state boards' peer review and positive enforcement programs, which have since become more formalized and widespread.[3]

The similarities of CPA self-regulation and statutory regulation open the door for analysis of private professional law in terms of criteria generally used for analyses of political-legislative law (ordinary legislation). In particular, the structure and operation of CPA self-regulation can be analyzed in comparison to regulatory statutes and criminal law, thus viewing CPA self-regulation more fully in the familiar context of the implementation and enforcement of law.

CPA self-regulation is firmly established in the United States. CPAs have been involved with regulation for more than 100 years, beginning with the first licensing laws. Codes of CPA ethics have existed for more than 70 years. Continuing education requirements spread throughout the AICPA and the states in the 1980s. Practice monitoring (quality review and peer review) began in earnest in 1977 when the AICPA Division for CPA Firms (SEC Practice Section and Private Companies Practice Section) was created. During the 1980s and 1990s, practice monitoring became a major activity in the state boards of accountancy, the state societies, and the AICPA.

CPAs are proud to call accountancy a "self-regulated" profession. However, other people sometimes observe that "self-regulation" is the same as "no regulation." Whether this implied criticism is fair is open to question, and is a matter to be considered. We next explore the nature of CPA self-regulation using concepts of sanctioning and compliance strategies.

ENFORCING REGULATION USING SANCTIONING AND COMPLIANCE STRATEGIES

To think about CPA self-regulation we draw on the socio-legal literature of regulatory enforcement, which so far has been concerned with the activities of statutory regulatory agencies involved in direct command-and-control regulation. Such agencies employ a combination of sanctioning and compliance strategies to enforce regulatory law. *Sanctioning strategy* is a term that refers to a set of enforcement activities designed to punish the breach of a rule. The term *compliance strategy* describes a set of enforcement activities designed by various means—education, persuasion, bargaining, bluffing, threatening (Hawkins 1983, 1984)—to induce the regulated persons and organizations to cooperate with the regulators and to conduct business according to the law.[4]

These two distinctive approaches imply two very different conceptions of law enforcement. The aim of *sanctioning strategy* is to punish a violation with formal prosecution, conviction, and penalty.[5] In contrast, the goal of *compliance strategy* is to seek to attain the aims of the broad legal mandate (e.g., cleaner water, safer workplaces, better quality of professional work and behavior).

Sanctioning Strategy

Sanctioning often has an *instrumental* purpose. It seeks to compel cooperation and to attain desired results by means of the apparatus of prosecution and penalty. These results are attained by exercising the power of deterrence. The social control of formal, legal deterrence is imposed by detecting, prosecuting, convicting, and penalizing violators (Beyleveld 1979). The purpose of deterrence, in the case of CPAs, is to control unprofessional behavior by holding out the threat of punishment. Deterrence has two aspects: (a) *individual deterrence* refers to punishing persons who break the rules so that they are not tempted to engage in further violations, and (b) *general deterrence* refers to punishing certain individuals or groups in an exemplary way to prevent other people, who might be similarly tempted, from engaging in violations.

However, sanctions also may be employed for an essentially *symbolic* purpose and may be used because the regulatory agency or its employees wish to be seen to be endorsing certain values or to display activity or "effectiveness" to an interested public (Edelman 1964). Sanctioning may occur in some cases, for example, where people have a philosophical view that those who break the law should be punished because they deserve it. Examples of instrumental and symbolic regulatory sanctioning are found in studies of tax administration (Long 1979), offshore oil production (Carson 1980, 1982), water pollution (Hawkins 1984), securities trading (Shapiro 1984, 1985), mining operations (Braithwaite 1985; Gunningham 1987), and occupational health and safety (Hawkins 1989). However, this discussion of sanctioning strategy should not obscure the fact that the dominant regulatory enforcement mode is compliance strategy.

Compliance Strategy

Although few detailed ethnographic studies are available that describe American regulatory practice, regulators in the United States appear to approach enforcement by adopting the same broad compliance-seeking strategy as do their U.K. counterparts.[6] These agencies regard their primary objective as the attainment of official goals largely without reliance on sanctioning and without any resort to the formalities of prosecution and court-administered punishment (Hawkins and Thomas 1984; Braithwaite, Walker, and Grabosky 1987; Grabosky and Braithwaite 1986). Their measure of success is the extent to which goals of prevention or repair are achieved, not the number of prosecutions (Galligan 1986, 129; Hawkins 1984). However, emphasis on compliance does not mean that the formal legal process and criminal prosecution are irrelevant. On the contrary, much compliance is achieved through bargaining between the regulators and the regulatees in the context of the background threat of prosecution. That is to say, the prospect of prosecution is suspended on the condition that the rule-breaker acts in cooperative and compliant ways.

Compliance strategy is encouraged by a number of important features. For example, regulatory officers (inspectors) vary in the extent to which they are in regular contact with regulated persons and businesses. In some regulatory arenas, such as the control of nuclear installations in the United Kingdom, they frequently encounter the people they regulate, and they know them extremely well on a personal level. Other regulatory settings, however, have such a large number of sites or potential sources of violation and so few inspectors to monitor and police them, that regulators find little opportunity to develop personal relationships. They enforce the law over a population of strangers. The Agriculture Inspectorate in the British Health and Safety Executive is a good example of a few inspectors regulating a large number of sites. Likewise in CPA regulation, regulators at the AICPA level and those in populous states are less likely to have a personal acquaintance with individual CPAs.

The degree of personal contact can be profoundly important for determining which enforcement strategy to adopt. Usually, the higher the degree of personal contact between the regulators and the regulated, the greater the opportunities for negotiation about the prevention of undesired events or the mitigation of untoward states of affairs, hence reliance upon compliance strategy. A population of strangers, who may be "here today and gone tomorrow," invites a sanctioning response because inspectors only come upon them when something unfortunate has already happened and there is essentially nothing left to negotiate, only an act or omission to punish.

Field officers and administrative officials operating with a compliance strategy also try to achieve technological or behavioral changes (e.g., water treatment, machine safety, CPA firms' technical performance) by negotiation because they are heavily dependent upon those they regulate. Officials need the friendly, albeit possibly grudging, cooperation of the regulated, because they depend upon them for information, for warnings of difficulties, and for their ultimate compliance. Regulated firms likewise depend upon regulatory enforcers for information, free expert advice, and especially for forbearance from enforcing the law to the extent that it could theoretically be enforced. The effect of this mutual dependency (a sort of symbiotic relationship in the enforcement of law) is to create the conditions for effective "contractualisation" of an enforcement relationship, in which the regulated agree to comply (more or less) with official requirements in return for a suspension of formal enforcement proceedings (Hawkins 1984). This approach to enforcement is often regarded by regulators as both more effective and efficient for attaining compliance, because regulators generally view it as a way of maintaining the good will of regulated persons while achieving the ends of the law with minimal expenditure of resources (Hawkins 1984).

Compliance Strategy in CPA Self-Regulation

In their compliance strategy, CPAs have professional licensing, continuing professional education, and practice monitoring. The first compliance feature is the state boards' process of screening and approving persons who apply to take the Uniform CPA Examination to ensure certain standards of character and education. The second is the requirement, common in other professions, to maintain the certificate and license by engaging in continuing professional education (CPE) to ensure maintenance of high standards of expertise. These two features of CPA self-regulation (albeit conducted through statutory state boards) are usually taken for granted as prerequisites for being a CPA, thereby making persons subject to

Table 1. Peer Review of Large CPA Firms

	Review Performed By				
	1994–96	*1992–93*	*1989–91*	*1986–88*	*1980–85*
Reviewed CPA Firms:					
Arthur Andersen & Co. (AA)	D&T	D&T	DHS	DHS	DHS
Ernst & Whinney (E&W)*	merge	merge	KPMG	KPMG	KPMG
Arthur Young & Co. (AY)*	merge	merge	PW	PW	PW
Ernst & Young (E&Y)*	KPMG	KPMG	-na-	-na-	-na-
BDO Seidman (BDO)	E&Y	E&Y	E&Y	AY	AY
Coopers & Lybrand (C&L)	E&Y	E&Y	E&Y	AY	AY
Deloitte,Haskins & Sells (DHS)**	merge	merge	merge	E&W	E&W
Touche Ross & Co. (TR)**	merge	merge	merge	PW	PW
Deloitte & Touche (D&T)**	E&Y	E&Y	E&Y	-na-	-na-
Grant Thornton (GT)	BDO	E&Y	E&Y	AY	AY
KPMG Peat Marwick (KPMG)	PW	PW	PW	AY	AY
Price Waterhouse	D&T	D&T	D&T	DHS	MainH***

Notes: *Ernst & Whinney and Arthur Young & Co. merged in October 1989, forming the firm of Ernst & Young.

**Deloitte, Haskins & Sells and Touche Ross & Co. merged in December 1989, forming the firm of Deloitte & Touche.

***MainH = Main Hurdman (later merged into KPMG).

the private professional self-regulatory activities. The third compliance feature is the peer review practice monitoring required by the state boards of accountancy and by the AICPA through its Division for CPA Firms. This peer review activity is similar in many respects to a regulatory inspection by independent officers. The largest CPA firms in the SEC Practice Section audit an overwhelming majority of U.S. public companies (approximately 95%). They choose their own reviewers from the other large firms, as shown in Table 1. These data show that Ernst & Young reviewed four of the largest eight firms (until Grant Thornton switched to BDO Seidman in 1995), Deloitte & Touche reviewed two, and Price Waterhouse and KPMG Peat Marwick reviewed one each (joined by BDO Seidman with its review of Grant Thornton in 1995). These long-term associations enable reviewers to get to know the reviewed firms well. Earlier, we noted that close relationships of this type might foster an unnecessarily tolerant approach to regulation.

The AICPA Peer Review Board standards (AICPA 1989) guide the peer review process. Reviewers have only the authority to report their findings concerning the reviewed firms' attestation services (not tax or management consulting services). While they may give consulting advice to a firm under review, they have no authority to negotiate change, in contrast to the authority vested in the AICPA peer review committees and in the state boards. However, most peer review reports contain comments on problems along with the reviewed firms' responses regarding efforts to cure them, and thus comply with quality control standards. Critics might say that the self-selection of reviewers and the continuing engagements are too cozy a relationship, since among these largest CPA firms, the possibility of implicit bargaining arises (i.e., "Let's not go too hard on each other.").

Compliance strategy is evident in the consulting/advising interchange between reviewed firms and reviewers during the peer review work. This interchange offers opportunities for bargaining at the field level. Reliance on bargaining—a central feature of compliance strategy—is endemic in law enforcement. It may exist, for instance, in the form of trading information for leniency or in pleading guilty to fewer or lesser charges to hasten the judicial process and secure lesser penalties (Heumann 1978; Feeley 1979). When they are informed of deficient practices, reviewed CPAs almost always promise to take corrective action. These responses are included in the reviewed firm's letter that accompanies the reviewer's comment letter (Wallace and Cravens 1994). Fairly significant practice shortcomings can be seen in these reviewers' comment letters submitted with the formal report (Wallace 1991, 64). Yet, the largest firms' formal reports have always been unqualified (good news).

No one other than reviewers and reviewed firms knows whether bargaining actually occurs. Indeed, it is not even necessary for any kind of bargain to be struck, merely that the players feel a sense for the conditions of mutual reciprocity (Gouldner 1960). Wallace and Cravens (1994) studied the 1980–1986 peer review files of CPA firms smaller than the largest 15 and noted that the SECPS peer review committee had required reviewed CPA firms to take particular remedial actions even though the firms received an unqualified ("good news") peer review report. They speculated that this type of resolution by the committee was a sort of compromise among the parties (reviewed firm, reviewers, and SECPS peer review committee) to achieve remedial action without the issuance of a ("bad news") qualified report (1994, 4). This form of compromise can be interpreted as the manifestation of bargaining in which the notice of deficiencies resides in the comment letter while the peer review report itself is unqualified.

However, in another analysis based on the 1980–1986 files, concentrating on 55 peer review reports containing commentary on independence-related deficiencies, Wallace (1988, 11, 13) offered data suggesting that the frequency of reviewers' independence and audit performance deficiency findings precluded a conclusion that "back-scratching" among reviewed firms and reviewers actually occurred.

In still another study using the 1980–1986 SECPS peer review files, Wallace (1991) analyzed the deficiency findings in peer review commentary letters. She acknowledged that nobody knows the normative benchmark for a number of deficiencies that "should be" reported (1991, 61), but she concluded that the peer review process appeared to be reasonably reliable (1991, 64). One reason for this conclusion (particularly apropos for the present analysis) was that the frequency of reviewers' deficiency findings was inconsistent with the contention that (1) reviewees' self-selection (for enrollment in the then-voluntary peer review program) would predetermine good results, or (2) reviewers would not report deficiency findings.

However, from our socio-legal regulation point of view, the important issue regarding bargaining and "back-scratching" is the number, type, and severity of the *unreported* review comments about deficiencies. Further research is needed to associate the reliability of peer review with other indicators of the quality of CPAs' accounting and auditing practices. These other indicators may include business press analyses and lawsuits or Securities and Exchange Commission actions alleging deficient audit performance or, on the positive side, reports of auditors performing well when companies disclose filing delays for the purpose of correcting their financial reports according to their auditors' requirements.

After the peer review field work is completed and the reviewer's report and comment letter are prepared, the AICPA practice sections' peer review committees examine the work. These peer review committees are volunteer CPAs, people who are supposed to have an unbiased interest in the practice monitoring process and who acknowledge its importance for the profession as a whole. The field reviewers might demonstrate a forgiving attitude of "there but for grace, go I," but the AICPA Division for CPA Firms and the public expect peer review committee members to have a more critical disposition. They are expected to notice the discretion a reviewer may have exercised in deciding to omit deficiency findings from the comment letter or to put practice quality deficiencies in a comment letter instead of giving a qualified or adverse report. These section committees possess the authority to require a reviewed firm to take corrective actions based on the results of a peer review. Indeed, the SECPS peer review committee has acted in this manner by requiring corrective action by firms that have received unqualified reports, apparently noticing the severity of deficiency findings in the comment letters (Wallace and Cravens 1994). If the reviewed firm fails to take corrective action, the firm can be sanctioned by being expelled from membership in the AICPA practice sections. If a firm refuses to take the corrective action required by a state board of accountancy in connection with peer review, the state boards can refuse to renew the firm's license to practice.

Sanctioning Strategy in CPA Self-Regulation

The peer review process can show some teeth which align it with a sanctioning strategy. From its work on approximately 3,500 peer reviews in the period 1979–1997, the SECPS peer review committee took sanctioning-type actions by requiring accounting firms: to have accelerated reviews taking place sooner than the normal three-year cycle (52 times), to employ consultants for pre-issuance reviews of financial statements or other procedures (84 times), to have revisits by peer reviewers for the purpose of ascertaining progress in implementing corrective actions (202 times), to have additional reviews of firms' internal inspection programs (341 times), to have additional reviews of firms' changes in control documents, manuals, and checklists (43 times), and to attend CPE in specified areas (47 times) (POB annual report 1996–1997).

In addition, acting through its Quality Control Inquiry Committee (QCIC), the SECPS can take other sanctioning-like actions.[7] After reviewing approximately 700 cases of litigation reported during the period 1979–1997, the QCIC required special reviews, expanded peer reviews, or specific corrective actions 185 times; and in 29 instances referred specific individuals' work to the AICPA Professional Ethics Division for disciplinary investigations (POB Annual Report 1996–97).

Sanctioning strategy may best be observed in the processes of enforcing (investigating and adjudicating) violations of the AICPA, state society, and state board rules of conduct. CPAs' codes of conduct exist to provide social control and give public notice of a commitment to compliance. The codes publicize CPAs' notification and enforcement of "right conduct" (Friedman 1977, 11). The rules of conduct and the accompanying enforcement mechanisms provide the basis for sanctioning strategy in CPA self-regulation.

CPAs often speak of regulatory enforcement activities in sociological terms as being either *proactive* or *reactive*. *Proactive* enforcement requires action that anticipates problems or violations, or otherwise prevents them by seeking out risks or potential difficulties and working on them to forestall the occurrence of something serious. *Reactive* enforcement occurs when an external information source provides notice of some problem or event which may trigger the enforcement process.

A proactive mode of regulatory enforcement requires an organized and active policing apparatus to search for rule violations and rule violators (as when traffic police use radar traps to catch speeding drivers). However, CPAs have no "accounting police force" in the self-regulation arena. A reactive mode of enforcement tends to be associated with sanctioning strategy in which action may be taken only after someone, usually someone external to the system, makes a report or complaint (as when a vehicle owner phones the police to report that a car has been stolen). CPAs' sanctioning strategy predominantly operates in a reactive mode. A possible proactive exception may be said to exist in the QCIC practice of occasionally referring possible violations to the AICPA Professional Ethics Division for consideration.

CPAS' SANCTIONING PROCESS

Space permits only a brief overview of two features of the CPA self-regulation sanctioning process. The following sections analyze (1) the enforcement system design, and (2) the types of sanctions. Criteria for evaluating law enforcement are used as a framework because of the similarities of private professional "law enforcement" and public law enforcement.

Enforcement System Design and Capacity

Effective law enforcement depends on having enough resources (system capacity) to achieve the goal of distributing justice equitably among citizens. Enforcement capacity, however, is a scarce resource. In general, institutions do not have enough to go around—not enough police officers to enforce the law, not enough officials to handle and process cases, not enough courts to resolve disputes, not enough prisons to hold convicted offenders, rarely enough regulatory officials, and so on. These limitations compel people working in the system to adapt in various ways. Sometimes new institutions are invented, such as the various forms of so-called "alternative dispute resolution" mechanisms devised during the last 20 or 30 years in the United Kingdom and United States (Marks, et al. 1984; Menkel-Meadow 1993). And, like it or not, the institutions and personnel of law also impose their own form of rationing so that cases can be diverted or cleared quickly. Police officers and other law enforcers exercise discretion not to invoke the formal criminal justice process in certain circumstances by turning a "blind eye" to certain sorts of offenses or offenders (Black 1980; Hawkins 1984). The bargaining that prosecutors and defenders conduct over charges and sentences is aimed at achieving a guilty plea and avoiding the cost, uncertainty, time, and trouble of going to full-blown criminal trial (Heumann 1978). The same feature is found in the civil legal process where, for example, the great majority of personal injury cases are settled out of court (Ross 1970; Harris, Maclean, Genn, Lloyd-Bostock, Corfield, and Brittan 1984; Genn 1987).

These are all informal ways of adjusting the capacity of the legal system to the demands placed upon it. The process of enforcing private professional rules of conduct can be effective in conducting investigations and finding violations only if the enforcement system can handle the load. The data in Table 2 show resources committed to regulatory activities by the AICPA, a state society (the Texas State Society of CPAs (TSCPA) is our example), and a state board of accountancy (for example, the Texas State Board of Public Accountancy (TSBPA)).

As shown in Table 2, the private professional organizations (AICPA and TSCPA) allocate far more resources of people and money to the peer review process of practice monitoring (compliance strategy) than to enforcing the rules of conduct (sanctioning strategy). Many more practice units are subject to peer review than there are complaints of rules violations. The question of whether sufficient resources are devoted to either function is a matter for debate.[8] The TSBPA, in contrast, allocates more resources to enforcement than to peer review. State boards are chronically underfunded, and they delegate practice peer review to the private professional organizations. They cannot delegate their enforcement activities to others.

Table 2. Selected CPA Regulation and Self-Regulation Resources

	Practice Monitoring			Ethics Enforcement		
	AICPA	*TSCPA*	*TSBPA*	*AICPA*	*TSCPA*	*TSBPA*
Personnel Resources:						
Staff	42	10	7	17	1	29
Volunteers	119	24	5	61	47	12
Private Companies Practice Section	4 (staff)					
SEC Practice Section	5 (staff)					
Public Oversight Board	11 (staff)					
Monetary Resources (000):						
Budget/expenditures	$5,325	$ 84	$ 70	$1,876	$ 48	$ 590
Private Companies Practice Section	$1,277					
SEC Practice Section	$ 434					
Public Oversight Board	$1,604					
Organizational Size:						
AICPA: 328,000 members. Total expenditures in FYE 1996				= $107 million		
TSCPA: 31,500 members. Total budget for 1995-96				= $ 4 million		
TSBPA: 60,000 licensees. Total expenditures in FYE 1995				= $ 3 million		

Notes and Sources: Personnel numbers and dollar amounts are approximate.
Budget and expenditure figures exclude continuing professional education expenditures for the AICPA and TSCPA.
American Institute of CPAs (AICPA) Annual Report 1994, 1995, 1996.
Texas Society of CPAs (TSCPA) Budget Information 1995-1996.
Texas State Board of Public Accountancy (TSBPA) Annual Report 1995.

In terms of the enforcement workload, case statistics reveal the infrequency of complaints made against CPAs relative to the total CPA population. The AICPA had 328,000 members in 1996, opened 344 investigations, and completed 186 cases with violations cited. The TSCPA had 31,500 members in 1996, opened 46 investigations, and completed 39 cases with violations cited. The TSBPA had 60,000 license-holders in 1995, opened 1,846 investigations (excluding 2,875 CPE and fee-payment cases), and completed 440 cases with violations cited.

The AICPA and the TSCPA have genuine resource limitations, both in terms of money and in staff and volunteer time. Uncomplicated complaints take 18 to 20 months from receipt of the complaint to final disposition. Cases that go to the AICPA Trial Board often take 36 to 44 months because of the care the AICPA takes to document and implement its due process procedures.[9] By comparison, the Texas State Board of Public Accountancy reports an average clearance time of five to 13 months.

In connection with members' voting on rule changes in the AICPA rules of conduct, neither the ability nor the capacity of enforcement resources has ever been mentioned in ballot information given to members (AICPA). CPAs appear to add rules, interpretations, and informal rulings with the implicit assumption that the existing enforcement bodies will be able to handle the workload. Hence, no concern is expressed about overloading the system. CPAs are expected to be "principled compliers"—people who voluntarily comply with rules as a matter of principle (Hawkins 1984; Kagan and Scholz 1984). However, the distinction between *instrumental compliance* (complying with rules to avoid penalties) and *normative compliance* (complying because it is the right thing to do) is important. Any assumptions about or evidence of the reason for compliance have the potential to influence enforcement resource allocations and enforcers' operational philosophies.

We hypothesize that the present state of CPAs' self-regulation is based on CPAs' assumption that normative compliance is in effect. The evidence is (1) the preponderance of AICPA and state society resources devoted to peer review where the goal is to advise and educate CPAs on ways and means of improving the quality of their practices, (2) the reactive mode of discovering violations by awaiting complaints, and (3) the general absence of an active "CPA police" devoted to discovery of violations (although State Boards in Florida, Missouri, and Texas use practitioners and consultants to sample and monitor CPAs' work products and otherwise be alert to report violations of practice standards—these being apparently the exception rather than the rule). These three features suggest that CPAs are willing to help each other with advice in a peer review but not to resort very much to active measures to discover violations. If CPA enforcers thought that noncompliance were widespread, perhaps they would change enforcement to be more proactive.

Whether the aversion to sanctions is self-serving or an accurate view of practice quality incentives is a matter for debate. The preface of an AICPA SEC Practice Section quality control (QC) survey report observed: "Member self-assessments are important because if members themselves do not believe QC works, it is unreasonable to expect the public to do so."[10] This assertion is questionable. That CPAs think self-regulation QC "works" is no guarantee the "public" thinks so as well. On the other hand, if sanctioning were the strategy with attendant imposition of stiff penalties, CPAs might think it "does not work" but the "public" might be quite satisfied.

CPAs apparently consider enforcement capacity to be adequate, mainly because CPAs in charge of the process seem willing to tolerate the fact that cases take months and years for closure. CPAs under investigation have little opportunity to speed the disciplinary process. They are caught in the web of due process (requests for responses to questions and production of documents) and hostage to the timing of AICPA and state society committee meeting schedules. They may even have little interest in speeding up the process because: (1) The proceedings are not public and nobody else knows about investigations in process, so no public reputational damage is done, (2) time offers opportunity to make remedial efforts that can be offered to deflect onerous penalties, and (3) serious penalties that become public knowledge can be delayed.

Types of Sanctions

After investigating a complaint, the AICPA, state societies, and state boards will find a CPA in violation or not in violation. Letters advising CPAs of investigation conclusions typically state: "The Professional Ethics Committee found evidence of prima facie violation of Rule X of the Code of Professional Conduct." The resulting sanction is a penalty the enforcers intend the CPA to find distasteful, uncomfortable, and embarrassing. Members of the enforcement committees believe they impose penalties that match the seriousness of the violations. The penalties range from requiring the CPA to take specified continuing education courses by a certain future date, suspension of membership in the AICPA and state society, and expulsion from membership. When the lesser penalties (e.g., required CPE courses) are imposed, neither the name of the CPA nor the penalty are made public. All the proceedings, including the imposition of the sanction, are confidential, thereby preventing any general deterrent effect.[11]

The greater penalties involving membership rights (suspension and expulsion) can be decided only by the Joint Trial Board or by an AICPA settlement proceeding that can impose equivalent penalties with the consent of the accused CPA. When suspension or expulsion is levied, the CPA's name and a brief description of the offense are published in an AICPA monthly newsletter (*The CPA Letter*). The Joint Trial Board has no discretion to decide not to publish the name and the suspension or expulsion penalty. However, this publicity is sent only to CPAs, and the U.S. general business newspapers and magazines rarely pick up this news for wider dissemination.

None of the AICPA or state society penalties affect a CPA's right to practice. They cannot suspend or revoke the license to practice, which is granted by a state board of accountancy. The state boards are the agencies whose sanctions can end a CPA's career. In most states, the licensing agency can limit a CPA's practice (e.g., forbidding performance of government audits when the case involved them), put a CPA on probation, suspend the legal license to practice, and revoke the license. The state boards can act on such violations as gross discreditable conduct (e.g., conviction on felony bribery, fraud, tax evasion charges), malpractice in audits, and malpractice in taxation services and consulting services. Suspension and revocation are sanctions of selective incapacitation—removing the offending CPA from practice temporarily or permanently. In Texas, the TSBPA publishes the names and a few particulars about the case in a state board newsletter which is sent to all license holders. Like the AICPA and state society public notifications, this news has limited distribution. However, the information is a matter of public record, and people can inquire about a particular CPA.

CPAs almost never receive the extreme penalties of membership suspension or expulsion, or license suspension or revocation for bad business practices like misleading advertising, aggressive solicitation, or rudeness (Tidrick 1992). Lesser penalties (e.g., reprimand and continuing education courses) are imposed because the enforcers probably view these offenses as less serious. Also, the AICPA and state societies may give lesser penalties so the CPA will remain a member and thus continue to be subject to their enforcement jurisdictions. The private professional organizations have no power to impose fines, although the TSBPA and other state boards can and do assess monetary costs and contributions in some cases.

Whether individual deterrence works well is a matter open to question and interpretation. Interviews with long-time members of the TSCPA enforcement committee elicited the recollection of five or six repeat offenders during the past 12 years—not many, but the TSCPA completes relatively few cases each year. On the other hand, Thomas and Seaman (1996, 257) found that of 404 CPAs disciplined by the TSBPA for violations of the rules of conduct in the period 1985–1991, 215 (53%) were repeat offenders. These TSBPA statistics do not speak well for the effectiveness of individual deterrence.

Whether general deterrence works, however, is more difficult to establish because lesser penalties conveyed in a Letter of Required Corrective Action (LRCA) are private and not known to the public or other CPAs. Enforcement committee members are enjoined by a confidentiality pledge not to "leak" information. Only the serious penalties involving membership suspension and expulsion are publicized in the AICPA's *CPA Letter* newsletter to members. (A broader range of penalties may be publicized by the state boards of accountancy in their newsletters.) To the extent that general deterrence works, it resides primarily in the fact that CPAs presumably know about the serious penalties and know that they are usually imposed in cases of technical malpractice.[12] Most CPAs know very little about the lesser penalties that can be imposed in an LRCA.

This situation suggests that serious violations (e.g., technical malpractice) might be generally deterred more effectively than the little-known minor violations. If so, observers might expect to see more behavioral penalties (related to violations of lesser rules concerning advertising, commissions, form of practice, and the like) than technical malpractice penalties. However, data presented by Thomas and Seaman (1996, 253–254) on the incidence of disciplinary action taken by the Texas State Board of Public Accountancy in the 1985–1991 period do not confirm this expectation. They found that of 805 violations for which TSBPA meted out punishment, 480 (60%) were related to the technical competence rules; and these violations were committed by 205 (51%) of the 404 CPAs involved in the cases they studied. Hence, insofar as TSBPA cases that were completed with actual punishment (thus excluding numerous technical and behavioral complaints that TSBPA dismissed in the disciplinary process), the more serious technical malpractice violations dominated the lesser behavioral violations.

SUMMARY AND CONCLUSIONS

CPA self-regulation reflects a mix of various socio-legal processes. The CPA self-regulation system is a complex process, operating at several levels and through several institutional agencies. No one should be surprised that it has never been comprehensively analyzed as a whole organism, though to be fair, not many analyses cover the criminal justice system and other regulatory systems in a holistic perspective either. The CPA system operates both with law (written rules) and with discretion (policies and case-by-case professional judgment). It has features both of compliance strategy (proactive encouragement towards compliance and commitment to remedy and repair) and sanctioning strategy (reactive enforcement and punishment).

At the beginning of this paper, we posited that effective CPA self-regulation depends on three features: (1) designing an effective system, (2) establishing the system in institutions and processes and providing sufficient resources, and (3) operating the system to the satisfaction of both the regulated persons and outside observers. We applied various elements of socio-legal theory and observations of practice to describe and analyze important elements of CPA self-regulation. Based thereon, we offer the following tentative conclusions.

CPA self-regulation is designed and established to operate with a combination of compliance strategy (peer review) and sanctioning strategy (enforcement of rules of conduct and occasional AICPA Quality Control Inquiry Committee intervention). The peer review process is multi-layered: CPA firms and review teams perform field reviews, the AICPA Division for CPA Firms peer review committee reviews the field reviews, the Public Oversight Board monitors the field work products and committee reviews, and the U.S. Securities and Exchange Commission reviews the POB work. The state societies of CPAs and the state boards of accountancy also conduct peer review programs with similar elements. Enforcement of various national and state rules of conduct resides in AICPA, state society, and state board enforcement committees. The QCIC can refer individuals' work for investigation of suspected rule of conduct violations.

This structure for self-regulation appears to be designed to accomplish remedial monitoring and disciplinary activity. Thus, the sharp issue is whether it actually operates satisfactorily—recognizing that the criterion of "operating satisfactorily" is as elusive in CPA self-regulation as it is in statutory regulation and law enforcement. CPAs appear to assume that the existing process works reasonably well. They have not felt the need to devote resources to the task of inventing a radically different one modeled along the lines of the statutory regulatory agencies or other agencies like the National Transportation Safety Board (as proposed by Wallace 1994). CPAs in the United States and Chartered Accountants in the United Kingdom generally regard statutory (government) regulation as a threat to professional autonomy (Parker 1994, 511).

Lacking a reliable benchmark for "satisfactory" self-regulation outcomes, we can only point to certain characteristics of system inputs. In this regard, we believe our socio-legal analysis enables us to express five major findings:

- *Evidence of institutionalized tolerance.* Peer reviewers in the field show some tendencies to require many very significant deficiency findings before giving qualified or adverse peer review reports, meanwhile relegating deficiencies to comment letters.
- *Indications of unjustifiably unqualified peer review reports.* Peer review committees sometimes require corrective action (based on information in comment letters) even when CPA firms receive unqualified peer review reports.
- *Insufficient enforcement resources.* Enforcement committees are underfunded[13] and rely heavily on otherwise busy volunteers, and their enforcement actions take a long time.
- *Insufficient sanctioning power.* Sanctions for violation of AICPA and state society rules of conduct are limited by their lack of variety and their lack of punishing effect.
- *Excessive Privacy.* The public and CPAs have access to little public information about penalties related to violations (because many State Society and AICPA disciplinary requirements are not reported), thus hindering effective deterrence.

Of course, each of these five identify areas for further empirical research.

Suggestions for change may be aligned with the forgoing five observations: (1) Provide for participation in peer reviews by knowledgeable non-CPAs or CPAs not in public practice, (2) develop more precise guides for the judgmental choices of unqualified, qualified, and adverse peer review reports, (3) devote more resources (money and full-time staff employees) to enforcement, and set quicker deadlines for dealing with enforcement investigations and resolutions, (4) develop an array of sanctions (perhaps in cooperation with state boards of accountancy) to impose more onerous penalties on errant CPAs, and (5) publish information designed for CPAs, general newspapers, and periodicals about the facts, circumstances, and outcomes of all enforcement sanctions (not just the ones that reach the AICPA Trial Board stage).

Each of these suggestions involves *input* for the self-regulation process. However, the most important facet is the *output*. The question of whether self-regulation output is satisfactorily effective might best be settled by research on CPAs' actual performance quality and especially on the cost to clients and external users resulting from malpractice. Even so, such research may be difficult because (1) the basic data presently available on actual performance quality resides in the peer review reports and comment letters, which may or may not be entirely objective; and (2) the available public information on injury (i.e., malpractice lawsuits and

Trial Board enforcement decisions) does not take into account the opportunity cost residing in unknown audit deficiencies (e.g., superficial audits with standard unqualified reports—apparently in conformity with auditing standards—that fail to find errors or frauds that no one yet knows about). So long as we lack this kind of research evidence on self-regulation outputs, we can only consider inputs.

This analysis and the tentative conclusions suggest that CPA self-regulation partially satisfies our three criteria. The socio-legal analytical perspective enabled us to show some little-acknowledged deficiencies in the ways CPAs conduct their self-regulation, and we believe that CPA self-regulation can benefit from the sorts of changes we suggest.

ACKNOWLEDGMENTS

The authors gratefully acknowledge the helpful comments and observations offered on earlier drafts by Matthew Weait of Birkbeck College, London, and Paul B.W. Miller of the University of Colorado at Colorado Springs.

NOTES

1. We have adopted the following definitions of professional self-regulation, statutory regulation, and law enforcement: "professional self-regulation" refers to regulation that is not rooted in constitutional government; "statutory regulation" refers to the more familiar view of command-and-control regulation by government agencies (e.g., EPA, OSHA); and we reserve the term "law enforcement" for the work of the police and courts in enforcing the traditional code of criminal behavior.

2. The relationship between public and private forms of law and regulation is an important topic about which relatively little is known, but see Smith (1994).

3. On the basis of a comparison of the State Board of Illinois (then a passive complaint-oriented program) with the State Board of Florida (a positive enforcement program), Wallace and Campbell (1988, 145–146) tentatively concluded that a peer review program (Florida) appeared to improve the quality of accountants' services. The contrast was to an enforcement program that dealt ex post with fraud and ethical problems that led to revocation of the CPA designation (Illinois).

4. This is in fact an oversimplified version of reality, since compliance exists in many different forms, including a form of "compliance for now," wherein a regulated person makes a statement of good intentions that regulators treat as bona fide and regard as "compliance" for all practical purposes, even though the violation continues for the time being (Hawkins 1984).

5. We use the term "sanctioning" throughout this paper to indicate an approach to enforcement whose purpose is to punish, without reference to the particular purpose of the punishment. Thus, the term is neutral and deliberately does not presuppose the goal or intended consequences of the application of punishment, as use of the term "deterrence" would imply. Reiss (1984) used the terms "compliance" and "deterrence" in speaking of social control *systems*, whereas our concern is primarily with enforcement *strategies*. Regulatory systems of control may not necessarily be deterrent in intent (though they may well be in certain circumstances). For instance, during the period of the research fieldwork in England for *Environment and Enforcement* (Hawkins 1984), the maximum fine for pollution violation convictions in the English Magistrates' Court was £100. Parliament could hardly have seen this small sanction as any kind of deterrent for all but the poorest industrialists and farmers.

Whether it had any deterrent effect in practice or even in legislative intent is questionable. (The corresponding maximum fine in 1997 was £20,000, which may serve to be a greater deterrent.)

6. However, a number of studies by political scientists (Vogel 1986; Kelman 1981) make general claims about regulatory styles and assert that U.S. regulatory enforcement is marked by a more legalistic and punitive approach than other countries'.

7. CPA firms in the SEC Practice Section are required to submit documents concerning litigation against them charging malpractice to the SECPS's Quality Control Inquiry Committee (QCIC). The QCIC reviews documents for evidence of systematic quality control failure but does not try to decide the merits of cases.

8. The State Bar of Texas spends about $5.9 million each year on enforcement of its rules of professional conduct and procedure, utilizing approximately 100 staff and 800 volunteers. The bar association has an active membership of 57,000 and a total annual budget of approximately $13.9 million (excluding continuing legal education expenditures).

9. In 1993, the AICPA enacted a significant change in its case handling procedure. CPAs can now reach a settlement agreement with the AICPA Ethics Division and avoid the lengthy process of taking a case to the Joint Trial Board. The CPA can (1) admit the allegations in a complaint, or (2) neither admit nor deny the allegations, and accept the remedial, corrective, or disciplinary action recommended by the Ethics Division. The intent of the settlement agreement option is to ease the workload of the Ethics Division and the Trial Board in the light of resource and time constraints.

10. A survey of members of the AICPA SEC Practice Section (SECPS) was conducted to elicit self-assessment of the quality control (QC) self-regulation system (Felix and Prawitt 1993). Members responded that QC programs are: vital to the profession's reputation, effective in maintaining audit quality, and expensive but worth the cost. The members also expressed the opinion that "SECPS membership requirements and QC are more effective than sanctions in reducing the risk of audit failure." Indeed, TSCPA practice monitoring officers have explicitly disavowed intentions to report violations discovered in practice reviews, stating their belief that CPAs might resign their membership or quit their accounting and audit practices (retaining taxation and consulting practices which are not subject to review) to try to avoid reviews if they thought reviewers would report violations of technical standards. (However, we note that Statement on Auditing Standards No. 46 "Consideration of Omitted Procedures After the Report Date" deals with ways and means of revisiting audits in which peer reviewers find signs of deficient technical work, but nothing in SAS 46 requires a referral to the self-regulatory discipline process.)

11. This is a very general description of AICPA and state society operating procedures. Various state societies and boards of accountancy may have different procedures. For example, the Texas State Board of Public Accountancy publishes the name and the penalty of all CPAs who are found to have violated the rules of conduct.

12. However, Weait (1995) found in a study of financial regulation in the City of London that lack of knowledge about regulation was a major reason for noncompliance, thus suggesting that an enforcement response based on general deterrence was inappropriate.

13. The membership size and the annual ethics enforcement budget/expenditure data in Table 2 show that the private self-regulatory organizations (TSCPA and AICPA) spend the least on enforcement that can lead to sanctions ($1.50 and $5.70 per member respectively), while the TSBPA spends almost $10 per licensee, and the State Bar of Texas spends slightly more than $100 per lawyer (see footnote 8).

REFERENCES

American Institute of Certified Public Accountants (AICPA). 1989. *Standards for performing and reporting on quality reviews*. New York: AICPA.

American Institute of Certified Public Accountants (AICPA). 1998. CPA Vision—2011 and beyond: Focus on the horizon. *Journal of Accountancy* (December): 1–48.

Baggott, R. 1989. Regulatory reform in Britain: The changing face of self-regulation. *Public Administration* 67: 435–54.

Baldwin, R. 1997 Regulation: After "command and control." In *The Human Face of Law: Essays in Honour of Donald Harris*, ed. K.O. Hawkins, 65–84. Oxford: Clarendon Press.

Beyleveld, D. 1979. Deterrence research as a basis for deterrent policies. *Howard Journal* 18: 135–49.

Black, D.J. 1980. *The Manners and Customs of the Police*. New York: Academic Press.

Black, J. 1997. *Rules and Regulators*. Oxford: Clarendon Press.

Braithwaite, J. 1985. *To Punish or Persuade: Enforcement of Coal Mine Safety*. Albany: SUNY Press.

Braithwaite, J., J. Walker, and P. Grabosky. 1987. An enforcement taxonomy of regulatory agencies. *Law and Policy* 9: 323–351.

Breyer, S. 1982. *Regulation and Its Reform*. Cambridge: Harvard University Press.

Burns, D.C., and W.J. Haga. 1977. Much ado about professionalism: a second look at accounting. *The Accounting Review* (July): 705–715.

Campbell, D.R., and L.M. Parker. 1992. SEC communications to the independent auditors: An analysis of enforcement actions. *Journal of Accounting and Public Policy* (Winter): 297–330.

Carey, J.L. 1947. The realities of professional ethics. *The Accounting Review* (April): 119–123.

Carson, W.G. 1982. *The Other Price of Britain's Oil*. Oxford: Martin Robertson.

Carson, W.G. 1980. The other price of Britain's oil: Regulating safety on offshore oil installations in the British sector of the North Sea. *Contemporary Crises* 4: 239–266.

Daintith, T. 1989. A regulatory space agency? *Oxford Journal Of Legal Studies* 9: 534.

Edelman, M. 1964. *The Symbolic Uses of Politics*. Urbana, IL: University of Illinois Press.

Feeley, M. 1979. *The Process is the Punishment: Handling Cases in a Lower Criminal Court*. New York: Russell Sage Foundation.

Felix, W.L., and D.F. Prawitt. 1993. Special report: Self-regulation—an assessment by SECPS members (AICPA monograph) *Journal of Accountancy* (July): 20–21.

Fogarty, T.J. 1996. The imagery and reality of peer review in the U.S.: Insights from institutional theory. *Accounting, Organizations and Society*. 21(2/3): 243–267.

Friedman, L.M. 1977. *Law and Society: An Introduction*. Englewood Cliffs, NJ: Prentice-Hall, Inc.

Galligan, D.J. 1986. *Discretionary Powers: A Legal Study of Official Discretion*. Oxford: Clarendon Press.

Genn, H. 1987. *Hard Bargaining: Out of Court Settlement in Personal Injury Actions*. Oxford: Clarendon Press.

Gouldner, A. 1960. The norm of reciprocity: A preliminary statement. *American Sociological Review* 25: 161–178.

Grabosky, P., and J. Braithwaite. 1986. *Of Manners Gentle: Enforcement Strategies of Australian Business Regulatory Agencies*. Melbourne: Oxford University Press.

Graham, C. 1994. Self-regulation. In *Administrative Law and Government Action*, eds. G. Richardson and H. Genn. Oxford: Clarendon Press.

Gunningham, N. 1987. Negotiated noncompliance: A case study of regulatory failure. *Law and Policy* 9: 69–97.

Harris, D.R., M. Maclean, H. Genn, S. Lloyd-Bostock, P. Corfield, and Y. Brittan. 1984. *Compensation and Support for Illness and Injury*. Oxford: Clarendon Press.

Hawkins, K. 1983. Bargain and bluff: Compliance strategy and deterrence in the enforcement of regulation. *Law and Policy Quarterly*. 5: 35–73.

Hawkins, K. 1984. *Environment and Enforcement: Regulation and the Social Definition of Pollution*. Oxford: Clarendon Press.

Hawkins, K. 1989. FATCATS and prosecution in a regulatory agency: A footnote on the social construction of risk. *Law and Policy* (July): 370–391.

Hawkins, K., and J.M. Thomas, eds. 1984. *Enforcing Regulation*. Boston: Kluwer-Nijhoff.

Heumann, M. 1978. *Plea Bargaining: The Experiences of Prosecutors, Judges, and Defense Attorneys*. Chicago: University of Chicago Press.

Kagan, R.A., and J.T. Scholz. 1984. The criminology of the corporation and regulatory enforcement strategies. In *Enforcing Regulation*, eds. K. Hawkins and J.M. Thomas, 67–95. Boston: Kluwer-Nijhoff.

Kelman, S. 1981. *Regulating America, Regulating Sweden: A Comparative Study of Occupational Safety and Health Policy*. Cambridge, MA: MIT Press.

Lipson, L., and S. Wheeler, eds. 1986. *Law and the Social Sciences*. New York: Russell Foundation.

Lempert, R., and J. Sanders. 1986. *An Invitation to Law and Social Science*. New York: Longman.

Loeb, S.E. 1983. A survey of ethical behavior in the accounting profession. *Journal of Accounting Research* (Autumn): 287–306.

Loeb, S.E. 1984. Codes of ethics and self regulation for non-public accountants: A public policy perspective. *Journal of Accounting and Public Policy* (Spring): 1–8.

Long, S. 1979. The Internal Revenue Service: Examining the exercise of discretion in tax enforcement. Law and Society Association meeting, Chicago, May.

Marks, J.B., E. Johnson, and P. Szanton. 1984. *Dispute Resolution in America: Processes in Evolution*. Washington, DC: National Institute of Dispute Resolution.

Mautz, R.K. 1983. Self-regulation: Perils and problems. *Journal of Accountancy* (May): 76–84.

Mautz, R.K. 1984. Self-regulation: Criticisms and a response. *Journal of Accountancy* (April): 56–66.

Menkel-Meadow, C. 1993. Lawyer negotiations: Theories and realities—What we learn from mediation. *Modern Law Review* 56: 3461–3479.

Mitnick, B. 1980. *The Political Economy of Regulation*. New York: Columbia University Press.

Ogus, A. 1994. *Regulation: Legal Form and Economic Theory*. Oxford: Clarendon Press.

Parker, L.D. 1994. Professional accounting body ethics: In search of the private interest. *Accounting, Organizations, and Society* 19(6): 507–525.

Ponemon, L.A. 1992. Ethical reasoning and selection-socialization in accounting. *Accounting, Organizations, and Society* 17(3/4): 239–258.

Public Oversight Board (POB). 1990–1996. Summary annual reports. New York: AICPA.

Rees, J.V. 1988. *Reforming the Workplace: A Study of Self-Regulation in Occupational Safety*. Philadelphia, PA: University of Pennsylvania Press.

Reiss, A.J., Jr. 1984. Selecting strategies of social control over organizational life. In *Enforcing Regulation*, ed. K. Hawkins and J.M. Thomas, 23–25. Boston: Kluwer-Nijhoff.

Ross, H.L. 1970. *Settled Out of Court: The Social Process of Insurance Claims Adjustment*. Chicago: Aldine.

Schauer, F. 1991. *Playing By the Rules: A Philosophical Examination of Rule-Based Decision-Making in Law and Life*. Oxford: Clarendon Press.

Shapiro, S. 1984. *Wayward Capitalists: Target of the Securities and Exchange Commission*. New Haven, CT: Yale University Press.

Shapiro, S. 1985. The road not taken: The elusive path to criminal prosecution for white collar offenders. *Law and Society Review* 19(2): 179–217.

Smith, R. 1994. *Medical Discipline: The Professional Conduct Jurisdiction of the General Medical Council 1858–1990*. Oxford: Clarendon Press.

Tamanaha, B.Z. 1997. *Realistic Socio-Legal Theory*. Oxford: Clarendon Press.

Thomas, C.W., and S.L. Seaman. 1996. Ethics violations in the accounting profession: An empirical investigation. *Research in Accounting Ethics* 2: 243–263.

Thomas, B.S. 1983. SEC oversight role in self-regulation. *The CPA Journal* (May): 10–15.

Thomas, J. 1998. The future: It is us. *Journal of Accountancy* (December): 23–24.

Tidrick, D.E. 1992. Disciplinary actions by the AICPA against individual members: 1980–1990. *Research in Accounting Regulation* (6): 163–177.

Vogel, D. 1986. *National Styles of Regulation. Environmental Policy in Great Britain and the United States*. Ithaca, NY: Cornell University Press.

Wallace, W.A., and K.S. Cravens. 1994. An exploratory content analysis of terminology in public accounting firms' responses to peer reviews. *Research in Accounting Regulation* 8: 3–32.

Wallace, W.A. 1994. The National Transportation Safety Board as a prototype for a more effective quality control inquiry committee. *Accounting Horizons* (March): 90–104.

Wallace, W.A. 1991. Peer review filings and their implications in evaluating self-regulation. *Auditing: A Journal of Practice and Theory* (Spring): 53–68.

Wallace, W.A. 1989. A historical view of the SEC's reports to Congress on oversight of the profession's self-regulatory process. *Accounting Horizons* 3(4): 24–39.

Wallace, W.A. 1988. Quality control problems related to independence: Evidence from AICPA peer review filings. *Proceedings of the DePaul University Research Symposium on A Profession in Transition: The Ethical and Legal Responsibilities of Accountants*, 1–29.

Wallace, W.A., and R.L. Campbell. 1988. State boards of accountancy: Quality review and positive enforcement programs. *Research in Accounting Regulation* 2: 123–154.

Weait, M.J., 1995. The role of the compliance officer in firms carrying on investment business in the City of London D. Phil. thesis, Department of Philosophy, Oxford University.

Wilson, J.Q. 1980. *The Politics of Regulation.* New York: Basic Books.

Zeff, S.A. 1987. Does the CPA belong to a profession? *Accounting Horizons* (June): 65–68.

REGULATION OF ACCOUNTANTS:
A TEST OF THE STIGLER-PELTZMAN THEORY

George D. Sanders

ABSTRACT

In 1969 a committee of the American Institute of Certified Public Accountants recommended that the education requirements for licensure for public accounting in the United States be increased from the equivalent of four years to the equivalent of five years of university education. This report represents the beginning of a lobbying effort by the Institute to persuade state legislators to change the licensing requirement in the various states. Through 1997, 37 states had adopted the new requirement. This study uses logistic regression and event history analysis of the adoption of the new educational requirements to test the economic theories of regulation developed by Stigler (1975) and Peltzman (1984). The results suggest that these theories have significant explanatory power with respect to the pattern of adoption, both cross-sectionally and over time. The number of AICPA members in a state relative to the population is the most significant predictor of adoption. The relative number of business proprietors is negatively associated with adoption and the relative number of local governments is positively associated with adoption.

Research in Accounting Regulation, Volume 13, pages 81-95.

ISBN: 0-7623-0520-7

SYNOPSIS AND INTRODUCTION

Since Stigler (1971) shifted the discussion of economic regulation from a normative price setting focus to one emphasizing the economic rent-seeking behavior of regulated industries and the responses of regulators, a large body of literature has expanded on and tested Stigler's theory that regulated industries attempt to control regulatory bodies to earn economic rents. Stigler (1975) and Peltzman (1984) extended Stigler's theory to include the role of consumers. Stigler (1975) recognized that groups that would be forced to bear the cost of a regulated industry's rents have incentives to oppose the regulatory capture and to make efforts to "weaken, delay, or prevent the regulation" (Stigler 1975, 129). Peltzman (1984) extended and generalized Stigler's work. Thus, the theory moved from a view in which a predatory industry attempts to influence the regulator to gain economic rents, to one in which producers and consumers struggle for control of the regulatory process.

A number of studies have tested Stigler's and Peltzman's hypotheses empirically against patterns of regulation across the United States. For example, Leffler (1978) examined the regulation of physicians; Primeaux, Filer, Herren, and Hollas (1984) examined the electric power industry; Becker (1986), dentists; and Kilbane and Beck (1990), optometrists. In general, the studies find support for the theory that both producer and consumer interests receive some weight in the regulatory process.

An alternate view of the regulatory process, specifically as directed toward professional licensing, holds that licensure provides a signal of quality where the quality of particular goods or services would otherwise be difficult to observe. Arrow (1963) argued that medical licensure was more likely a result of informational asymmetries involving the quality of the service purchased rather than rent-seeking by the profession. Leffler (1978) provided empirical evidence about physician licensure that indicates that the variance in licensing standards is consistent with an informational explanation. However, he also found that the refusal of nine states to accept the national board exam for physicians functioned as an entry barrier, and that the existence of the barrier could not be explained by the demand variables he used to surrogate demand for quality. He concluded that his results are consistent with the view that regulators attempt to balance the competing demands of interest groups.

The regulation of the accounting profession provides an interesting case for the study of the regulatory process. All states in the U.S. regulate the certification of public accountants (CPAs), but the licensing requirements, including educational and experience requirements, vary among the states.

In 1969, an AICPA Committee, the Beamer Committee, issued a report that recommended five years of college study to obtain the common body of knowledge for CPAs and, therefore, recommended that states adopt a five-year educational requirement as a prerequisite to licensing (AICPA 1969). In due course, the

Institute adopted a rule that limits membership in the Institute after the year 2000 to CPAs who have completed at least 150 semester hours of college education. Between 1969 and 1995, the last year for which data were available for this study, 32 state boards of accountancy adopted the five-year requirement.

Without prejudice to the merits of the AICPA's case for a minimum five-year educational requirement, it seems clear that increasing the cost of an accounting education will erect a higher barrier to entry into the profession and that the supply of qualified practitioners is likely to shrink, ceteris paribus. Because of mandatory audit requirements for many business entities, particularly publicly owned corporations and many governmental units, aggregate demand for audits is likely to be relatively inelastic; as a result, a reduction in supply can be expected to increase the price of CPA services, to the benefit of existing practitioners.

Previous studies of regulatory behavior have tested the Stigler-Peltzman hypotheses using cross-sectional samples. Becker (1986), for example, models the adoption of a reciprocity rule by state legislatures using probit analysis. The difficulty with this approach is that it does not allow the investigator to test the length of the time that the independent variables need to produce an effect, nor does it allow the investigator to consider changes in the predictors and response variables over time. As Stigler (1975, 129) recognized, it seems likely that the intensity of the lobbying effort is related to the length of time required for a legislature or a regulatory body to respond. By analyzing cross-sectional differences only, the researcher loses information about the time required to produce a response. Survival, also known as event history analysis, can use this information to provide insight into factors that affect the time dimension.

In recent years, a number of researchers in the social sciences have turned to a technique adapted from the biomedical literature to capture the information represented by the time dimension of events. This statistical method, known as survival analysis, also known as duration analysis or event history analysis, has been used to model economic events such as bank failures (Lane, Looney, and Wansley 1986), employee turnover (Morita, Lee, and Mowday 1989), and new firm survival (Audretsch and Mahmood 1995). The decision by a state to adopt a five-year education requirement for CPAs is a regulatory action that is particularly amenable to event history analysis because the time from the beginning of the lobbying effort can be measured relatively accurately to obtain an empirical assessment of the time dimension suggested in Stigler's analysis.

This study uses membership data from the AICPA and census sources to analyze the five-year adoption decision as a function of the number of AICPA members relative to the population of each state, the number of business proprietors in each state relative to the population, per capita income, and the number of cities with populations in excess of 20,000 relative to population. A cross-sectional logit analysis and two survival analyses, one based on an accelerated failure time model, and one based on a Cox proportional hazards model, is provided. All three approaches show results that are consistent with the Stigler-Peltzman model.

The remainder of this paper is organized as follows. The first section briefly summarizes the history and current state of accounting regulation in the United States. The second section develops the theory investigated in this paper. The third section explains the research method. The fourth section presents research findings. And the fifth section presents a summary and conclusions.

ACCOUNTING REGULATION IN THE UNITED STATES

Attempts to control access to the accounting profession in the United States date from the late 1800s. In 1895, a bill was introduced in the New York legislature providing for the licensing of CPAs. The bill, introduced on behalf of the Institute of Accountants and Bookkeepers, then the major professional association of public accountants, provided that CPAs must be citizens of the United States and that only CPAs of the state of New York should be appointed to act as examiners of accounts, expert accountants or paid auditors by courts, receivers, and government officers (Previts and Merino 1979). The bill failed, perhaps because the language clearly excluded the large number of British accountants practicing in New York who dominated a rival organization, the American Association of Public Accountants (AAPA). However, as Previts and Merino (1979, 98) note, professional accountants were successful in promoting a bill that passed in 1896, permitting the licensing of those who had declared an intention to become U.S. citizens. The lobbying success certainly reflected that the size of the group favoring the legislation had been increased with the support of the AAPA (Flesher, Miranti, and Previts 1996) and the size of the group that would be damaged most directly (foreign accountants) had been decreased. Previts and Merino (1979, 98) also note that the barrier was effective; after the passage of the legislation, many British accountants who did not wish to relinquish their British citizenship moved to other states.

Efforts to develop stringent licensing requirements continued during the next few years. By 1900, Pennsylvania, Maryland, and California had passed legislation modeled on the New York law. However, in the South and Midwest, these efforts often foundered in hostile state legislatures where the argument that a higher standard of service was needed failed to prevail against charges that the legislation was intended to keep out competition (Previts and Merino 1979, 141). In 1908, the President of the Fourth National Bank of New York publicly accused public accountants of conspiring to create a monopoly (Previts and Merino 1979, 141). Previts and Merino (1979, 147) note an article in the *Chicago Herald* that, in Illinois between 1903 and 1908, out of 111 candidates who sat for the examination, only six actually passed, while 98 certificates were awarded by waiver. However, despite the opposition, public accountants ultimately prevailed in their attempts to enact legislation requiring licensure. Flesher, Merino, and Previts (1996) note that by 1921, with the adoption of legislation by the State of New

Mexico, the professionalization of public accounting had spread through the United States.

The most recent attempt to set minimum educational requirements similarly has been met with resistance from legislators who interpreted the requirements as attempts to restrict entry into the profession (see for example Wolf 1996). Accountants, however, argue that the call for increased educational requirements reflect increased professionalization of accounting, the growth in the body of professional knowledge, and the need for greater technical skills.

The history of public accounting regulation as sketched above reflects the economic incentives outlined by Stigler and Peltzman: existing practitioners seek to control entrance by competitors, often citing a real or perceived need to improve the quality of services offered to the public; legislators are lobbied over a period of time to persuade them that the need is real and that it can be addressed by specifying certain minimum requirements that those individuals wishing to offer a service must meet; and legislators realize that other constituents may be affected adversely and attempt to balance the demands of their constituents in such as way as to maximize voter support. Over time, a well-organized and persistent group faced with more diffuse and less well organized opposition was able to prevail.

In the next section, a set of specific hypotheses for the adoption of the new education requirements by the states is developed using the Stigler–Peltzman model.

HYPOTHESES DEVELOPMENT

The literature reviewed above suggests that current CPA practitioners will have the strongest incentive to lobby for higher educational requirements, and that the persuasiveness of lobbying and its effectiveness, as measured by time to adoption is likely to be related not to the absolute number of CPAs but to the number of CPAs relative to the population.[1] A larger relative number of CPAs also increases the incentive to lobby for restrictions on the entry of new competitors. One would expect, therefore, that:

> **H1.** The likelihood of adoption is positively related to the number of CPAs per capita in a state. The length of time to adoption is negatively related to the number of CPAs per capita in a state.

The primary users of CPA services are businesses, state and local governments, and individuals who require a relatively high level of accounting and tax expertise. If current quality and quantity is satisfactory, and a barrier to entry is expected to reduce the supply of CPA practitioners resulting in an increase in CPA fees, or the elimination of some demanded quantity–quality combinations, these users are likely to oppose the legislation. Again, it is assumed that group lobbying influence and resources are proportional to group size relative to population. Thus:

H2. The likelihood of adoption is negatively related to the number of businesses and governments per capita and to the income per capita in a state. The length of time to adoption is positively related to the number of businesses and governments per capita and to the income per capita in a state.

Stigler (1975) suggests that the cost of lobbying is positively related to the size of the legislature. To secure favorable legislation, a lobbying group must convince a majority of legislators to vote in favor of its proposal. The larger the legislature, the greater the resources that must be devoted to winning conversions, and the longer the time needed to persuade them to do so. Therefore:

H3. The likelihood of adoption is negatively related to the size of the state legislature. The length of time to adoption is positively related to the size of the state legislature.

DATA

The AICPA furnished the number of members residing in each state for the years 1978–1995. For the years 1970–1979, only national totals are available.[2] The number of business users of audit services in a state is difficult to measure. Business operations that are branches or subsidiaries of larger firms may be audited by the parent corporation's auditors, and not by local CPAs. Therefore, as a surrogate measure for business demand, I use the number of business proprietors in a state as reported by the BEA's Regional Economic Information System, for 1969–1994 (Bureau of Economic Analysis 1998). Per capita income is from the same source. The number of local governments is drawn from the County and City Data Book (Bureau of the Census 1994), and the size of the state legislature is drawn from the U.S. Statistical Abstract on CD-ROM (Bureau of the Census 1996).

STATISTICAL METHOD

Logistic regression is used to test whether variations in the explanatory variables discussed above can explain the adoption of the 150-hour education requirement in or before 1995. Survival analysis is used to test whether the time to adoption for all states from 1969 to 1995 can be explained by variations in the explanatory variables.

Logistic Regression

Logistic regression estimates the relationship between a categorical response variable and a set of predictor variables. In this case, the response variable is binary, adoption or nonadoption of the new education requirement. Logistic regression allows the estimation of the likelihood that a state has adopted the requirement, given the observed values of the predictor variables, at some time in the past. Logistic regression is well known in the accounting literature, so it will not be described further.

Survival Analysis

Survival analysis is a statistical method developed in the biomedical sciences to test hypotheses about the length of survival of experimental subjects. However, the technique has been extended to examine questions in the physical and social sciences involving hypotheses about other phenomena, where the lengths of time periods from some defined point of time to the occurrence of some well defined event are of interest. Available statistical techniques allow for the analysis of either the probability of survival to at least time t or the first derivative of this survival function, termed the hazard function. If an experimental subject has not experienced the event of interest by the end of the

Table 1. Year of Adoption of a 150-Hour Education Requirement

State	*Year of Adoption*	*State*	*Year of Adoption*
Alabama	1989	Missouri	1993
Alaska	1991	Montana	1989
Arkansas	1990	Nebraska	1991
Connecticut	1992	Nevada	1993
Florida	1979	New Jersey	1995
Georgia	1991	North Dakota	1993
Hawaii	1977	Ohio	1992
Idaho	1993	Rhode Island	1992
Illinois	1991	South Carolina	1991
Indiana	1992	South Dakota	1992
Iowa	1992	Tennessee	1987
Kansas	1990	Texas	1989
Kentucky	1990	Utah	1981
Louisiana	1990	West Virginia	1989
Maryland	1993	Washington	1995
Mississippi	1990	Wyoming	1993

experiment or observation period, the subject is said to be censored. One of the advantages of survival analysis is the ability to use the information that the subject has survived at least as long as the censoring time. In this case, a state is treated as censored if it has not adopted the 150-hour requirement at the end of 1995. A more technical description of survival analysis is provided in the Appendix.

RESULTS

Descriptive Statistics

Table 1 presents a list of states and the year of adoption of the 150-semester hour requirement for those who have adopted to date through 1995.

Table 2 presents descriptive statistics for the predictor variables and the response variable for the survival analysis. The average number of years to adoption is 22, the minimum is seven years, and 18 states had not adopted by the end of 1995. The table shows that adopters have a higher number of CPAs per 1,000 population, a smaller number of business proprietors, higher income, a smaller number of local governments, and larger legislatures.

Table 3 presents the pairwise correlation among the study variables. To test for collinearities involving several predictors, condition indices were calculated for the predictors. The largest index was 19.4. Factors in excess of 30 are considered indicative of poorly estimated regression coefficients (Montgomery

Table 2. Descriptive Statistics

Variable	*Description*	*Adopt*	*Mean*	*Standard Deviation*	*Minimum*	*Maximum*
DUR	Years to adoption		22.22	4.33	7.00	26.00
CPAPC	CPAs per 1000 population	0	1.045	0.347	0.564	2.062
		1	1.160	0.236	0.778	1.787
PROPPC	Business Proprietors per 1000 population	0	92.279	25.742	63.628	146.493
		1	91.402	17.703	66.828	123.672
INCOM	Per capita income (000)	0	16.478	4.860	7.458	27.729
		1	22.370	2.515	17.781	26.802
PCGOVS	Number of governments per 1000 population	0	3.681	3.339	0.437	15.266
		1	1.818	1.377	0.635	6.551
LEGIS	Size of legislature	0	138.969	42.069	49.000	236.000
		1	164.278	81.284	62.000	422.000

Note: Adopt = 0 for states that had not adopted as of the end of 1995 (n = 18).
Adopt = 1 for states that had adopted as of the end of 1995 (n = 32).

Table 3. Pearson Correlation Coefficients
(*Prob* > |*R*| under *Ho*: *Rho* = 0)

	CPAPC	*PROPPC*	*INCOM*	*PCGOVS*	*LEGIS*
DUR	0.356 (0.011)	0.219 (0.126)	0.840 (0.000)	−0.082 (0.570)	0.181 (0.208)
CPAPC		0.008 (0.955)	0.643 (0.000)	−0.234 (0.102)	0.104 (0.471)
PROPPC			0.051 (0.725)	0.702 (0.000)	−0.154 (0.285)
INCOM				−0.239 (0.094)	0.231 (0.106)
PCGOVS					−0.050 (0.729)

and Peck 1982). Table 3 shows no evidence of serious collinearities among the predictors.

Logistic Regression Analysis

Table 4 presents the results of the logistic regression analysis. All of the predictors, except *PCGOVS*, the relative number of local governments, have the expected sign and all except the size of the legislature, *LEGIS*, are significant at conventional significance levels. The predictors are jointly significant at $p < .001$; the results are consistent with the Stigler–Peltzman model—regulatory bodies consider the needs of consumers and producers and are not simply controlled by the regulated industry.

Table 4. Effect of Predictor Variables On Adoption of Education Requirement Logistic Regression

Variable	*DF*	*Parameter Estimate*	*Standard Error*	*Wald Chi-Square*	*p-Chi-Square*
INTERCEPT	1	12.261	4.800	6.525	0.011
CPAPC	1	5.098	2.039	6.249	0.012
PROPPC	1	−0.074	0.038	3.684	0.055
INCOM	1	−0.589	0.210	7.859	0.005
PCGOVS	1	1.064	0.521	4.171	0.041
LEGIS	1	−0.009	0.008	1.386	0.239

Notes: Adjusted Generalized R^2 (Nagelkerke 1991) = 0.673; n = 50.
Goodness-of-Fit (Hosmer and Lemeshow 1989) = 10.09 (18 d.f., p-value 0.92) Model $p < .001$.

Survival Analysis

Accelerated Failure Time Model

The accelerated failure time model (AFT) requires that a particular distribution of survival times and, therefore, hazard, be assumed.[3] The plots and log likelihood statistics suggested that either a Weibull or generalized gamma distribution would provide the best fit to the data. Table 5 reports the results of the fit of a Weibull model to the data.

The results reported in Table 5 are similar to the results for the logistic regression model. Note, however, that the coefficient signs have changed. The AFT analysis estimates the survival function, the length of time to adoption; and the logistic regression estimates the log-odds of adoption, which can be interpreted as the likelihood that a state will have adopted at the end of 1995. Time to adoption should be inversely related to the log-odds of adoption at any given point in time and, therefore, the coefficient signs are reversed in the two analyses. Considering the sign change, the signs of three of the coefficients are consistent with expectations and with the earlier analysis. Increasing values for CPAPC are associated with a shorter time to adoption, increasing values for *PROPPC* and *INCOM* are associated with longer times to adoption. *PROPPC* has a p-value just under 0.10.

Proportional Hazards Model

Proportional hazards survival analysis or Cox regression is a nonparametric technique for analyzing hazard. The method assumes that hazard is constant over time. It has the advantage, however, of allowing the use of time dependent covariates; that is, changing values of predictor variables over time can be incorporated in the analysis.

Table 5. Effect of Predictor Variables On Adoption of Education Requirement Accelerated Failure Time Model

Variable	*DF*	*Parameter Estimate*	*Standard Error*	*Chi-Square*	*p–Chi-square*
INTERCEPT	1	2.199	0.170	162.829	0.000
CPAPC	1	−0.329	0.101	10.51	0.002
PROPPC	1	0.002	0.001	2.825	0.093
INCOM	1	0.057	0.008	47.916	0.000
PCGOVS	1	−0.010	0.010	1.171	0.279
LEGIS	1	0.001	0.001	1.230	0.267
SCALE	1	0.113	0.017		

Notes: Log likelihood for Weibull = 7.308 (Weibull model with no covariates = −23.687)
Generalized R^2 = 0.711; n = 50.

Table 6. Effect of Predictor Variables On Adoption of Education Requirement Proportional Hazards Model

Variable	*DF*	*Parameter Estimate*	*Standard Error*	*Wald Chi-Square*	*p– Chi-Square*	*Risk Ratio*
CPAPC	1	0.158	0.053	8.699	0.003	1.171
PROPPC	1	−0.022	0.013	2.756	0.097	0.978
INCOM	1	−0.221	0.113	3.847	0.050	0.801
LEGIS	1	−0.003	0.004	0.700	0.403	0.997
PCGOVS	1	0.140	0.074	3.549	0.060	1.15
CPATIME	1	−0.012	0.004	9.823	0.002	0.989
CPATIM2	1	8.28E-07	2.69E-07	9.507	0.002	1

Notes: −2 log Likelihood = 151.593 (p = 0.0071). Without covariates, −2 log Likelihood = 170.955. Generalized R^2 = 0.5391; n = 50.

The AFT model reported above suggests that the hazard is not constant over time, as is assumed by the proportional hazards model. Allison (1995) suggests that if the hazard is not thought to be constant over time, the inclusion of an interaction term composed of a time measure and a time-dependent covariate provides both a test of the time dependence and a method of controlling for the time dependence while still allowing the use of time varying covariates. To allow for both linear and nonlinear time dependence, two interaction terms, defined as the product of CPAPC and DUR (identified as CPATIM), and its square, CPATIM2, are used as predictor variables. The results of the regression are presented in Table 6.

The results in Table 6 are similar to the Weibull analysis with respect to the significance of the variables. However, note that the coefficient signs are reversed because Cox regression estimates the hazard function, not the survival function. The Cox–Snell generalized R^2 (Cox and Snell 1989) for the proportional hazards model is 0.5391, somewhat lower than for the AFT model.

SUMMARY AND CONCLUSIONS

The results reported above are generally consistent with the theory that regulation is a process in which the regulator attempts to balance the demands of competing interests. The finding in two models that the relative number of AICPA members in a state is the largest and most significant predictor is consistent with the view that a well-organized lobbying group, though small relative to a more diffuse group of opponents, is likely to prevail in the process over time. The interests of more diffused groups, business proprietors and high income individuals, seem not to affect the outcome of the process as strongly, but there is evidence that they do affect the process. The size of the legislature is not statistically significant in any model. The results are broadly similar across the three statistical methods.

It must be noted that the effects of the predictors on the dependent variables, while they are statistically significant, are modest. The risk ratio, reported in Table 6 for the proportional hazards model, provides the most direct method for comparing the influence of the predictors. The risk ratio of the variable *CPAPC* is 1.171, indicating a 17.1 percent increase in the hazard for every additional AICPA member per 1,000 population. *PROPPC* only results in a 2.2 percent decrease in hazard for every additional proprietor per 1,000. A $1,000 increase in per capita income reduces the hazard by 19.9 percent; however, the standard error of the estimate also is relatively large, and the coefficient is large relative to *CPAPC* only in this model.

The only coefficient that consistently has a sign that is counter to expectations is *PCGOVS*, the number of local governments relative to population. It is possible that this result reflects the widespread concern about the quality of governmental financial reporting and auditing. Local officials may feel that the increased educational requirements will translate into an increase in auditing quality and may support the new educational requirement.[4] On the other hand, the variable may not be an adequate proxy for local government preferences and willingness to lobby.[5]

The negative coefficient for per capita income is opposite to the expectation that would be drawn from the information asymmetry hypothesis if Leffler (1978) is correct and the quality of service demanded is positively related to income. However, if higher income individuals are able to procure a desired level of service under the present regulatory regime, and if they expect higher costs under the new regime, they should oppose the change, so the expectation would be for a positive effect on survival (the AFT model), a negative effect on hazard (the proportional hazard model), and a negative effect on the log-odds of adoption (the logistic regression model), all consistent with these results.

The patterns of adoption we observe are consistent with the predictions from the Stigler–Peltzman theory. In addition, this is the first study to provide evidence consistent with Stigler's (1975) hypothesis about the effect of lobbying over time. Levels of statistical significance for the models are quite high, but statistical analysis paints a rather broad picture and further research on this question would be interesting. One might analyze the events in particular states in detail and with finer tools than was possible in this study. In addition, the adoption of the Uniform Accountancy Act (UAA) by the states will provide a unique opportunity to test aspects of the economic theory of regulation and aspects of the economic theory of public choice.[6]

APPENDIX

Statistical Method

Survival analysis assumes that the time to event (survival time) is a stochastic variable, T, characterized by a cumulative distribution function, $F(t)$, such that $F(t) = Pr[T<t], t \geq 0$. The survival function, $S(t) = 1 - F(t)$, defines the probability that the time to event is at least t. The first derivative of $S(t)$, $S'(t) = -F'(t)$, provides another useful characterization of the time to event, termed the hazard function. The hazard function is the instantaneous rate of change of the probability of the event, given that an experimental subject has not yet experienced the event.

Survival analysis is generally concerned with the effect that an experimental variable has on the time to the occurrence of the event, the survival time. While this effect can be modeled several ways by assuming different distributional characteristics for T, this analysis is restricted to two types of survival models, a proportional hazards (PH) model, and an accelerated failure time (AFT) model.

The PH model assumes that the hazard faced by subject j is always proportional to the hazard faced by subject k, with a constant of proportionality determined by the values of the predictor variables. An important advantage of the *PH* model is that it can be estimated using Cox, or partial likelihood regression (Cox 1972), a nonparametric technique that does not require additional assumptions about the distribution of survival times.

The AFT model assumes that the effect of the predictors is to increase or decrease the survival time by a constant, conditional on the values of the predictor variables.

The event of interest in this study is the adoption by a state of the 150-hour education requirement for CPA licensing. The study period begins in 1970 and ends at the end of 1995. The study period was determined by data availability, and states that had not adopted the new education requirement by the end of 1995 are treated as censored.

ACKNOWLEDGMENTS

Helpful comments on earlier drafts from Arthur Allen, John H. Beck, Michael Dugan, Regg Mathews, Rodney K. Rogers, Stephen Senge, the editor, and two anonymous reviewers; assistance with data from Michael R. Ruble; and research support from Western Washington University are gratefully acknowledged.

NOTES

1. The organization of a lobbying group is a complex phenomenon. A larger group can muster more lobbying resources; however, the benefits derived from legislation will have to be shared among

a larger number of participants. In addition, if a lobbying coalition is large, it may experience more of a free rider problem. Because a relatively well organized, durable, and effective lobbying organization exists for CPAs, I hypothesize that its effectiveness in any given state is likely to be related to the number of votes and to the lobbying resources that can be provided by the membership, relative to the number of votes and resources that can be mustered by those who are likely to oppose the effort.

2. For purposes of the proportional hazards survival analysis, the years 1970–1979 are extrapolated using the AICPA national totals and the state population.

3. The simplest assumption about hazard is that it is constant over time. Assuming a constant hazard implies that survival times follow an exponential distribution. If the hazard varies over time, the Weibull model, a log-normal model, a log-logistic model, or a gamma model may be appropriate. To choose a distribution, a plot of the Cox–Snell residuals was prepared using the method described in Allison (1995). The Weibull is used for the statistical testing.

4. It is interesting to note that fiscal problems, and service delivery problems experienced by several large U.S. cities in the late 1970s have been blamed, in part, on poor accounting and financial reporting practices (Securities and Exchange Commission 1977). The U.S. General Accounting Office (1986), the chief Federal government accounting rule maker, has also been critical of state and local auditing and financial reporting.

5. It has been suggested that the variable *PCGOVS* may proxy for urban concentration, a variable that is used in a number of studies to represent the cost of organizing a lobbying group (see, for example, Kilbane and Beck 1990). Because of the greater physical proximity of potential members, it is hypothesized that coalitions form more easily in urban areas. Substitution of a Census urbanization measure for *PCGOVS*, however, did not result in a significant coefficient on the urbanization measure.

6. I am grateful to the editor for suggesting the study of the UAA; for those interested in the study of professional regulation, it should provide very interesting research possibilities.

REFERENCES

American Institute of Certified Public Accountants (AICPA). 1969. *Report of the Committee on Education and Experience Requirements for CPAs*. New York: AICPA.

Allison, P.D. 1995. *Survival Analysis Using the SAS System*, 1st ed. Cary, NC: SAS Institute, Inc.

Arrow, K. 1963. Uncertainty and the economics of medical care. *American Economic Review* 53: 941–966.

Audretsch, D.B., and T. Mahmood. 1995. New firm survival: New results using a hazard function. *Review of Economics and Statistics* 77(February): 97–103.

Becker, G. 1986. The public interest hypothesis revisited: A new test of Peltzman's theory of regulation. *Public Choice* 49: 223–234.

Bureau of Economic Analysis. 1998. *Regional Economic Information System*. Washington, DC: U.S. Department of Commerce.

Bureau of the Census, Data User Services Division. 1994. *County and City Data Book: Files on Diskette*. Washington, DC: The Bureau of the Census.

Cox, D.R. 1972. Regression models and life tables. *Journal of the Royal Statistical Society* 34: 187–220.

Cox, D.R., and E.J. Snell. 1989. *The Analysis of Binary Data,* 2nd ed. London: Chapman & Hall.

Flesher, D.L., P.J. Miranti, and G.J. Previts. 1996. The first century of the CPA. *Journal of Accountancy* 182(4): 51–57.

Hosmer, D.W., and S. Lemeshow. 1989. *Applied Logistic Regression.* New York: John Wiley & Sons.

Kilbane, S.C., and J.H. Beck. 1990. Professional associations and the free rider problem: The case of optometry. *Public Choice* 65: 181–187.

Lane, W.R., S.W. Looney, and J.W. Wansley. 1986. An application of the Cox proportional hazards model to bank failure. *Journal of Banking and Finance* 10(December): 511–531.

Leffler, K.B. 1978. Physician licensure: competition and monopoly in American medicine. *Journal of Law and Economics* 21: 165–186.
Montgomery, D.C., and E.A. Peck. 1982. *Introduction to Linear Regression Analysis.* New York: John Wiley & Sons.
Morita, J.G., T.W. Lee, and R.T. Mowday. 1989. Introducing survival analysis to organizational researchers: A selected application to turnover research. *Journal of Applied Psychology* 74: 280–292.
Nagelkerke, N.J.D. 1991. A note on a general definition of the coefficient of determination. *Biometrica* 78: 691–692.
Peltzman, S. 1984. Constituent interest and Congressional voting. *Journal of Law and Economics* 27(April): 181–210.
Primeaux, W.J., J.E. Filer, R.S. Herren, and D.R. Hollas. 1984. Determinants of regulatory policies toward competition in the electric utility industry. *Public Choice* 43: 173–186.
Previts, G.J., and B.D. Merino. 1979. *A History of Accounting in America* New York: John Wiley & Sons.
Securities and Exchange Commission. 1977. *Staff Report on Transactions in Securities of the City of New York.* Washington, DC: Subcommittee on Economic Stabilization of the Committee on Banking, Finance and Urban Affairs.
Stigler, G.J. 1971. The theory of economic regulation. *Bell Journal of Economics and Management Science* 2: 137–146.
Stigler, G.J. 1975. The theory of economic regulation. In *The Citizen and the State: Essays on Regulation,* 114–141. Chicago and London: The University of Chicago Press.
U.S. General Accounting Office. 1986. *CPA Audit Quality: Many Government Audits Do Not Comply with Professional Standards.* Washington, D.C.: U.S. General Accounting Office.
Wolf, M. 1996. State board adopts a fifth-year requirement for CPAs. *Columbian* (October 15): 1.

THE IMPACT OF SCHOLARLY RESEARCH ON THE REGULATION OF GOVERNMENTAL ACCOUNTING AND AUDITING

Richard E. Brown

ABSTRACT

For several years the business media and business community have been critical of schools of management for a number of perceived ills, including what is often viewed as irrelevant research by university faculty members. More recently a number of scholars have voiced similar concerns. This paper, prepared by an author with a background in both the practice and academic worlds, focuses on governmental accounting and auditing to examine the relevance of scholarly research to a series of fundamental accounting and auditing issues that are presently either under study or in use in public financial management. All relevant papers from *The Accounting Review* and the *Journal of Accounting Research*, two of the profession's premier academic journals, were reviewed to determine the relevance and contribution of these papers to the current debate surrounding generally accepted accounting principles and generally accepted auditing standards for government. Findings suggest

Research in Accounting Regulation, Volume 13, pages 97-110.

ISBN: 0-7623-0520-7

that, at least since the late 1960s or early 1970s, relatively few scholarly papers have advanced insights or information which would appear useful or relevant to the current debate. Moreover, when they are cited in other journals, the published papers overwhelmingly tend to appear only in other academic journals. This paper explores some of the possible reasons for this development, and its costs, and also offers suggestions to reverse the trend.

INTRODUCTION

During the past decade, scholarly business research, including academic accounting research, has begun to receive a substantial amount of study and even criticism from a wide array of reviewers, including some of its own. Even the American Assembly of Collegiate Schools of Business (AACSB) has joined the debate. In its Summer 1996 issue of *Newsline*, the AACSB included a discussion of "Remaking Doctoral Education: The Missing Link to Customer Satisfaction." Under the caption, "Relevant Research," the article quotes a vice dean and faculty director at UCLA as stating:

> To succeed at the schools that hire them, they [faculty] have to produce and publish knowledge, not in practitioner journals, but in the journals of their fields. Much of the work would be considered relevant by many of the peers evaluating them, and much of it would be considered irrelevant by many practitioners (AACSB 1996, 2).

The Dean at the Simon School at the University of Rochester put it succinctly: "A question we ask ourselves, our colleagues, and our students is 'Why?' Why should we care about what you write? If the answer to your question doesn't matter to anybody, then maybe you'd better think of another question" (AACSB 1996, 3).

One might expect that the discipline of accounting, with its heavy applied orientation would not be subject to the same degree of concern, at least not on the part of its own, accounting academics. But this is not the case. Upon his induction into the Accounting Hall of Fame in 1995, W.W. Cooper had this to say:

> This is not to say that the contemporary research I am describing is bereft of interest in the problems of our profession. It is to say that this research often takes a form that can be described as "theory driven applications" rather then "applications driven theory." The latter is needed...if we are to maintain fruitful contact with the rapidly changing scenarios of contemporary practice.... This is what is intended by "applications driven theory." The application is driven by problems of actual practice with a solution that is also extended and stated with sufficient rigor and generality to be understood by others (Cooper 1995, 2–3).

Later in his paper Cooper provides a specific illustration of the kind of development which is prompting his concern:

> I would be remiss if I did not also mention auditing.... Here, too, I am struck by the fact that a major development like "performance auditing" has developed both in governmental and internal auditing with very little attention in the research literature (Cooper 1995, 6).

Several years ago Robert Freeman, a well-known accounting scholar who has also comfortably bridged the gap with the practice world as a member of the Governmental Accounting Standards Board (GASB), stated in a paper he authored: "In sum, relatively little of the type of research that is published in the leading contemporary academic journals appears to be of value to standards setters or practitioners" (Freeman 1990, 45).

This growing concern about the relevance of accounting research especially intrigued this author, who has spent a more than thirty year career almost evenly divided between being an accounting practitioner and an academic. The practice years included service creating a performance audit capability for the New York State Legislature, service as Legislative State Auditor of Kansas, and a stint as a Price Waterhouse consultant to state and local governments; the academic side has included, in addition to my current position as Professor of Accounting at Kent State University, visiting assignments at the College of William and Mary and the University of Kansas. As one who has assisted numerous state governments in developing and using a performance audit capability, for example, it always seemed puzzling that so little guidance and assistance were to be found in the academic literature on fundamental practice issues. Thus, at both a professional and personal level, an inquiry into the nature and relevance of accounting research seemed intriguing.

FOCUS AND METHODOLOGY

Given this abundance of fundamental criticism and concern over the impact and value of academic accounting research, it seemed appropriate to attempt to examine in greater detail the validity of the arguments. The case of the regulation of governmental accounting and auditing was selected since it is a discrete and manageable subfield within accounting, an area which, as we have seen, has received the same specific criticism as management research in general. Moreover, the evolution and development of governmental accounting principles and auditing standards have lagged well behind the private sector and are, at this moment, undergoing fundamental discussion debate, and change. Thus, the opportunity to test the extent of the linkages between scholarly research and these current issues in governmental accounting and auditing was most attractive.[1]

An effort was next made to identify, based on GASB's own newsletters and various releases, several of the more basic issues currently under discussion and study by the GASB, i.e., issues now being discussed by GASB with scholars and practitioners as a prelude to their possible release as generally accepted accounting principles, or GAAP for government. The following issues were identified for review:

1. The basis of accounting, including the concept of reporting depreciation. GASB has been struggling with the switch from modified accrual to full accrual accounting since its inception (GASB 1992, 1995, 1997).
2. The appropriate financial reporting presentation, including the number and combination of funds. This topic would also include the structure of the Comprehensive Annual Financial Report (CAFR), and how this relates to alternative reporting formats, including "Popular Reporting" (GASB 1995, 1997).
3. Service Efforts and Accomplishments Reporting, or SEA. GASB's concept statement No. 1, released in 1985, included a discussion of the importance of nontraditional financial (or performance) measures, and this concern was further underscored in GASB's 1994 concept statement No 2. Indeed GASB is now more than midway through a 10-year experimentation period in SEA reporting as a precursor to possible required SEA reporting (GASB 1985, 1994).

A fourth item was added to this list, the topic touched on in the Cooper paper cited earlier: performance auditing. Performance auditing, of course, is less the concern of GASB than it is of the U.S. General Accounting Office (GAO). SEA is the reporting side of performance data, while performance auditing deals with the standards and techniques for auditing such nontraditional data. Performance auditing was first codified in the GAO's *Governmental Auditing Standards*, dubbed the "Yellow Book," in 1972. However, its roots go back to performance budgeting of the 1930s and even earlier. The GAO, state and local auditors, and a small number of CPA firms have been conducting performance audits since the 1960s (USGAO 1994; Brown, Gallagher, and Williams 1982; Brown and Pethtel 1974).

The research issues raised in this paper are the following. What has academic research contributed to these four very fundamental concerns of governmental accounting and auditing? To what extent have academics helped to shape the evolution and development of the field? Methodology now becomes a factor in addressing these issues. If all academic accounting journals were consulted to identify relevant papers since the beginning of such journals, or even over the past few decades, researchers would be quickly overwhelmed with the resulting volume of material, and rendered incapable of analyzing the papers in any depth. So a decision was made to select two of the leading academic accounting journals—arguably the top two academic accounting journals—and review since their beginnings all papers dealing with governmental accounting and auditing research. *The Accounting Review*, the lead publication of the American Accounting Association, and the *Journal of Accounting Research* are widely recognized as two prestigious academic journals in accounting, and so they became the focus of this study. Specifically, to what extent have these two journals, and those publishing in them, shed light on the four current fundamental concerns of governmental accounting and auditing identified above? With the help of graduate assistants, every issue of *The Accounting Review* and the *Journal of Accounting Research* was reviewed for all published papers on governmental accounting and auditing since the journals' inception through 1994. Abstracts, if available, were used; if not, abstracts were prepared. If a particular paper seemed to merit closer inspection, a copy of the entire paper was obtained for review. When possible, relevant databases were examined through computer technology.

FINDINGS

Journal of Accounting Research

The first issue of the *Journal of Accounting Research* (*JAR*) appeared in spring 1963. During the better than thirty year span covered by our review, close to twenty papers dealt exclusively with governmental accounting and auditing. This would constitute about one paper every one and one-half years. If we assume that each issue of *JAR* carried only five research papers, that would total about 600 papers (5 papers per issue x 4 issues per year x 30 years).

This lack of coverage of the governmental area will be discussed later, but the key point of this research is the content of the papers published in *JAR*. A few of the papers might be of interest to practitioners, but were not on the issues we have isolated. For example, the spring 1990 paper, "Determinants of Auditor Change In The Public Sector," might fall into this category (Roberts, Glezen, and Jones 1990). It was admittedly difficult to see, without much further investigation, the relevance of several papers. "Governmental Accounting In China During the Chou Dynasty (1122–256 B.C.)" is a leading example of this problem (Fu 1971). A few other papers might possibly have offered value to individuals other than academics on topics outside our concern, but seemed to disguise their relevance by writing in a specialized (academic) language almost designed to discourage practitioner readers.

Beginning in 1981 and through the middle of that decade, several papers analyzed a similar theme: the association between municipal market measures and reporting practices. This research theme seems to have been begun by Wallace in the August 1981 issue of *JAR*, but a series of papers followed that either extended or redirected Wallace's work (Wallace 1981). This series included papers by Copeland and Ingram (1982); and Wilson and Howard (1984). Wallace (and it would seem, most of the other researchers) concludes that:

> This evidence suggests that accounting variables have a significant association with net interest cost and auditing variables have a significant association with municipal bond ratings.... With respect to alternative reporting practices, the analysis of individual coefficients indicates

> that benefits in the form of lower interest costs and higher bond ratings accrue to municipalities when they comply with GAAFR, hire a national auditor, and have a clean audit report (Wallace 1981, 513).

Important as this would seem, it still does not directly address the key topics confronting GASB and the GAO today, including the composition of GAAP.

In short, the scholar or practitioner attempting to do his or her own research in *JAR* prior to taking a public position on current concerns relating to the work of GASB or the GAO would find little there of benefit. In 1984 *JAR* published a paper entitled, "Two Decades of the Journal of Accounting Research." In the paper the authors attempted to gauge the contribution of *JAR* during its first 20 years (1963–1982). It is significant to note that little or no mention is made of *JAR*'s contribution to the field of governmental accounting and auditing (Dyckman and Zeff 1984).

The Accounting Review

The story of *The Accounting Review* is a more complex one. First of all, the journal has a much longer history; it began as a journal in 1926. Second, while in more recent years the *Review*'s contribution to the formation of government GAAP and related issues is quite similar to that of the *Journal of Accounting Research*, the *Review* was not always directed in that vein.

From its inception and for close to five decades thereafter, the issues of *The Accounting Review* contained numerous papers of an applied nature, often shedding light on issues of continuing interest. The papers rarely constituted a significant proportion of the journal's total research output. However, papers on governmental accounting were frequent, were of practical benefit, and were relevant. Between 1917 and 1970 more than 100 papers were published on governmental topics, which is an average of about two papers per year. While the volume is not remarkable for such an important sector of society and business, the content of the papers—at least by today's standards—is. Again, these early papers were highly pragmatic.

Without concern for precise identification of content, the titles of the papers offer evidence as to their applied nature, for example: "Fund and Proprietary Accounts in Governmental Accounting" (Morey 1926); "Principles of Municipal Accounting" (Morey 1934); "Classification of Municipal Income and Expenditures" (Lorig 1937); "The Application of Governmental Accounting Principles" (Frisbee 1939); "Internal Auditing For the State of New York" (Seldon 1943); "Determining the Current Financial Position of A City" (Lorig 1941); "New Developments and Simplified Approaches to Municipal Accounting" (Newton 1954); "Reporting and Interpreting the Cost of State Government" (Freeman 1955); "Modern Accounting Methods for Governmental Units" (Herbert 1956);

and "Needed: More Information and Understandable Financial Statements from Governmental Units" (Hylton 1957).

An important observation must be made at this point: the titles of these papers do reflect their contents accurately. They are practical papers about (then) current shortcomings in governmental accounting and how to change those things to make them better. Moreover, while of course there are more theoretical or abstract papers included in the more than 100 papers published during this roughly 50-year period, they are indeed truly exceptions. The titles offered above seem representative of those which appeared during this period. Published paper after published paper throughout the 1950s and, to a lesser extent, the 1960s, elaborate on what ought to constitute generally accepted accounting principles for government. While discussion does take place on auditing in general and internal auditing, there is little or no mention of performance auditing. And, while performance measures are mentioned from time to time, no author in this era seems to have foreseen the growing importance of SEA reporting.

The Last Two Decades of The Accounting Review

In about the mid-1970s, coverage of research in governmental accounting and auditing began to take on a different emphasis. First of all, fewer applied papers were published. Published research began to resemble that published in *JAR*. Moreover, the academic form and tone of the papers becomes such that their benefits would not be readily apparent to most decision makers.

In sum, during this period of two decades or more, there is little usable research which contributes to the current dialogue. Almost nothing is published directly on accounting procedures and GAAP. And only a few highly theoretical papers do appear on performance measurement which relate indirectly to SEA reporting and performance auditing.

Much of the published research during this period mirrored *JAR* as to topics: financial reporting practices and municipal bond rating changes. Indeed, many of same authors appeared on the same topics in the pages of both journals.

The contributions of *The Accounting Review*, at least in more recent years, to governmental accounting and auditing, are best summed up in a paper by Banker, Cooper, and Potter in July 1992 entitled, "A Perspective On Research In Governmental Accounting." Their comments include the following:

> The magnitudes involved are huge, and the issues to be addressed are important...state and local governments now account for some 11 percent of gross national product. The total of public expenditures...approaches 40 percent.
>
> Continuing this evolution to broadened realms of accountability, GASB has recently issued a research report, which is also a call to research, entitled "Service Efforts and Accomplishments Reporting: Its Time Has Come."

> Still referred to as "GAO-type audits," these audits have a variety of other names, such as performance audits...
>
> We do not want to leave the impression of blaming *The Accounting Review* for lacunae in the research activities reported in its pages.... Researchers in accounting, it seems, have not been responsive to the problems and opportunities associated with developments in governmental accounting...
>
> The main desiderata lie in the development of attitudes that will encourage accounting researchers to respond to problems in the profession and practice of auditing and accountancy (Banker, Cooper, and Potter 1992, 506–509).

ANALYSIS AND INTERPRETATION

The issue before us then is the extent to which the academic accounting journals, using the *Journal of Accounting Research* and *The Accounting Review* as a test case, have contributed to practice and related policy formulation for government GAAP as well as newer forms of governmental auditing as identified in our four test issues. Deemed relevant were papers dealing with the basis of accounting (modified vs. full accrual), the presentation of financial reports, service efforts and accomplishments reporting, and performance auditing.

For about the first 50 years of its existence, the pages of *The Accounting Review* carried limited numbers of papers dealing with public sector accounting. However, in general, the papers that were published did tend to deal specifically with many of the practical problems of financial accounting and reporting for government. Those who assisted in preparing and releasing the initial reports on government GAAP, first in 1934 by the National Committee on Municipal Accounting, and then in 1979 by the National Council on Governmental Accounting, were surely the beneficiaries of this dialogue in the pages of *The Accounting Review*. Among the first actions of GASB, created in 1984, was the adoption of the NCGA's report. Thus, it may be said, current government GAAP benefited from this early work in the pages of *The Review*.[2]

However, even though many of the papers contained in *The Review*'s pages were quite relevant to current GAAP issues, there was little or no attention given to SEA reporting or to performance auditing. Moreover, as seen above, for about the past two decades few papers published in *The Accounting Review* dealt directly with the issues we are examining. Further, few, if any, of the papers published in the *Journal of Accounting Research* would be useful to today's decision makers who must develop or implement current government GAAP or auditing. Added research might address the issue of what, specifically, occurred in academic circles in the 1960s and 1970s, which seems to have fundamentally shifted the essence of scholarly research from the more applied to the highly theoretical. An earlier paper in this journal sheds considerable light on the issue. In his important work, "Regulating Research: Relevance Versus Elegance?," Maher examines the evolution of managerial accounting research and traces significant changes in that research to the impact of the Ford Foundation's business school reform efforts in the 1950s. Specifically, Maher finds that due in part to those reform efforts, managerial accounting research currently focuses on narrow, tractable problems, instead of on issues relevant to the practice of accounting; uses more sophisticated research methods from mathematics, the social sciences, and other disciplines; and reflects a significant reduction in practitioner authorship. The paper also notes that the University of Chicago, home to *JAR*, was one of five research universities targeted by the Ford Foundation to spearhead the business school reform movement (Maher 1997). Thus, for good or ill it would appear that the Ford Foundation was one of the driving forces behind accounting research's shift from the applied to the theoretical.

Two associated questions arise when one examines this dearth of practice-related material in the academic journals reviewed: first, is it fair to judge the journals on this lack of applied content if this is not the mission of the journals; and second, is it not possible that practice-related papers were not published because such papers were never submitted to the journals in the first place?

To some extent the responses to these questions must necessarily be circular. For example, with regard to journal mission, perhaps it is time to reconsider the established journal mission. The reasons for such reassessment are fairly numerous and are raised in a powerful paper by Bricker and Previts, published in 1990, called "The Sociology of Accounting: A Study of Academic and Practice Community Schisms." In this paper, the authors meticulously trace the evolution of the current schism between the accounting practice and academic communities, including the role of accounting research. They suggest that accounting academics, from about 1946 on, were persuaded to follow the social science research model rather than emulating the research models of faculty associated with a specific profession. On this point the paper continues:

> As an applied field-science and a learned profession, accountancy's academic community would derive research questions from a socially responsible view of the scope of services which the discipline offers to society. It is [as] anomalous for accountancy researchers to be uninterested in the concerns and issues of practitioners as it would be for medical researchers to hold such an attitude about research related to cancer, or...AIDS (Bricker and Previts 1990, 10–11).

If, indeed, accountancy and accounting-related research were for a time served by its focus on more theoretical or conceptual research, it may be that it is now time for a more mature profession to reexamine that focus.

The second question, relating to the kinds of papers initially submitted to *JAR* and *The Accounting Review*, is equally important and also difficult to answer satisfactorily. In short, did the journals not publish practice-related papers because such papers were never submitted? The only definitive way to answer this question would be to examine the papers received by the journals and rejected, which would be a formidable task if it could be accomplished at all. On the other hand, it is well known among academic researchers, who view themselves as being in a publishing and literary marketplace, what journals do and do not publish; (i.e., the missions of respective journals). These insights are gained by reading journal guidelines, through experience, and through networking. Moreover, it is a well-known fact among academics that if a journal wishes to publish certain kinds of materials and/or special issues, it merely publicizes this fact and the marketplace responds. Thus, it is reasonable to conclude that to a considerable degree *JAR* and *The Accounting Review* attracted the kinds of research papers that they both sought and routinely published. This issue is explored further in a study published by Previts and Brown in *The Accounting Historians* where they examine coverage of governmental accounting by *The Journal of Accountancy* (Previts and Brown 1993).

The research conducted for this paper surfaced an additional, related issue which was not the focus of the initial inquiry—the extent to which academic researchers, inadvertently or not, end up writing exclusively for other academics. This issue was suggested by the tangential finding that frequently papers on governmental accounting topics first appearing in either *JAR* or *The Accounting Review* would, before long, surface in the other journal, either as an extension of the paper by the same or other authors, or as a reference source used in the preparation of the second paper. This, in turn, raised a question as to the extent to which the research represented by the published papers that were the focus of this study was picked up in some fashion by applications or practice journals.

To respond to this question a decision was made to use the Social Science Citation Index to determine the extent to which a selection of papers published in *JAR* and *The Review* were cited in other academic and practitioner journals. The published articles selected and tested were several papers which, while covering important governmental accounting topics, are not directly related to the four issues being examined in this paper. The published articles include those cited in the reference section of this paper and authored by Copeland and Ingram (1982); Hayes and Millar (1990); Ingram (1984); Mensah and Li (1993); Robbins and Austin (1986); Roberts, Glezen, and Jones (1990); Sorensen and Grove (1977); Wallace (1981); and Wilson and Howard (1984).

Of a total of 63 citations shown in the SSCI, all citations appeared in academic journals. Thus, this look at a selection of governmentally-related papers published in *JAR* and *The Accounting Review* would seem to indicate that such research primarily, perhaps exclusively, benefits an academic audience since all located citations appear in other academic journals. Especially notable for its absence is *The Journal of Accountancy*, the journal of the American Institute of Certified Public Accountants. This journal was included as a covered journal by the Social Science Citation Index during most of the years of our search, from 1977 until coverage ended in 1994. The absence of citation in what is arguably the profession's leading practice journal, *The Journal of Accountancy*, is a telling point.

CLOSING OBSERVATIONS

Our finding is that two of the more established, prestigious accounting journals receive, at best, a mixed rating for their ability in recent years to cover relevant and timely governmental accounting topics This lack of relevant content of the academic journals is not without costs.

For one thing, the practice marketplace changes quickly. It will not delay for the decade or more that is necessary for scholars and journals to respond. A great cost may be the growing perception that scholarly, theoretical research does not lead, but rather that it follows. This seems to be the case for governmental accounting and auditing where, for example, accounting scholars are only now becoming interested in SEA and performance auditing, a generation or more after practitioners began to use the concepts in their daily work. The societal cost is that the value of the thinking of many good minds is lost to the process. And, practitioners understandably begin to doubt the value of academic research.

Nor should the actual dollar costs of this breakdown be overlooked. Several years ago *Business Week* stated that "The top B-schools alone spend nearly $240 million on research.... The bulk of the money supports faculty time not dedicated to teaching" (Cover Story 1990, 62). Viewed at a more modest level, let us take the case of an accounting faculty of ten tenured and tenure-track faculty members at a large state university, where the department has graduate programs. Faculty members who are actively engaged in research are permitted teaching loads of five courses, rather than the eight they would otherwise teach. This, in essence, constitutes a reduction of 37.5 percent from the normal teaching load. Accounting faculty salaries are high, especially at this type of school. Thus, an average salary of $90,000, including fringe benefits, would not be unrealistic ($72,000 base salary × .25 fringe benefits). This accounting department, in effect, is costing and, hopefully, contributing, about $337,500 each academic year to accounting research ($90,000 × 10 × .375). In addition, added costs would likely be incurred to hire temporary or adjunct faculty to teach any unstaffed course work, to dedicate graduate assistants to aid faculty in their research, to acquire research (computer) equipment, to provide word processing, and so on. And, note that this is only for one department, at one university, for one year.

If we are to assume, then, that there is indeed no "free lunch," is it reasonable, even responsible, to ask: What are the taxpayers getting for this investment? Surely it must be more than professors, writing only for a handful of other professors, who then recommend tenure for a job well done. A dean quoted in this paper's opening stated it clearly: "Why should we care about what you write? If the answer...doesn't matter to anybody then maybe you'd better think of another question." It would seem that the question (and the possible answers) are the last thing many researchers think about. Tenure, promotion, respect of colleagues, what the "good" journals publish, the availability of data, the ability to demonstrate techniques and methods—all these seem to be considered over the question itself.

The current dilemma in academic accounting research may merely indicate that most scholars are unwilling or unable to "buck the trend" and are acting rationally within the system they are handed. Thus, the system itself needs to be changed. Robert Freeman has observed:

> In case you haven't noticed, many of the leading academic accounting journals appear to be statistical methodology journals rather than accounting journals. Indeed, the editors of many of these journals seem to be more concerned with elaborate statistical methodology and jargon than with the relevance of the research topic or whether meaningful conclusions are drawn and useful recommendations are made.... The rigor often seems to be more in the methodology than in the relevance of the research topic or the rigor of the analyses made.
>
> Moreover, if professors like Bill Paton, Bill Vatter, Robert Sprouse, Bob Mautz, or Bob Anthony were beginning their careers today, their outstanding analytical work would be *rejected* by most or all of today's leading academic journals (Freeman 1990, 45).

Some of the ingredients of a new system of scholarly research might include the following. Either current journals need to reshape their mission, or new journals ought to be created to bring together the worlds of theory and practice, of scholars and practitioners. More journal editors need to team with practitioners as co-editors, and be certain to include large numbers of practitioners as reviewers. Professor-authors need to reach out to practitioners as co-authors, and journals ought to increasingly insist on such team manuscripts. Deans and chairs need to insist on relevant research. Funding organizations must demand potential usefulness as a leading funding criteria. And everyone in the cycle needs to increasingly ask: "Why should we care about what you write?"

ACKNOWLEDGMENTS

I am grateful to participants at the University of Akron–Kent State University 1998–99 Research Symposium, to Gary John Previts, and to the journal reviewers for their constructive comments.

NOTES

1. The Governmental Accounting Standards Board (GASB), created in 1984, followed the creation of FASB by more than a decade. GASB's current research agenda includes several fundamental accounting issues, some of which have been long settled in the private sector.

2. The basic principles in GASB's current codification of GAAP clearly evolved from the original 1934 pronouncements of the National Committee on Municipal Accounting.

REFERENCES

American Assembly of Collegiate Schools of Business (AACSB). 1996. Remaking doctoral education: The missing link to customer satisfaction? *Newsline* 26(Summer): 1–6.

Banker, R.D., W.W. Cooper, and G. Potter. 1992. A perspective on research in governmental accounting. *The Accounting Review* 67(July): 496–510.

Bricker, R.J., and G.J. Previts. 1990. The sociology of accountancy: A study of academic and practice community schisms. *Accounting Horizons* 4(March): 1–14.

Brown, R.E., T.P. Gallagher, and M.C. Williams. 1982. *Auditing Performance in Government*. New York: John Wiley & Sons.

Brown, R.E., and R.D. Pethtel. 1974. A matter of facts: State legislative performance auditing. *Public Administration Review* 34(July/August): 318–327.

Cooper, W.W. 1995. Research and practice in contemporary accounting. *Speech For Induction Into Accounting Hall of Fame* (August 14): 1–6.

Copeland, R.M., and R.W. Ingram. 1982. The association between municipal accounting information and bond rating changes. *Journal of Accounting Research* 20(Autumn): 275–289.

Cover Story. 1990. Is Research In the Ivory Tower Fuzzy, Irrelevant, Pretentious? *Business Week* (October 29): 62–66.

Dyckman, T.R., and S.A. Zeff. 1984. Two decades of the *Journal of Accounting Research*. *Journal of Accounting Research* 22(Spring): 225–297.

Freeman, R.A. 1955. Reporting and interpreting the cost of state government. *The Accounting Review* 30(April): 232–239.

Freeman R.J. 1990. Public sector research in the universities: Significant research efforts. *The Government Accountants Journal* 38(Winter): 43–49.

Frisbee, I.N. 1939. The application of governmental accounting principles. *The Accounting Review* 14(March): 27–33.

Fu, P. 1971. Governmental accounting in China during the Chou Dynasty (1122 BC–256 BC). *Journal of Accounting Research* 9(Spring): 40–51.

Governmental Accounting Standards Board (GASB). 1985. *Concepts Statement No. 1: Objectives of Financial Reporting*. Norwalk, CT: GASB.

Governmental Accounting Standards Board (GASB). 1992. *Proposed Statement: Measurement Focus and Basis of Accounting (Statement No. 11)*. Norwalk, CT: GASB.

Governmental Accounting Standards Board (GASB). 1994. *Concepts Statement No. 2: Service Efforts and Accomplishments Reporting*. Norwalk, CT: GASB.

Governmental Accounting Standards Board (GASB). 1995. *Preliminary Views: Governmental Financial Reporting Model—Core Financial Statements*. Norwalk, CT: GASB.

Governmental Accounting Standards Board (GASB). 1997. *Exposure Draft: Basic Financial Statements—and Management's Discussion and Analysis—for State and Local Governments*. Norwalk, CT: GASB.

Hayes, R.D., and J.A. Millar. 1990. Measuring production efficiency in a not-for-profit setting. *The Accounting Review* 65(July): 505–519.

Herbert, L. 1956. Modern accounting methods for governmental units. *The Accounting Review* 31(October): 628–631.

Hylton, D.P. 1957. Needed: More information and understandable financial statements from governmental units. *The Accounting Review* 32(January): 51–54.

Ingram, R.W. 1984. Economic incentives and the choice of state government accounting practices. *Journal of Accounting Research* 22(Spring): 126–144.

Lorig, A.N. 1937. Classification of municipal income and expenditures. *The Accounting Review* 12(June): 163–173.

Lorig, A.N. 1941. Determining the current financial position of a city. *The Accounting Review* 16(March): 41–49.

Maher, M.W. 1997. Regulating research: Relevance versus elegance? *Research In Accounting Regulation* 11: 47–72.

Mensah, J.M., and S.H. Li. 1993. Measuring production efficiency in a not-for-profit setting: An extension. *The Accounting Review* 68(January): 66–88.

Morey, L. 1926. Fund and proprietary accounts in governmental accounting. *The Accounting Review* 1(June): 77–84.

Morey, L. 1934. Principles of municipal accounting. *The Accounting Review* 9(December): 319–325.

Newton, W.K. 1954. New developments and simplified approaches to municipal accounting. *The Accounting Review* 29(October): 656–660.

Previts, G.J., and R.E. Brown. 1993. The development of government accounting. *The Accounting Historians Journal* 20(December): 119–138.

Robbins, W.A., and K.R. Austin. 1986. Disclosure quality in governmental financial reports: An assessment of the appropriateness of a compound measure. *Journal of Accounting Research* 24(Autumn): 412–421.

Roberts, R.W., G.W. Glezen, and T.W. Jones. 1990. Determinants of auditor change in the public sector. *Journal of Accounting Research* 28(Spring): 220–228.

Seldon, S. 1943. Internal auditing for the state of New York. *The Accounting Review* 18(July): 239–244.

Sorensen, J.E. and H.D. Grove. 1977. Cost-outcome and cost-effectiveness analysis: Emerging nonprofit performance evaluation techniques. *The Accounting Review* 52(July): 658–675.

U.S. General Accounting Office. 1994. *Government Auditing Standards*. Washington, DC: U.S. Government Printing Office.

Wallace, W.A. 1981. The association between municipal market measures and selected financial reporting practices. *Journal of Accounting Research* 19(Autumn): 502–520.

Wilson, E.R., and T.P. Howard. 1984. The association between municipal market measures and selected financial reporting practices: Additional evidence. *Journal of Accounting Research* 22(Spring): 207–224.

THE IMPACT OF ACCOUNTING INFORMATION ON CONTRIBUTIONS TO CHARITABLE ORGANIZATIONS

Janet S. Greenlee and Karen L. Brown

ABSTRACT

Although numerous studies have examined the impact of accounting information on investments in publicly traded corporations, few have addressed the ways in which accounting information affects contributions to nonprofit organizations. The two types of organizations are similar in at least one important respect: Both rely on external sources of scarce capital. Only a limited amount of funds are available to nonprofit organizations, and each organization must somehow convince resource providers that it deserves financial support.

This paper explores the relationship between selected information and contributions to charitable organizations. Specifically, cross-sectional regression analysis is used to see if any relationships exist between administrative cost ratios, fund-raising cost ratios, and contributions to charitable organizations registered in the Commonwealth of Pennsylvania between 1991 and 1994. The results indicate that an inverse relationship exists between administrative cost ratios and contributions: More

Research in Accounting Regulation, Volume 13, pages 111-125.

ISBN: 0-7623-0520-7

contributions were received by those charities with smaller administrative cost ratios. A positive relationship was found between fund-raising ratios and contributions: More contributions were received by those charities with larger fund-raising cost ratios.

INTRODUCTION

Numerous studies have examined the impact of accounting and other information on investments in publicly traded corporations. Little comparable research has addressed the ways in which such information affects the funding of nonprofit organizations. The two types of organizations are similar in at least one important respect: Both rely on external sources of scarce capital. Only a limited amount of resources (whether private donations or government funding) is available to nonprofit organizations, and each organization must somehow convince resource providers that it deserves financial support (Gronbjerg 1993).

The Financial Accounting Standards Board (FASB) determined that non-business organizations should provide information useful to both present and potential funding sources as a basis for resource allocation decisions (1980). Charitable organizations are required to disclose increasing quantities of accounting and other information at significant cost to them in both time and money. A 1989 American Accounting Association (AAA) report on nonprofit organization performance measures, however, stated that "We currently know relatively little about how important decision makers in the voluntary sector use basic financial information" (AAA 1989, 109). In an era of scarce resources, an empirical examination of the impact of that information could be beneficial in discovering the extent to which the FASB's "usefulness" objective is being met.

We conducted a study to explore the relationship between selected accounting information and charitable contributions, specifically the impact of administrative and fund-raising costs on contributions to charitable organizations registered in Pennsylvania between 1991 and 1994. Contributors *claim* to use financial information in making contribution decisions (Reynolds 1981; Sarver 1994; Swarden 1996). Although laboratory experiments have provided some verification that contributors use such information (Reed and Koch 1989; Stout 1997; Khumawala and Gordon 1997), the sparse empirical evidence on the impact of financial information on actual contributions has been mixed (Steinberg 1985; Weisbrod and Dominguez 1986; Greenlee and Knoblett 1993; Tinkelman 1997).

The remainder of this paper is organized as follows. The next section examines the economic context of the nonprofit sector, and the characteristics and operating environment of charities. The theoretical foundation of the study is then considered. The hypotheses and study method are presented, and the study results are reported. The final section presents a summary and conclusion.

CONCEPTUAL FRAMEWORK

The Nonprofit Sector

A nonprofit is formally defined as an organization that has officially registered with the Internal Revenue Service (IRS) as a section 501, tax-exempt organization. Nonprofits are given tax-exempt status in part because "no part of the net earnings" shall inure to the benefit of, or be distributed to, its members, trustee, officers, or other private persons" (§501). The FASB's (1980) definition corresponds to that of the IRS by formally describing a nonprofit organization as one that receives a significant amount of resources from providers who do not expect a return on those resources, does not operate to earn a profit, and does not have defined ownership interests that can be redeemed, transferred, or sold (SFAC 4, para. 6). Although both the IRS and the FASB specifically exclude governmental organizations, they do include nonprofits as diverse as social service agencies, museums, cemetery organizations, unions, private schools, country clubs, and public radio stations. Nonprofits examined in this study are charities which fall within the 501(c)(3) section of the IRS tax code. These organizations are ones which are "organized and operated exclusively for religious, charitable, scientific, literary, educational, or similar purposes" (Hodgkinson and Weitzman 1996, 321).

The nonprofit sector is a "hybrid" that provides public goods (the primary function of government) through private organizations (typical of the commercial sector), and hence is not immune to many of the constraints of the economy. The nonprofit sector tends to supply those sorts of public goods for which there is not a demand from the majority of its citizens (Weisbrod 1988). These organizations exist to provide services rather than to generate profits (Salamon and Anheier 1996). Profits measure effectiveness and efficiency of business organizations. The lack of a profit motive in the charitable sector makes measurement of their effectiveness and efficiency extremely difficult (Anthony 1988; Chang and Tuckman 1993). Several normative studies have attempted to develop practical measures of the effectiveness or efficiency of nonprofit organizations (AAA 1989; AICPA 1972; Elkin and Molitor 1984; Gambino and Reardon 1981; Lohmann 1980); however, none have been widely accepted (AAA 1989; Gronbjerg 1993).

Nonprofits are subject to a myriad of increasingly complex reporting requirements. Many are multi-funded, receiving funds from such sources as local community fund-raising efforts (such as United Way), client fees, governmental grants, private foundations, and individual and/or corporate contributions (Lohmann 1980; Gronbjerg 1993). One result of the multiplicity of funding sources can be an abundance of complex reporting and accountability requirements. Each resource provider may require different year-ends, distinctive charts of accounts, and unique procedures for allocating indirect costs (AAA 1989). (Universities' problems with the allocation of allowable indirect costs to be reimbursed by federal grants have been well documented in the popular media.)

Although both institutionally separate from government and self-governing, nonprofits operate in an atmosphere of increasing governmental regulation and public scrutiny. For example, in the second and third quarter of 1994 alone, 11 states either instituted or increased nonprofit regulation and reporting requirements (Bush 1994). Although this pace has slowed somewhat, the trend continues. One section of the 1996 Taxpayer Bill of Rights requires significantly increased nonprofit disclosure. Under this law, nonprofits are required not only to supply a copy of their informational tax returns (Form 990) to any requesting party, but to make these returns "widely available" (*Nonprofit Times* 1996).[1] The National Council for Charitable Statistics (NCCS) plans to place the Form 990 information from all tax-exempt organizations on the Internet (Gordon, Greenlee, and Nitterhouse 1999). The expense and time required to implement these new regulations further emphasizes the importance of discovering whether or not financial information is used.

Signaling Theory and Charitable Organizations

Signaling theory was initially developed in an attempt to provide one explanation for some of the imperfections in the supposedly efficient capital market (Ross 1978). In an efficient market, a "good news," or high quality signal, such as the voluntary early disclosure of earnings, or the choice of a "big" audit firm, should be reflected in higher security prices (Bar-Yosef and Livnat 1984, Palmrose 1986, Pownall and Waymire 1989, Roberts, Glezen, and Jones 1990, Yeo 1995). In the competitive nonprofit environment, a contributor may have difficulty measuring the value of the organization to the community (Gronbjerg 1993; Gui 1991). Consequently, a potential donor may not be able to differentiate between charities providing similar services. The charity that credibly signals its superior quality should be rewarded with a higher "price," i.e., increased contributions. The effect cannot be reflected instantaneously, as it has been assumed to for corporations, because contribution decisions cannot be changed retroactively. It can, however, be reflected in a subsequent funding cycle: Contributors can choose to allocate their resources elsewhere or not contribute at all. Accordingly, a charity sending a high quality signal should receive more resources than one sending a low quality signal or one that is not signaling.

Research Question Development

Previous research on the importance of financial information in this sector has been predominantly normative (AAA 1989; AICPA 1972; Elkin and Molitor 1984; Gambino and Reardon 1981), but some empirical research has been conducted.

Studies have explored the *perceived* importance of financial information by contributors and potential contributors. An early survey by Reynolds (1981) asked three resource provider groups, corporate, foundation, and United Way executives, what information they used in making resource decisions. All three groups indicated that they used financial statement information when making contribution decisions. Income statement information was ranked as particularly useful and important.

This early finding of the perceived importance of financial information to donors was confirmed by four more recent studies. Interestingly, all four studies found that contributors were interested in program cost ratios. Respondents to two 1994 surveys conducted by the *Nonprofit Times* claimed to use information regarding the proportion of charities' income going to programs when making a contribution decision (Sarver 1994). A focus group study conducted by the Council of Federations found that employees participating in workplace campaigns desired data on the proportion of total expenses going toward administrative costs (*Nonprofit Times* 1994). Finally, the Charities' Review Council of Minnesota asked a panel of randomly selected contributors what information they needed to make contribution decisions. They found that contributors needed to know financial information, particularly the proportion of contributions used to provide services (Swarden 1996).

Three studies used laboratory settings to examine the impact of budgeted financial information on donor allocations. Reed and Koch (1989) studied paid United Way employees in a laboratory setting. They found a link between budgeted financial information and resource allocation decisions. A more recent laboratory experiment using United Way volunteer budget allocation committee members considered materiality in United Way resource allocation decisions (Stout 1997). Budgeted financial information did impact resources allocated, although not as much as nonfinancial information (such as the commission of illegal acts by management). Finally, a laboratory experiment conducted by Khumawala and Gordon (1997) used accounting students to study the importance placed on various financial and nonfinancial disclosures by potential donors. They found that although the subjects claimed that (primarily expense-related) financial information was important, disclosures relating to the primary purpose, or mission, of the charity outweighed all other information in their "actual" decisions.

While these studies investigated the *perceived* importance of financial information to potential contributors, other studies focusing on the impact of information on *actual* contributions have yielded mixed results. Weisbrod and Dominguez (1986) looked at the IRS Form 990 informational returns of 7,444 charitable organizations and found a positive relationship between the level of contributions and the level of fund-raising expenditures. Steinberg's (1985) examination of Form 990 returns submitted by 2,266 charitable organizations found no relationship between non-program costs and the level of contributions. Greenlee and Knoblett (1993) integrated a multi-year database provided by United Way of America with a survey mailed to a sample of charities included in the United Way database to examine the impact of both financial and nonfinancial budgeted information on actual resource allocations. They found no relationship between budgeted administrative costs and resource allocations. Tinkelman (1997) used data filed by charities with New York State between 1992 and 1994. He confirmed Weisbrod and Dominguez's findings of a positive relationship between the level of fund-raising expense and the level of contributions. However, the negative relationship he found between total non-program costs and level of contributions disputes Steinberg's findings.

Thus, in spite of the growing number of studies in this field, the AAA's (1989) statement regarding the lack of awareness of decision maker use of financial information in this sector remains largely accurate.

This study explores the effect of selected information on actual contributions to charities. If contributors are sensitive to signals, they will change the size of their contribution. This study differs from earlier empirical research by examining two signals simultaneously: administrative costs and fund-raising costs. In theory, contributors should be sensitive to both signals. Larger proportions of administrative and fund-raising costs (as a percentage of total costs) necessarily result in a lower proportion of spending on the charitable purpose, which is often the primary motivating factor for contributors (Weisbrod and Rodriquez 1986; Hodgkinson and Weitzman 1996).

Administrative (AD) and Fund-Raising (FR) Costs

Because no measures have been developed that accurately assess effectiveness and efficiency of service, reported administrative and fund-raising costs may be perceived as signals of quality by contributors in this sector. A charity that is organized more efficiently (has lower administrative costs) or is more effective in generating revenues (and thus has lower fund-raising costs) may be perceived as being a higher quality charity than one that is less effective or efficient in these areas. Two national organizations recognize the importance of the relationship between administrative and fund-raising costs, and quality. The Better Business Bureau (BBB) declares that fund-raising costs should not exceed 35 percent of related contributions and total non-program expenses should not be greater than 50 percent of total income (BBB 1991). The National Charities Information Bureau (NCIB) requires that its approved charities spend no more than 40 percent of total expenditures on the sum of administrative and fund-raising costs (NCIB 1991).

Gambino and Reardon (1981, 7) define administrative costs for a nonprofit organization as "those that relate to the maintenance of the organization and not directly to program services." Fund-raising costs, also unrelated to program services, are expenses incurred in raising money. The smaller the proportion of funds a charity spends on administrative or fund-raising costs (and hence, the larger the proportion it allocates to program service costs), the more efficient and effective the charity may be perceived to be, and the larger the allocation of contributions the charity should receive. Our two research questions are:

Q1. Does a relationship exist between reported administrative cost signals and contributions?

Q2. Does a relationship exist between reported fund-raising cost signals and contributions?

THE STUDY

Research Design

The purpose of this study is to explore whether a relationship exists between signals and contributions to charitable organizations. A cross-sectional regression model developed to examine the research questions generated earlier in this paper examines the impact of both administrative and fund-raising costs on contributions. The model reflects the normative beliefs of the NCIB in assuming that contributors *should* respond to signals of the ratios of non-program expenditures to total expenditures regardless of charitable purpose. The conceptual model is as follows:

$$\text{Contributions}_t = f\,[\text{Administrative Cost Ratio}_{t-1}, \text{Fund-Raising Cost Ratio}_{t-1}, \text{Total Contributions}_{t-1}]$$

This model suggests that contributors are sensitive to the prior year ratios of administrative costs and fund-raising costs to total costs. The relationship will be positive if contributors are convinced of the necessity of the costs, and negative or nonsignificant if they are not. We use prior year costs because this information is evident to contributors only after the fiscal year end. If contributors use this information, an inverse relationship should exist between contributions and both administrative and fund-raising ratios. We include prior year total contributions to control for size.

Data Collection and Measurement

The data for the study were obtained from a database provided by the Pennsylvania Bureau of Charitable Organizations (hereafter, the Bureau), operating under the aegis of the Secretary of State of the Commonwealth of Pennsylvania. The agency has, since 1989, required all charities that raise more than $25,000 in non-governmental revenues within the boundaries of the Commonwealth, or who pay a fund raiser any amount of money (and not otherwise excluded by statute) to register and file annual financial statements with the Bureau.[2] Charities with more than $100,000 in annual revenues, and not otherwise exempt from registering, are required to file a "long form" financial statement (hereafter, BCO-23) and to submit audited financial statements within 180 days of each fiscal year end.[3] From a database of 952 charities, 251 reported no activity within the 1991–1994 period under consideration, leaving a base of 701 charities for examination.

We extracted the following information to generate the variables for the study: general contributions,[4] administrative expenditures,[5] fund-raising expenditures[6] and total expenditures[7] (BCO-23). While the NCIB (1991) used total expenditures as the denominator in both administrative and fund-raising ratios, we used this total in the fund-raising ratio only. The administrative ratio in this study was calculated by dividing administrative expenditures by the sum of administrative and program expenditures. In this manner, we avoid the statistical problem of collinearity; in a zero-sum context, an elevated level of one variable would inherently imply a lower level in the other.

Determination of the specific costs included in both administrative costs (Nitterhouse and Sharp 1988) and fund-raising costs (Chitnis 1996) is a complex issue that was not considered in this study. Both administrative and fund-raising costs are those not directly resulting in program services, *as defined by the Bureau and recognized/reported by the charity*. The possible propensity to understate these costs was not considered, as the purpose of the study was to explore the relationship between *reported* information and contributions, rather than to investigate the *accuracy* of that information.

DATA DESCRIPTION

Table 1 displays summary statistics of the relevant information gleaned from the database. Between 1991 and 1994, mean total expenditures grew steadily from $4.532 million to $5.249 million. Median expenditures were significantly smaller, but increased from $501,174 to $583,248 during the same period. Total expenses for all 701 charities in the study grew from $3.177 billion in 1991 to $3.679 billion in 1994.

Mean total contributions were $2.006 million in 1991, decreased slightly in 1992, but increased during each of the next two years, reaching $2.149 million in 1994. Total contributions received by all 701 charities increased from $1.406 billion in 1991 to $1.506 billion in 1994. The $500 million increase in total expenses reported by charities during this period is far greater than this $100 million increase in contributions, indicating that these charities also relied on alternative sources of funding.

Throughout this period mean Administrative Ratio remained at approximately 16.8 percent; mean Fund-raising Ratio declined from 12 percent to 9.82 percent. A mean of 50 charities reported no administrative expenditures, and 166 charities reported no fund-raising expenditures in any given year. An average of 22 organizations per year reported incurring neither of these costs during any given year, with eight charities reporting neither cost for the entire 1991–1994 period. We were not surprised by the number of charities not reporting these expenses,

Table 1. Descriptive Statistics Charitable Organizations Registered in the Commonwealth of Pennsylvania 1991–1994

	Year	*n*	*Mean*	*Median*	*s.d.*	*Non-Reporters**
Total Contributions						
	1991	701	$2,006,149	$171,840	7,380,151	8
	1992	701	$1,988,804	$168,764	7,319,878	8
	1993	701	$2,119,794	$186,065	7,723,575	10
	1994	701	$2,148,964	$189,179	7,717,148	11
Total Expenses						
	1991	701	$4,531,847	$501,174	18,550,887	5
	1992	701	$4,913,884	$518,321	21,289,669	1
	1993	701	$5,089,301	$559,768	21,952,608	1
	1994	701	$5,248,599	$583,248	22,103,562	0
Administrative Ratio						
	1991	696	16.62%	12.01%	17.24%	57
	1992	700	16.88%	12.11%	17.49%	52
	1993	700	16.85%	12.58%	16.84%	46
	1994	701	16.81%	11.85%	17.39%	44
Fundraising Ratio						
	1991	696	12.00%	4.65%	18.97%	167
	1992	700	10.22%	4.24%	16.47%	166
	1993	700	10.35%	4.04%	16.54%	169
	1994	701	9.82%	3.73%	16.04%	173

Note: *n reported as "0" or "system missing"

because researchers have found, for example, that approximately 40 percent of the publicly supported charities registered with the IRS did not report any fund-raising expense in their most recent IRS Form 990 filings (Guidestar Directory of American Charities 1996). Again, our study is concerned with *reported* expenses, not with the accurate reporting of these expenses.

By contrast, a mean of 15 charities reported incurring 100 percent of total expenditures in the administrative and fund-raising categories. While eight organizations reported this full 100 percent total on non-program expenditures for three of the four years under consideration, two reported 100 percent for the entire four-year period. However, the majority of charities (approximately 81 percent each year) reported total expenditures for these categories within the NCIB's recommended 40-percent guideline.

For the information displayed in Table 1, missing values were coded as zero-dollar amounts. However, where these missing values were in the denominator of the calculation of Administrative and Fund-Raising Ratios, the value of these ratios was not defined. This problem existed primarily in the ratios for 1991, where five charities reported no expenditures. In addition, an observation was omitted from analysis if *any* of the values between the two years under consideration at the time was undefined. Last, the natural log transformation of the dependent variable, total contributions, was used to adjust the highly skewed distribution of the variables. Thus, the dependent variable was undefined in a small number of cases, from eight in 1992 to 11 in 1994.

Cross-Sectional Model

In this section, we test the following model:

$Ln(CONTRIB_t)^8 \quad = \quad B_0 + B_1 ADPCT_{t-1} + B2FRPCT_{t-1} + TOTCON_{t-1} + e_t$

where:

$Ln(CONTRIB_t)$	=	natural logarithm of total contributions in current year
$ADPCT_{t-1}$	=	ratio of prior year administrative expense to total expense in prior year
$FRPCT_{t-1}$	=	ratio of prior year fund-raising expense to total expense in prior year
$TOTCON_{t-1}$	=	total contributions in prior year
e_x	=	error term

This model suggests first that contributors are sensitive to the prior year ratios of administrative costs (ACPCT) and fund-raising costs (FRPCT) to total expenditure costs in the prior year (Total Expenditures). We use prior year costs because this signaling information is evident to potential contributors only after the fiscal year end. If contributors are sensitive to administrative or fund-raising costs, as suggested by both the NCIB and BBB, an inverse relationship should exist.

Second, by including prior year contributions, this model controls for the possible passivity of contributors. If the purpose of the particular organization appeals to contributors, they may tend to continue to provide resources in subsequent years, despite reported performance ratio signals. Indeed, potential donors may not even look at expenditure ratios if they are otherwise satisfied with the charity. Alternatively, if performance ratios are unacceptable, these potential donors may choose to contribute to a different organization or withhold contributions altogether. Either of these latter alternatives will negatively affect the subsequent contributions to the original charity.

Because the model depends on prior year information, analysis is limited to the 1992–1994 contribution period. Standardized (beta) coefficients from least squares regression and the related two-tailed probabilities appear in Table 2. The model was significant for all three years of analysis, with the adjusted R^2 exceeding 0.32 for all years. A normal probability plot for all three years of analysis indicated that the residuals were normally distributed, supporting the use of the natural logarithm of the dependent variable.

Table 2. Cross-sectional Regression Results: Charitable Organizations Registered in the Commonwealth of Pennsylvania, 1992-1994

	Standardized Beta (t-value)	*Standardized Beta (t-value)*	*Standardized Beta (t-value)*
Year	*1992*	*1993*	*1994*
	Dependent Variable: Ln (Total Contributions$_t$)		
n	679	678	681
Administrative Ratio$_{t-1}$	−0.117	−0.150	−0.156
	(−3.580)**	(−4.738)**	(−4.847)**
Fundraising Ratio$_{t-1}$	0.086	0.073	0.116
	(2.662)*	(2.320)*	(3.632)**
Total Contributions$_{t-1}$	0.537	0.553	0.542
	(16.822)**	(17.704)**	(17.306)**
F-value	109.131**	124.917**	122.858**
Adjusted R^2	0.323	0.354	0.347

Notes: *Significant at the 0.05 level
**Significant at the 0.001 level

As expected, the coefficient for the control variable TOTCON was both positive and significant. For whatever reason the charity appealed to contributors in any given year, it appears to have maintained this appeal in ensuing years.

Q1: Does a relationship exist between administrative ratio signals and contributions? Prior literature suggests that administrative cost ratios should be inversely related to contributions. Administrative Ratio (ADPCT) was significant ($p < 0.001$) with the expected sign for all three years of analysis. Contributors do appear to respond to administrative cost ratios, with higher ratios resulting in smaller total contributions.

Q2: Does a relationship exist between fund-raising ratio signals and contributions? While theory suggests that fund-raising cost ratios should also be inversely related to contributions, we found this not to be the case; the positive relationship between lagged fund-raising *ratios* and contributions is in contrast to the inverse relationship between lagged fund-raising *levels* and contributions found by Weisbrod and Dominguez (1986) and Tinkelman (1997). The relationship in all three years was positive, indicating that contributors tend to contribute more to charities with larger fund-raising ratios. While this positive relationship was somewhat less significant for the 1992 and 1993 contributions [$p = 0.021$ and $p = 0.008$, respectively], it was highly statistically significant ($p = 0.001$) for the 1994 fiscal year.

SUMMARY AND CONCLUSION

The FASB suggests that one important attribute of information in the non-business sector is its usefulness to both present and potential funding sources in resource allocation decisions. Our study empirically examined the impact of selected information on one such funding source, contributions, in the charitable sector. We used cross-sectional regression analysis to see if any relationships exist between prior year administrative cost ratios, prior year fund-raising cost ratios, and current year contributions. Significant inverse relationships were found between administrative cost ratios and contributions for all three years, and a significant positive relationship emerged between fund-raising ratios and contributions.

The findings of this exploratory study have implications for both the charitable sector and the accounting profession. The prior literature indicating that both administrative and fund-raising cost ratio signals are potentially useful to contributors was partially confirmed. Contributors do seem to pay attention to administrative costs by contributing more to those charities with lower administrative cost ratios. The implication for smaller charities is not auspicious, since the large fixed component of administration (which includes such costs as management salaries, rent, and utilities) may result in higher administrative ratios for smaller charities than for larger ones.

Our findings contrast with those of both Weisbrod and Dominguez (1986) and Tinkelman (1997). They found a positive relationship between current fund-raising levels and contributions, but an inverse relationship between lagged fund-raising levels and contributions. We found significant positive relationships between lagged fund-raising ratios and contributions for all three years of the study. This positive relationship between lagged fund-raising ratios and contributions implies that donors do not penalize charities with higher reported fund-raising ratios. In addition, because prior year contributions are the greatest predictor of current year contributions in the model, increasing fund-raising cost ratios in the current year appears to enhance future contributions. Thus, a fund raiser may be appropriate for a new or stagnant charity. A challenge to nonprofit management is to determine at what point resources can and should be allocated to program expenditures, rather than further fund-raising efforts, to support the mission for which the charity was established.

While our results confirm some prior empirical analyses of the charitable sector, some limitations inhibit the generalizability of the conclusions. First, the data do not include some organizations (such as nonprofit hospitals and educational institutions). Smaller charities may be under-represented, as these organizations are not required to fill out the BCO-23. In addition, the large number of charities reporting no administrative expenditures suggests that this category of costs is variously interpreted, as may also be true for fund-raising expenditures.

Little empirical research has been conducted on the impact of information on contributions to charitable organizations. As a result, many avenues are open for future research. Other areas warranting further investigation include the addition of such variables as organization purpose or type of service. From the perspective of the contributor, studies of decision-making mechanisms in a variety of arenas (private, corporate, governmental, foundation) would be a significant extension of this study.

NOTES

1. Originally, the bill would have required significantly greater disclosure. Nonprofits would have been required to disclose publicly (1) any change in governing board or CPA firm, (2) IRS tax exemption applications, and (3) the payment of professional fund-raising fees (Hock 1994).

2. Exempted from this filing requirement are those charities (a) specifically exempted by name, (b) that solicit only within the membership of the organization by members of that organization, (c) that use only volunteers, members, or permanent employees to conduct fund-raising activities, (d) receive less than $25,000 in any year in contributions, and (e) for specific classes of organizations (typically volunteer fire companies, veteran's organizations, rescue organizations) (Commonwealth of Pennsylvania 1994, 7).

3. Froelich and Knoepfle's (1996) comparison of information reported in Form 990 filings with audited financial statements found a high degree of correlation between these two reports. However, the correlations were higher for charities with total annual revenues greater than $100,000.

4. General contributions (source of the dependent variable) are "total contributions from individuals, commercial co-venturers, corporations and other businesses, unrelated exempt organizations, trusts, legacies, bequests, donated land, buildings, property, equipment, and materials" and the "gross amount received from all special fund-raising events activities conducted either by the organization or on its behalf." The variable does not include revenues from the following sources: governmental grants and contracts, federated fund-raising organizations (such as the United Way), membership dues, investments or sale of assets other than inventory, or revenues earned for "providing services or performing activities for which the organization was created to conduct" (BCO-23, 17).

5. Administrative expenditures include "all management and general expenses of a charitable organization, not identifiable with a single program or fund-raising activity, but indispensable to the conduct of such programs and activities and to an organization's existence, including expenses for the overall direction of the organization, business management, general record keeping, financial reporting and related activities, salaries, rent, supplies, equipment, and general overhead" (BCO-23, 17).

6. Fund-raising expenditures include "those expenses incurred in inducing others to make contributions to a charitable organization for which the contributors will receive no direct economic benefit" and all expenses "related to special fund-raising events." Fund-raising expenses normally include "salaries, rent, acquiring and maintaining mailing lists, printing, mailing, and all direct or indirect costs of soliciting" (BCO-23, 18).

7. Total expenditures include administrative, fund-raising, program, and miscellaneous expenses for the charitable organization. This value was used as the denominator in the Administrative Ratio and Fund-Raising Ratio used in the regression model, following the model used by the NCIB (1991). The BBB uses total revenues as the denominator to determine administrative and fund-raising expenditure percentages (1991). However, we found that total expenditures and revenues were highly correlated in this study (Pearson product moment correlation (0.997 for all years); thus, the arbitrary choice should have little effect on the analysis.

8. The natural log of the independent variable was chosen for three reasons. First, preliminary analysis indicated that proximate years' total contributions were highly correlated (Pearson $r > 0.90$).

The lagged contributions dominated the relationship; however, it was the intent of the authors to use this as a variable to control for size, stability, reputation, and other potentially omitted variables. Second, the natural log preserved the monotonic relationship in the total contributions from year to year. Third, use of the transformed dependent variable resulted in a highly normal distribution of the residuals, one of the underlying assumptions of linear regression.

REFERENCES

American Accounting Association (AAA). 1989. *Measuring the Performance of Nonprofit Organizations: The State of the Art*. Sarasota, FL: AAA.

American Institute of Certified Public Accountants (AICPA). 1972. *Objectives of Financial Statements for Governmental and Not-for-Profit Organizations*. New York: AICPA.

Anthony, R. 1988. *Financial Accounting in Non-Business Organizations*. Stamford, CT: Financial Accounting Standards Board.

Bar-Yosef, S., and J. Livnat. 1984. Auditor selection: An incentive signaling approach. *Accounting and Business Research* Autumn: 301–309.

Better Business Bureau (BBB). 1991. *Standards for Charitable Solicitations*. New York: Council of Better Business Bureaus Inc.

Bush, B. 1994. Regulation watch. *Nonprofit Times*. April–September.

Chang, C., and Tuckman, H. 1993. Financial vulnerability and attrition as measures of nonprofit performance. In A. Ben-Ner and B. Gui (Eds.), *The Nonprofit Sector in the Mixed Economy*: 163-180. Ann Arbor: The University of Michigan Press.

Chitnis, B. 1996. *Two Faces of Charity*, Northwest Publishing, Inc., Salt Lake City, UT.

Commonwealth of Pennsylvania. 1994. *Registration Forms for Charitable Organizations*. Harrisburg, PA: Commonwealth of Pennsylvania, Department of State, Bureau of Charitable Organizations.

Elkin, R., and M. Molitor. 1984. *Management Indicators in Nonprofit Organizations: Guidelines to Selection and Implementation*. New York: Peat Marwick.

Financial Accounting Standards Board (FASB). 1980. Objectives of financial reporting by nonbusiness enterprises. *Statement of Financial Concepts No. 4*. Stamford, CT: FASB.

Froelich, K., and T. Knoepfle. 1996. Internal Revenue Service Data: Fact or Fiction? *Nonprofit and Voluntary Sector Quarterly* March: 40–52.

Gambino, A., and T. Reardon. 1981. *Financial Planning and Evaluation for the Nonprofit Organization*. New York: National Association of Accountants.

Gordon, T., J. Greenlee, and D. Nitterhouse. 1999. Tax-exempt organization data: Availability and limitations. *Accounting Horizons* June: 113–128.

Greenlee, J., and J. Knoblett. 1993. The use of accounting and other information in determining the allocation of resources to private nonprofit organizations: An empirical analysis. Presented at *American Accounting Association Annual Meeting*, San Francisco, CA, August.

Gronbjerg, K. 1993. *Understanding Nonprofit Funding*. San Francisco: Jossey-Bass.

Gui, B. 1991. The economic rationale for the third sector. *Annals of Public and Cooperative Economy* 62(4): 551–572.

Guidestar Directory of American Charities, 1996 Index. Williamsburg, VA: Philanthropic Research Inc.

Hock, S. 1994. House marks nonprofits for new tax disclosures. *Accounting Today* June 6: 3, 36–38.

Hodgkinson, V., and M. Weitzman. 1996. *Nonprofit Almanac 1996–1997*. San Francisco: Jossey-Bass Publishers.

Khumawala, S., and T. Gordon. 1997. Bridging the credibility of GAAP: Individual donors and the new accounting standards for nonprofit organizations. *Accounting Horizons* 11(September): 45–68.

Lohmann, R. 1980. *Breaking Even: Financial Management in Human Service Organizations*. Philadelphia, PA: Temple University Press.

National Charities Information Bureau (NCIB). 1991. *Wise Giving Guide*. New York: NCIB.

National Center on Charitable Statistics (NCCS). 1997. Presented at *Association for Nonprofit Organizations and Voluntary Action Annual Meeting*, Indianapolis, IN, December.

Nitterhouse, D., and F. Sharp. 1988. Allocation of joint costs: Special audit problems for nonprofits. *Today's CPA*, January–February: 24–27.

Nonprofit Times. 1994. Donors want choice, study finds. (October): 8.

Nonprofit Times. 1996. The taxpayer bill of rights. (September): 6.

Palmrose, Z. 1986. Audit fees and auditor size: Further evidence. *Journal of Accounting Research* (Spring): 97–110.

Pownall, G., and G. Waymire. 1989. Voluntary disclosure credibility and securities prices: Evidence from management earnings forecasts, 1969–1973. *Journal of Accounting Research* (Autumn): 227–245.

Reed, S., and B. Koch. 1989. Resource allocation decisions by charitable organizations: An experiment. *Research in Government and Nonprofit Accounting* Vol???: 99–122.

Reynolds, R. 1981. Resource providers' and practicing accountants' perceptions of the importance and quality of accounting information on voluntary health and welfare agencies. Unpublished Ph.D. dissertation, Georgia State University.

Roberts, R., G. Glezen, and T. Jones. 1990. Determinants of auditor change in the public sector. *Journal of Accounting Research* (Spring): 220–228.

Ross, S. 1978. The determination of financial structure: The incentive-signaling approach. *The Bell Journal of Economics* (Fall): 23–40.

Salamon, L., and H. Anheier. 1996. *The Emerging Nonprofit Sector: An Overview*. New York: St. Martin's Press.

Sarver, P. 1994. Charity efficiency: The public's view. *Nonprofit Times* (April): 1.

Sinclair, M. 1996. Bill of rights mandates executive comp restrictions: Additional 990 reporting. *Nonprofit Times* (September): 6.

Steinberg, R. 1985. Optimal fundraising by nonprofit firms. In *Giving and Volunteering: New Frontiers of Knowledge*, 411–446. Washington, DC: Independent Sector and United Way of America.

Stout, W. 1997. Some empirical evidence of nonprofit financial statement users' materiality thresholds. In *Proceedings of the American Accounting Association Mid-Atlantic Regional Meeting*: 66.

Swarden, C. 1996. Guilty or not guilty? Donor jury seeks answers. *Nonprofit Times* (September): 14, 24.

Tinkelman, D. 1997. An empirical study of the effect of accounting disclosures upon donations to nonprofit organizations. Unpublished dissertation, New York University.

United Way of America. 1990. *1988 Local United Way Fund Distribution Results*. Alexandria, VA: United Way of America Research Services Division.

Weisbrod, B. 1988. *The Nonprofit Economy*. Cambridge, MA: Harvard University Press.

Weisbrod, B., and N.D. Dominguez. 1986. Demand for collective goods in private markets: Can fundraising expenditures overcome free-rider behavior? *Journal of Public Economics* 30: 83–96.

Yeo, G. 1995. An empirical test of the signaling effect of management's earnings forecasts: A decomposition of the earnings surprise and forecast surprise effects. *Journal of Accounting, Auditing, and Finance* (Fall): 787–802.

POLITICAL COST INCENTIVES FOR EARNINGS MANAGEMENT IN THE PHARMACEUTICAL INDUSTRY DURING THE 1993 CAMPAIGN FOR HEALTH CARE REFORM

Obeua S. Persons

ABSTRACT

This study investigates political cost incentives for earnings management among pharmaceutical companies during President Clinton's health care reform campaign in 1993. Two hypotheses are examined. First, pharmaceutical firms are hypothesized to engage in income-decreasing management in order to alleviate the political costs associated with health care reform. Second, pharmaceutical firms with higher political visibility (i.e., those that are larger and more profitable) are hypothesized to engage in more income-decreasing management than those with lower political visibility (i.e., those that are smaller and less profitable). Earnings management is

Research in Accounting Regulation, Volume 13, pages 127-148.

ISBN: 0-7623-0520-7

measured by discretionary (unexpected) accruals (Dechow, Sloan, and Sweeney 1995).

Results indicate that pharmaceutical firms engaged in income-decreasing management in 1993. Regression results also suggest that pharmaceutical firms with higher political visibility have more income-decreasing discretionary accruals than those with lower political visibility. Further analysis reveals that pharmaceutical firms also used discretionary noncash write-offs to manage earnings downward.

This study has three major contributions. First, it contributes to the literature of earnings management by providing additional evidence in support of the political cost hypothesis. Second, it contributes to the law and economics literature by documenting the effects of regulation on the financial reporting strategies of the pharmaceutical industry. And third, it provides an evidence of earnings management consistent with the SEC's concerns. Two implications for the SEC, other regulators, and investors are: (1) they should look out for any potential income-decreasing schemes among those companies facing political pressure; and (2) they should focus their scrutiny on larger and more profitable firms.

INTRODUCTION

President Clinton's 1993 campaign for health care reform targeted the pharmaceutical industry as a major contributor to rising health care costs. His campaign blamed the industry for raising drug prices much faster than the increase in Americans' incomes and for charging Americans many times more than people in foreign countries where drug prices are regulated. One of his campaign objectives was to reduce prescription drug prices through price controls (Luce and Dutton 1993).

The purpose of this study is to examine whether pharmaceutical companies managed their earnings in response to the political pressure from the health care reform campaign. The political cost hypothesis, advanced by Watts and Zimmerman (1978), posits that managers of entities under intense public scrutiny will choose discretionary financial reporting methods and practices that reduce their reported profits to attract sympathy from politicians, to mitigate unwanted political costs, or to influence the outcome of the political process.

In particular, this study tests two research questions: (1) whether estimated discretionary accruals of pharmaceutical companies tended to be income-decreasing during the health care reform campaign, and (2) whether larger and more profitable pharmaceutical firms had more income-decreasing accruals than smaller and less profitable firms. Results suggest that pharmaceutical firms used discretionary accruals to decrease profits during the period. A cross-sectional analysis indicates more income-decreasing accruals among larger firms and firms with higher profitability. The analysis controls for time period and the debt-to-equity ratio.

Additional investigation reveals that pharmaceutical firms also used discretionary non-cash write-offs to decrease earnings. The conclusion that pharmaceutical companies managed their earnings in response to the political pressure is further substantiated by the insignificant results of earnings management among the control firms, that is, chemical companies.

This study extends prior research of the political cost hypothesis by focusing on an industry that was the actual target of a particular political action, that is, health care reform. This explicit link to a particular political event enables the study to clearly define the incentives facing managers and to make testable predictions. In particular, the President of the United States was actively involved in the reform campaign, and the reform's debates and movements were nationally televised on a regular basis. Because the reform campaign placed pharmaceutical firms in the national political spotlight, managers of these firms may have been reluctant to engage in earnings management. It is therefore interesting to investigate whether the political cost hypothesis would apply to this exceptionally high political pressure situation. This investigation is quite timely given the SEC's increasing concerns over the widespread, but too little-challenged practices of earnings management (Levitt 1998).

The remainder of this chapter is organized into five sections. The first section describes arguments for and against health care reform. This section, which documents political scrutiny of the reform campaign and the reactions of pharmaceutical firms, provides necessary background for developing the hypotheses. The second section discusses hypothesis development. The third section presents methodology. The fourth section reports results and the fifth section describes conclusions.

ARGUMENTS FOR AND AGAINST REFORM

Arguments For Reform

Unreasonably high drug prices was one of President Clinton's arguments for the health care reform. The practice of maintaining high prices among pharmaceutical companies can be dated back to the 1940s. Prices of prescription drugs increased and per capita drug expenditures nearly doubled between 1950 and 1960. Congress expressed concern over the lack of competition in the industry, and, in 1959, the Kefauver hearings revealed the industry's sizable profits, exploitive pricing practices and lack of price competition. Regardless of extensive investigations over the past 30–40 years, the pharmaceutical industry has done little to change its practices. Since the 1960s, the industry has blamed its high prices on the escalating costs of research and development (R&D).[1]

Certain characteristics of the drug industry set it apart from other industries and help explain its ability to steadily increase prices and profits. One is the lack of consumer control over the selection of the products. Consumers have very little access to information about the safety and effectiveness of prescription drugs and must rely on the experience and knowledge of physicians and pharmacists. Another characteristic is the lack of price competition stemming from a variety of factors such as the prevalence of patent-protected products and the proliferation of brand-name products. A drug is typically priced as high as the market will bear, taking into consideration the therapeutic advantages of the drug and the cost of alternative therapies, rather than setting prices based on the amount of revenue needed to recoup the cost of investment in R&D. Price increases usually occur in the first few years when the drug is introduced to the market because this is the period of fastest sales growth.[2] The U.S. Senate (1993a) *Earning a failing grade: A report card on 1992 drug manufacturer price inflation* contends that "during the period 1980–1992, while overall inflation was 21.7%, pharmaceutical inflation was 128.4%, six times this amount." Although some economists dispute these statistics, the public and political impression remains that drug prices are rising too rapidly, and that the pharmaceutical industry is getting rich while contributing to the health care cost crisis in America.

One of President Clinton's 1993 health care reform objectives was to cope with these unreasonable increases in drug prices. On January 25, 1993, the President appointed his wife, Hillary Rodham Clinton, to lead a cabinet-level health care reform task force. The reform campaign portrayed the pharmaceutical industry as the "bad guys" who contribute to excessive increases in health care costs.[3] Hillary Rodham Clinton singled out the industry for special rebuke at a health care forum: "It is true we have the finest pharmaceutical companies in the world, but they are charging Americans twice, three times, 10 to 15 times more than in foreign countries where drug prices are regulated." Sen. David Pryor (D, Ark.), the Chairman of the Senate Committee on Aging, also made an assault on the pharmaceutical industry saying that drug prices have increased at a rate far in excess of that of other commodities and are the fastest growing component of medical costs—rising at a time when the industry is *enjoying profits substantially higher* than most other sectors of the manufacturing community. He suggested a number of legislative remedies including regulation of pharmaceutical companies as public utilities, establishing price controls, and creating an excess profits tax.[4]

Arguments Against Reform

The Pharmaceutical Manufacturers Association (PMA), which represents virtually all of America's innovative pharmaceutical firms and biotechnology companies, responded that the government's numbers were seriously flawed, and that the implementation of any price controls would undermine the biomedical research from which most medical advances come. Gerald Mossinghoff, President of PMA, argued that the industry's price-increase patterns have slowed substantially during 1990s and moderated sharply in 1993. He said that the Producer

Price Index increase was "the lowest since 1974." He also said that the industry was painfully adjusting to market-driven forces and did not need "new layers of government price regulation" (Conlan 1994).

During testimonies at Congressional hearings (U.S. House 1993a, 1993b; U.S. Senate 1993b), PMA consistently stressed that government regulation of the pharmaceutical market would have extremely adverse effects. The fear of price and cost controls did hurt the pharmaceutical business: stock prices of pharmaceutical firms, especially biotechnology companies, plummeted, financing dried up, and plans for expansion were put on hold. PMA further reminded Congress that the pharmaceutical industry is America's most internationally competitive industry which has consistently maintained a positive balance of trade, even with Japan. PMA attributes the industry's success to the impressive productivity of research and development (R&D) and to the fact that the United States has not to date implemented price controls on pharmaceuticals.

PMA also pointed out that the industry's huge investments in R&D mean more new medicines which not only save lives but also save billions of dollars in health care costs. It further posited that 17 PMA members which make up about two-thirds of the market had voluntarily pledged to keep their price increases at or below the level of general inflation. As a result, in the 12-month period ending in May 1993, the increase in drug-price inflation and general inflation were virtually the same. In addition to the industry's commitment to decrease pharmaceutical prices, PMA contended that prices had already been restrained by competitive market pressures from the growing number of managed care systems and generic drugs. PMA's argument for relying on competitive market forces, rather than price controls, was also shared by several media and many economists. Particularly, Abbott (1995) and Grabowski and Vernon (1994) conclude that there is little evidence of excessive prices or profits among the pharmaceutical firms, and there is no reason to believe that price regulation of any kind would be successful in stabilizing prices while providing adequate incentives for future R&D.

HYPOTHESIS DEVELOPMENT

The above discussions indicate that the pharmaceutical industry strongly opposed the government price regulation proposed in President Clinton's health care reform. The industry did attempt to influence politicians through testimonies at several congressional hearings. Throughout the stages of scrutiny, there is ample evidence that parties to the political process used accounting information. In some instances there are actual data and calculations cited, and in other instances terminology is used which implies the importance of accounting information. Profits and prices of pharmaceuticals are frequently cited in congressional hearings and reports. Revenues, costs, and investments also received attention in the process and are present in the legislative documents.

The use of accounting information during political scrutiny supports the prediction of political cost hypothesis (Watts and Zimmerman 1978, 1986) that managers will choose accounting strategies that lower profits to alleviate unwanted political costs. Watts and Zimmerman (1978) argue that politicians and their constituents equate high profits with monopolies and either lack incentive or are unable to undo accounting numbers completely. Similarly, Larcker and Revsine (1983) reason that if accounting earnings influence public opinion, reducing the earnings may alter public opinion. This change in public opinion could translate into reduced pressure on regulatory and legislative bodies to increase regulation. These arguments lead to the first hypothesis.

H1. Pharmaceutical companies managed earnings by using discretionary accruals to decrease income during the 1993 health care reform campaign.

It appears that the extent of any political backlash depends in part on the political visibility of a company. Mensah, Considine, and Oakes (1994), and Hall (1993) suggest companies' reported profits as a measure of political visibility. Several earlier studies use firm size as the measure.[5] This study uses both firm size and profit as proxies for political visibility because larger firms, and firms with higher profits are likely to be more visible to regulators and bear more political criticism than smaller firms with lower profits. The use of these two variables is supported by the U.S. Senate (1993a) *Earning a failing grade: A report card on 1992 drug manufacturer price inflation* which highlights the top ten drug manufacturers with highest price increases. These ten firms are larger and more profitable firms. Therefore, larger firms and higher-profit firms are likely to be particularly vulnerable to wealth-extracting political impact in the form of legislation and/or regulation. Managers of these firms will have more incentives to use accounting procedures that reduce earnings. This leads to the second hypothesis.

H2. High-political-visibility pharmaceutical companies had more income-decreasing discretionary accruals in 1993 than low-political-visibility companies.

This study does not include 1992 and 1994 in the hypothesized earnings management period for the following reasons. Although Clinton first mentioned health care reform in his 1992 presidential campaign, pharmaceutical firms were not sure that he would win the election. Therefore, these firms should not be expected to seriously engage in earnings management until 1993 when his reform was widely debated and its details (particularly drug price controls) were revealed publicly. The year 1994 marks the death of Clinton's health care reform. Many Republicans in the Congress opposed the reform, and several Democrats gave up under pressure of the negative response from the public and the interest group lobbying efforts, including that from the pharmaceutical industry. In August 1994, the Senate, together with House Speaker Foley, conceded that perhaps health care reform was an untimely issue that would be better served at a later date and limited to minimal health insurance reforms with modest coverage expansion. Eventually, in September 1994, House Energy and Commerce Committee Chair Dingell, one of Clinton's feisty fighters and his principal ally for health care reform, called for Clinton to "call it quits" (Jacks and Jacks 1995). The years 1992 and 1994 are, however, used as control years in this study.

METHODOLOGY

Past studies and the SEC Chairman's speech (Levitt 1998) suggest that managers may use any of the following three accounting alternatives to decrease earnings. They are discretionary accruals (Jones 1991; Hall 1993; DeAngelo, DeAngelo, and Skinner 1994; Mensah, Considine, and Oakes 1994), discretionary non-cash write-offs (DeAngelo, DeAngelo, and Skinner 1994), and discretionary accounting method changes (Hall 1993). Although this study focuses on the use of discretionary accruals, it also examines the use of discretionary non-cash write-offs, and discretionary accounting method changes. An advantage of discretionary accruals is that they are less visible and less likely to be undone by political decision makers. Undoing the income differences caused by discretionary accruals can be difficult because the information required to make these adjustments may not be publicly available (Schipper 1989). However, if discretionary accruals are not sufficient for decreasing earnings to a desired level, managers may also use discretionary non-cash write-offs and accounting method changes. Although these two alternatives are more visible and could be undone by regulators, Scholes, Wilson, and Wolfson (1989) contend that regulators rationally use simple decision models because of limited processing time and ability, and therefore, may not make any adjustments. Similarly, Jones (1991) posits that regulators may not have incentives to adjust for managers' earnings manipulations since there is no direct payoff for such adjustments.

The methodology section is divided into four parts. The first part discusses sample selection. The second part includes tests of the first hypothesis, while the third part describes tests of the second hypothesis. Finally, the fourth part discusses tests of discretionary write-offs and accounting method changes.

Sample Selection

Hypothesis testing for the year 1993 is based on 103 pharmaceutical companies which meet two criteria:

1. They are listed on the Compustat tapes under the four-digit SIC codes, 2834–Pharmaceutical Preparations and 2836–Biological Products Except Diagnostic. Prescription drugs, which are the main products of firms with SIC code 2834, were the main target of the price controls proposed by President Clinton's 1993 health care reform. In addition, arguments of the Pharmaceutical Manufacturers Association (PMA) indicated that firms with SIC code 2836 would also be adversely affected because they are regarded as biotechnology firms which are involved in new prescription drug development.[6] Most members of PMA, which represents pharmaceutical firms in opposing health care reform, are firms with SIC codes 2834 and 2836. Therefore, it is expected that the negative relation between discretionary accruals and political visibility pertain primarily to these two groups of pharmaceutical companies. There are 236 firms with these SIC codes: 169 firms for code 2834 and 67 firms for code 2836.[7]
2. They have the necessary financial statement data for estimating discretionary accruals. Financial statement data were collected from Compustat tapes, Moody's manuals, and annual reports. Sample firms are required to have at least eight time-series observations for estimating discretionary accruals after excluding an observation for the year 1982.[8] The year 1982 was the deliberation period of the Possessions Corporation (PC) tax changes which were enacted by the Tax Equity and Fiscal Responsibility Act of 1982 (TEFRA). This legislation affected the pharmaceutical industry by primarily reducing current and future cash flows of pharmaceutical companies through higher taxes, that is, more fully taxable income was shifted from their Puerto Rico subsidiaries to the parent companies.[9] Because TEFRA affected the revenues, profits, and cash flows of pharmaceutical firms substantially, it is plausible that these firms would have managed their earnings to mitigate negative effects of this legislation. Including 1982 observation would violate the stationary assumption of the accrual generating process during the estimation period. In all, this second sample criterion eliminated 133 firms, resulting in the final sample of 103 firms (75 firms for SIC-2834 and 28 firms for SIC-2836).

This study then examines whether these 103 firms have necessary financial statement data in 1994 and also have at least eight observations for estimating 1992 accruals. These two years are the control years. All 103 firms have necessary data in 1994, but only 101 firms have at least eight observations in 1992.

Testing H1: Pharmaceutical Companies Managed Earnings by Using Discretionary Accruals to Decrease Income During the 1993 Health Care Reform Campaign

H1 will be supported if discretionary accruals of pharmaceutical firms in 1993 are significantly negative (income decreasing). Discretionary accruals are computed as total accruals minus expected accruals in the absence of earnings management. Total accruals are calculated as the change in noncash working capital less total depreciation expense (Gaver, Gaver, and Austin 1995). Expected accruals in the absence of earnings management is based on Dechow, Sloan, and Sweeney (1995). The detailed computation of total accruals and expected accruals is described in the appendix.

The hypothesis that pharmaceutical firms use discretionary accruals to decrease income in 1993 will be supported if discretionary accruals are significantly negative. To assure that the hypothesized earnings management pertains only to 1993, the year of Clinton's health care reform campaign, this study also computes discretionary accruals for 1992 and 1994. Discretionary accruals for these two years are not expected to be significantly negative, i.e., drug firms are unlikely to engage in income-decreasing management in 1992 and 1994.

Testing H2: High-Political-Visibility Pharmaceutical Companies Had More Income-Decreasing Discretionary Accruals in 1993 than Low-Political-Visibility Companies

This study uses cross-sectional regression analysis to examine this hypothesis. Estimated discretionary accruals are regressed on the two proxies for political visibility: firm size and profitability. Firm size is measured by natural log of the beginning total assets. Profitability is measured by the prior year's return on stockholders' equity (ROE). An examination of congressional documents reveals that politicians most frequently used ROE as a measure of profitability. The coefficients of firm size and profitability are expected to be negative, i.e., the larger the size and profitability, the more income-decreasing discretionary accruals.

The regression model also includes a control variable for the debt covenant hypothesis. Corporate lending contracts typically contain accounting-based covenants that alleviate the bondholder-stockholder conflict within the borrowing firm (Smith 1993). Debt covenants generally require borrowing firms to maintain specified levels of accounting-based ratios (e.g., the ratio of net income to interest expense). A covenant that becomes binding imposes costs on a firm, either in renegotiating to remove the covenant or in restricting its financing and investing activities (e.g., dividend payments and issuance of new debt). This study uses a ratio of long-term debt to stockholders' equity to measure the existence of accounting-based constraints. This variable is expected to have a positive coefficient because the higher this ratio, the closer a firm is to the violation of accounting-based constraints, and the more likely it is that a firm will engage in income-increasing management.[10] This cross-sectional regression model is further described in the appendix.

Discretionary Non-cash Write-offs and Accounting Method Changes

In addition to exercising discretion over operating accruals, managers may also use discretionary write-offs and accounting method changes to decrease earnings. To identify discretionary write-offs and accounting changes, this study examines 1992–1994 annual reports for sample firms after initially identifying write-offs and accounting changes from Compustat items 17 (special items) and 48 (extraordinary items plus discontinued operations). Following a conservative approach of DeAngelo, DeAngelo, and Skinner (1994), this study excludes as non-discretionary all amounts from actual transactions such as pension terminations and debt/equity swaps. The number and magnitude of discretionary write-offs in 1993 are compared to those in 1992 and 1994. Accounting method changes are treated as discretionary if they are voluntary changes or early adoption of new Statements of Financial Accounting Standards (SFAS).

RESULTS

This section is divided into three parts. The first part is a highlight of relevant accounting numbers. The second part reports test results of the two hypotheses. The third part presents discretionary non-cash write-offs and accounting changes.

Highlight of Relevant Accounting Numbers

Table 1 presents mean and median changes in revenues, expenses, earnings, cash flow, and total accruals for 1993, the hypothesized earnings management year, and 1992 and 1994, the two control years. These changes are the differences between the variables in year t and year t-1 and are scaled by beginning total assets. Since the mean and median of these changes are quite different, a nonparametric Wilcoxon signed rank test is used to test whether the changes differ significantly from zero. The Wilcoxon p values suggest that revenues and operating expenses increased significantly in each of the three years. However, according to the Wilcoxon two–sample test, the revenue increase in 1993 is significantly smaller than in 1992. This smaller increase in 1993 may reflect the public and political pressure on pricing of pharmaceutical firms after the release of the U.S. Senate's 1993 report, *Earning a failing grade: A report card on 1992 drug manufacturer price inflation* (1993a). This report claimed that "Drug makers broke their promise to hold down prices in 1992. During 1992, drug prices increased at more than four times the rate of inflation, although manufacturers had agreed

Table 1. Revenue Changes, Operating Expense Changes, Earnings Changes, Cash Flow Changes, and Total-Accrual Changes During 1992–1994 Scaled by Beginning Total Assets[a]

	1992 (N = 101)		*1993 (N = 103)*		*1994 (N = 103)*
Revenue Changes					
Mean	0.1936		0.1569		0.1042
Median	0.1027		0.0414		0.0622
Wilcoxon *p*-value	0.0001		0.0001		0.0001
Wilcoxon two-sample *p*-value		0.0043		0.4612	
Operating Expense Changes					
Mean	0.0876		0.2044		0.1071
Median	0.0737		0.1023		0.0502
Wilcoxon *p*-value	0.0001		0.0001		0.0001
Wilcoxon two-sample *p*-value		0.0356		0.0523	
Earnings Changes					
Mean	0.0292		–0.0562		0.0508
Median	0.0060		–0.0197		0.0077
Wilcoxon *p*-value	0.6277		0.0334		0.9651
Wilcoxon two-sample *p*-value		0.0458		0.0541	
Cash Flow Changes					
Mean	0.0118		–0.0121		0.0085
Median	0.0025		–0.0046		0.0050
Wilcoxon *p*-value	0.3256		0.2576		0.4183
Wilcoxon two-sample *p*-value		0.4554		0.6375	
Accrual Changes					
Mean	–0.0207		–0.1545		–0.0623
Median	–0.0040		–0.0965		–0.0081
Wilcoxon *p*-value	0.7269		0.0307		0.3889
Wilcoxon two-sample *p*-value		0.0287		0.0409	

Note: [a]These changes are computed as year *t* item minus year *t*-1 item.

voluntarily to hold price increases to the rate of inflation." As a response to the report, pharmaceutical firms may have slowed down price increases in 1993 to mitigate the public discontent. On the other hand, the operating expense increase in 1993 is significantly larger than in 1992 and 1994. Because cash flow change is not statistically significant, this larger expense increase may reflect an increase in discretionary accruals through expense accounts.[11]

Another significant change is a decrease in 1993 earnings before extraordinary items. This change in earnings is significantly lower in 1993 than in 1992 and 1994. This decrease in earnings, together with smaller revenue increase and larger expense increase in 1993, seems to indicate that pharmaceutical firms may have managed earnings in response to the political pressure of 1993 health care reform. In line with the significant decrease in 1993 earnings, a decrease in 1993 total

Table 2. Mean of Descriptive Statistics for Firm-Specific Expected Accruals Model*

	1992	*1993*	*1994*
a	7.1981	5.2135	6.6504
t-statistic	0.1572	0.1467	0.1396
b_1	0.1086	0.0958	0.0963
t-statistic	1.6520	1.6253	1.6047
b_2	−0.0631	−0.0646	−0.0597
t-statistic	−0.9572	−1.0605	−1.0234
Adjusted R^2	0.4329	0.4512	0.4075
Autocorrelation	−0.2410	−0.2523	−0.2628
Durbin-Watson	23175	2.2824	2.3267
Number of years	11.508	12.464	13.451

Notes: *$TA_{it} = a_1 + b_{1i}(\Delta REV_{it} - \Delta REC_{it}) + b_{2i}\,PPE_{it} + e_{it}$ where TA_{it} = Total accruals in year *t* for firm *i* as defined in equation (1); ΔREV_{it} = Revenues in year *t* less revenues in year *t*-1, ΔREC_{it} = Receivables in year *t* less receivables in year *t*-1, PPE_{it} = Gross property, plant and equipment at the end of year *t*, e = Error term. All variables are scaled by beginning total assets.

accruals is also significantly negative (income-decreasing accruals). Although this decrease in total accruals is significantly larger than those in 1992 and 1994, total accruals include both nondiscretionary and discretionary accruals. These two accrual components must be separated in order to test whether managers used discretionary accruals to manage earnings. For 1992 and 1994, changes in earnings and total accruals are not statistically significant.

Test Results of the Two Hypotheses

Table 2 reports the results of estimating expected accrual models for 1992, 1993 and 1994. For 1993, the average adjusted R^2 for the 103 firm-year regressions is 45.12 percent. The average estimated coefficient for the change in revenues is, as expected, positive (0.0958) and the average estimated coefficient for property, plant, and equipment is, as expected, negative (−0.0646). The average residual first-order autocorrelation is −0.2523. The average Durbin-Watson two-tailed test statistic is 2.2824, indicating that, on average, the first-order autocorrelation is not significant. The expected accrual models for 1992 and 1994 also indicate similar results. In sum, these statistics suggest that, on average, the control for changes in nondiscretionary accruals is achieved.

Table 3 reports discretionary (unexpected) accruals for 1992, 1993, and 1994. The average discretionary accrual for 1993 is negative (−0.0755) and statistically significant at < 0.01 level, whereas the average discretionary accruals for 1992 and 1994 are not statistically significant. The Wilcoxon non-parametric test also indicates similar inferences. These results strongly support the first hypothesis

Table 3. Discretionary Accruals for Pharmaceutical Firms During 1993, the Hypothesized Earnings Management Year, and During 1992 and 1994, the Control Years

	1992 (*N* = *101*)	*1993* (*N* = *103*)	*1994* (*N* = *103*)
Mean	0.0239	−0.0755	−0.0164
Median	0.0087	−0.0632	0.0025
Std. Dev.	0.2960	0.3403	0.3721
% Negative	45.3219	70.7531	48.8602
t-statistic	0.8115	−2.2517***	−0.4473
Wilcoxon *p*-value	0.7293	0.0085	0.6549

Notes: Discretionary accrual is the difference between total accrual and expected accrual (equation 3).

***Significant at < 0.01 level, one-tailed significance test.

that pharmaceutical firms use discretionary accruals to decrease earnings in response to political pressure of the 1993 health care reform campaign.

Table 4 presents cross-sectional regression analysis for testing the association between discretionary accruals and firms' political visibility. Regression results shown in the table are based on the estimation after excluding outliers (i.e., observations with a large influence on the estimated coefficients). Outliers are identified by the statistics proposed by Belsley, Kuh, and Welsch (1980).[12] There are 98, 101, and 100 observations for estimating 1992, 1993, and 1994 models, respectively.

The results indicate negative and highly significant coefficients of ROE and firm size in 1993. These results support the hypothesis that high-political-visibility (larger and more profitable) pharmaceutical firms had more income-decreasing discretionary accruals in 1993 than low-political-visibility (smaller and less profitable) firms. The insignificant coefficients of ROE and firm size in 1992 and 1994 further support the hypothesis.

The coefficient of long-term debt to equity ratio (DE) is positive and significant at 0.05 level in the 1993 model. This result supports the debt-covenant hypothesis that firms which are closer to violation of debt covenants are more likely to engage in income-increasing management. DE's coefficient is not statistically significant in 1992 and 1994. The significant result only in 1993 of DE may be attributable to a large increase in drug firms' cost of capital as a result of a sharp increase in the uncertainty about their future prospects related to the 1993 health care reform.[13] This large increase in cost of capital made it more difficult and more costly for drug firms to raise needed funds for financing its operations. Insufficient or more costly funds could adversely affect drug firms' operating results. This, in turn, could increase the likelihood of debt covenant violation in 1993. Because political pressure of the health care reform on drug firms was much

Table 4. Cross-Sectional Regression Results for Testing the Association Between Discretionary Accruals and Firms' Political Visibility. Estimated Coefficients and Their t-statistics (in the Parentheses) Are Reported

Variables	*Expected Sign*	*1992*	*1993*	*1994*
Intercept	?	0.2081	0.3815	−0.2465
		(0.306)	(0.482)	(−0.279)
ROE	−	−0.0205	−0.1826	−0.0189
		(−0.681)	(−6.920)****	(−0.306)
SIZE	−	−0.0389	−1.0321	−0.0256
		(−0.285)	(−3.514)***	(−0.241)
DE	+	0.0374	0.3816	0.0523
		(0.352)	(1.685)**	(0.496)
Adjusted R^2		0.0216	0.4523	0.0254
F-statistic		0.6917	26.701****	0.8340
Number of firms		101	103	103

Notes: $DA_{it} = a + b_1\, ROE_{it-1} + b_2\, SIZE_{it-1} + b_3\, DE_{it}$ where DA_{it} = Discretionary accruals for firm i in year t ROE_{it-1} = Year t-1 income before extraordinary/year t-1 stockholders' equity, $SIZE_{it-1}$ = Natural log of beginning total assets, DE_{it} = Long-term debt divided by total stockholders' equity.

**Significant at < 0.05 level, one-tailed significance test.

***Significant at < 0.001 level, one-tailed significance test.

****Significant at < 0.0001 level, one-tailed significance test.

lower in 1992 and 1994, the adverse effect of this pressure on their cost of capital and the likelihood of debt covenant violation were likely to be lower in these two years. This explains the insignificant result of DE's coefficient in 1992 and 1994.

A high adjusted R^2 of 0.4523 and a highly significant F-statistic of 26.701 for 1993 regression, together with insignificant F-statistics for 1992 and 1994 regressions, strengthens the inferences regarding the 1993 negative association between discretionary accruals and political visibility among pharmaceutical firms. Re-estimating the model after replacing ROE by earnings per share and income before discretionary accruals yields virtually the same inferences. A test for collinearity based on Belsley, Kuh, and Welsch (1980) does not reveal a multi-collinearity problem. A test for heteroskedasticity based on White (1980) does not indicate that a problem exists.

This study also examines whether the significantly negative coefficients of political visibility variables are not primarily attributed to low-political-visibility firms' managing earnings upward through positive discretionary accruals. This examination is achieved by ranking firms on the basis of the two political visibility variables, and grouping them into quintiles. As reported in Table 5, in 1993, a higher quintile for both size and ROE has more negative discretionary accruals than those in a lower quintile. In addition, all quintiles except for the lowest one have negative discretionary accruals. A two sample t-test indicates that the

Table 5. Quintiles of Political Visibility and Their Associated Discretionary Accruals (DA) in the Years 1992, 1993, and 1994 (1993 is the Hypothesized Earnings Management Year)

Quintiles	*1992*		*1993*		*1994*	
(1 = Largest)	*ROE or Size*	*DA*	*ROE or Size*	*DA*	*ROE or Size*	*DA*
Panel A: Profitability (ROE)						
1	0.2415	0.0267	0.2246	−0.1334	0.2390	−0.0374
2	0.1823	−0.0523	0.1667	−0.0875	0.1705	0.0148
3	0.1361	0.0341	0.1081	−0.0661	0.1216	−0.0215
4	0.0789	−0.0078	0.0573	−0.0383	0.0727	−0.0687
5	0.0275	0.0495	0.0035	0.0145	0.0280	0.0287
t-statistic[a]	0.4018		−4.5416		−0.3625	
Panel B: Size (Beginning Total Assets in Millions)						
1	17,725	−0.0170	19,928	−0.1268	21,857	−0.0297
2	8,812	0.0236	9,560	−0.0747	10,242	0.0773
3	3,810	−0.0478	4,182	−0.0563	4,561	−0.0164
4	1,795	0.0150	2,045	−0.0195	2,385	−0.0821
5	671	−0.0245	758	0.0151	836	0.0425
t-statistic[a]	0.3275		−3.4572		−0.2813	

Note: [a]Two-samle *t*-test for the difference in mean discretionary accruals of quintiles 1 and 2 versus quintiles 4 and 5.

average discretionary accruals of the top two quintiles is significantly more negative than that of the bottom two quintiles. Such results do not exist in 1992 and 1994. Therefore, these simple univariate tests support the inferences based on the earlier regression analysis.

Validity Test for the Discretionary Accrual Hypotheses

To verify that the above discretionary accrual results pertain only to the pharmaceutical industry, this study uses firms in the chemical industry (three-digit SIC codes 280, 281, and 282) as a control group. The chemical industry seems to be closely related to the pharmaceutical industry because it supplies particular chemicals used as raw materials for drug manufacturing by pharmaceutical companies. According to Dietrich and Olsen (1985), suppliers' stock returns are positively related to the customers' sales announcements. Their study implies that customers and suppliers such as the pharmaceutical and the chemical industries generally share a similar trend in revenues, expenses, and earnings. This similar trend makes the chemical industry an appropriate control group for testing the earnings management of the pharmaceutical industry. The two hypotheses will be further supported if chemical firms did not have significantly negative income-decreasing accruals in any of the three years, especially 1993.

The estimation of discretionary accruals using chemical firms indicates that these firms do not have significant discretionary accruals in any of the three years (results not tabulated here). This study also uses chemical firms in the cross-sectional regression analysis for testing the association between discretionary accruals and firms' political visibility. The regression results do not indicate any significant coefficient estimates. These insignificant results for the chemical industry add more validity to the political cost hypothesis as an explanation for earning management in 1993 by the pharmaceutical industry.

Discretionary Non-cash Write-offs and Accounting Method Changes

In addition to using income-decreasing discretion over operating accruals, pharmaceutical firms may also use discretionary non-cash write-offs to lower earnings. Table 6 indicates that, in 1993, 29 (28.2%) of 103 sample firms had discretionary write-offs, whereas in 1992 and 1994, a total of 38 (18.6%) firms had discretionary write-offs.[14] Besides higher frequency of write-offs in 1993, the Wilcoxon two-sample test indicates that 1993 write-offs are significantly larger than write-offs in 1992 and 1994. This finding suggests that, on average, pharmaceutical firms used discretionary non-cash write-offs to decrease their earnings in 1993 to alleviate the political pressure from President Clinton's health care reform.

Panel B of the table describes the nature of 29 discretionary write-offs in 1993. The categories of these write-offs are the same as those in DeAngelo, DeAngelo, and Skinner (1994). In all, there are ten firms with provision for restructuring

Table 6. Summary Statistics of 29 Discretionary Non-Cash Write-Offs in 1993 versus 39 Discretionary Non-Cash Write-Offs in 1992 and 1994 (In Millions)

Panel A	*Mean*	*Std. Dev.*	*Median*	*Min.*	*Max.*
1993	154.328	201.634	12.351	0.265	1,172.7
1992 & 1994	68.721	148.892	5.123	0.097	912.0

Wilcoxon two-sample test *p*-value = 0.0463

Panel B

Nature of Discretionary Write-offs in 1993	*# of Cases*	*% of Write-offs*
Provision for restructuring costs	10	34.5%
Writedown of productive assets	9	31.0%
Provision for plant closing	8	27.6%
Provision for losses on operations to be sold	1	3.5%
Writedown of investments	1	3.4%
Total	29	100.0%

costs, nine firms with writedown of productive assets, eight firms with provision for plant closing, one firm with provision for losses on operations to be sold, and one firm with writedown of investment. Most of these discretionary write-offs (24 out of 29) occurred in the fourth quarter.[15] Seven out of these 29 discretionary write-offs belong to seven very large firms (in the top 10% of the sample based on their total assets and profits). The total write-offs of these seven firms amount to 64 percent of all write-offs.

Another possibility for earnings management is the use of accounting method changes to decrease earnings. An examination of 1993 annual reports reveals 19 accounting changes made by 16 firms out of 103 sample firms. Only one of these changes was voluntary, i.e., a change in inventory method from LIFO to FIFO. This voluntary change resulted in an increase in earnings. The other 18 accounting changes were mandatory, involving an adoption of SFAS No. 106 (Post-retirement Benefits: four firms), SFAS No. 109 (Income Taxes: 9 firms), SFAS No. 112 (Postemployment Benefits: four firms), and SFAS No. 115 (Investments in Debt and Equity Securities: one firm). Since SFAS No. 106 and No. 109 are effective for fiscal years beginning after December 15, 1992, an adoption of these two statements in 1993 is not a discretionary decision. On the other hand, the effective date of SFAS No. 112 and No. 115 is for fiscal years beginning after December 15, 1993. Therefore, an adoption of these two statements in 1993 is an early adoption which is a discretionary decision of a firm's management. The one firm that adopted SFAS No. 115 in 1993 did not experience any effect of the change on its earnings. All four firms adopting SFAS No. 112 in 1993 experienced a decrease in earnings as a result of the adoption. These four firms are very large firms, that is, their size and profit are in the top 10 percent of the sample. Although these four firms may make an early adoption of income-decreasing mandatory accounting change in order to reduce their political visibility, such a small number of firms (four out of 103) prohibits a conclusion that the pharmaceutical industry made discretionary accounting changes in 1993 in response to political pressure of the health care reform.

CONCLUSIONS

This study investigates whether pharmaceutical firms engaged in income-decreasing management in response to the political costs related to President Clinton's 1993 health care reform campaign. Earnings management is primarily measured by discretionary (unexpected) accruals (Dechow, Sloan, and Sweeney 1995). This study also examines whether earnings management is associated with firms' political visibility. Data analyses yield the following major findings:

1. Pharmaceutical firms engaged in income-decreasing management in 1993 through the use of discretionary accruals.
2. Firms with higher political visibility (i.e., larger and more profitable firms) had more income-decreasing discretionary accruals than firms with lower political visibility (i.e., smaller and less profitable firms).
3. Pharmaceutical firms had more discretionary non-cash write-offs in 1993 than they did in 1992 and 1994.

In summary, these results lend support to the political cost hypothesis that firms that are subject to political scrutiny will manage earnings downward to mitigate unwanted political costs. These results also suggest that the political cost hypothesis prevails even in the situation where political scrutiny places firms in the national spotlight. This study contributes to the earnings management literature and to the law and economics literature by documenting the effects of regulation on financial reporting strategies among pharmaceutical firms.

The study has two important implications for regulators and investors. First, they may want to scrutinize the financial reports of firms that are under political pressure. Second, more of this scrutiny should be focused on larger and more profitable firms.

APPENDIX

Definition of the Total Accruals (TA)

$$\begin{aligned} TA = {} & [\Delta\text{Current Assets (4)} - \Delta\text{Cash (1)}] - [\Delta\text{Current Liabilities (5)} \\ & - \Delta\text{Current Maturities of Long-Term Debt (44)} \\ & - \Delta\text{Taxes Payable (71)}] - \text{Depreciation Expense (14)} \end{aligned} \qquad (1)$$

The change, Δ, is computed between time t and t-1. Compustat data item numbers are in parentheses. Note that decreases in non-cash working capital and increases in depreciation expense are associated with reductions in income.

Definition of the Expected Accruals

The expected accruals are estimated by the modified version of Jones's 1991 model proposed by Dechow, Sloan, and Sweeney (1995). This modified version includes two variables: (a) changes in revenues less changes in receivables, and (b) the level of gross property, plant, and equipment. These variables control for changes in expected accruals due to economic conditions during the test period. Changes in revenues less changes in receivables account for non-discretionary changes in working capital accounts. Gross property, plant, and equipment account for non-discretionary depreciation expense. This modified version measures earnings manipulation with less error in the presence of revenue manipulation. If managers inflate revenues by inflating receivables, the typical relationship between revenue and receivables will be altered and detected by this modified version. The original Jones model implicitly assumes no revenue manipulation. To reduce heteroskedasticity in the data, all variables are scaled by the beginning total assets.

$$TA_{it} = a_i + b_{1i}(\Delta REV_{it} - \Delta REC_{it}) + b_{2i}PPE_{it} + e_{it} \qquad (2)$$

where TA_{it} = total accruals in year t for firm i as defined in equation (1),
ΔREV_{it} = revenues in year t less revenues in year t-1 for firm i,
ΔREC_{it} = receivables in year t less receivables in year t-1 for firm i,
PPE_{it} = gross property, plant and equipment at the end of year t for firm i,
a_i, b_{1i}, b_{2i} = estimated coefficients for expected accruals for firm i,
e = error term in year t for firm i,
i = 1,..., N firms (N = 103),
t = 1,..., T years (T, the estimation period of firm i ranges from 8 to 17 years).

Estimates of a_i, b_{1i}, and b_{2i} are obtained by ordinary least-square (OLS) regression analysis for each of the 103 pharmaceutical firms. Based on the definition of total accruals and expected accruals above, discretionary or unexpected accruals (DA) are defined below. All variables are scaled by the beginning total assets.

$$DA_{it} = TA_{it} - [\, a_i + b_{1i}(\Delta REV_{it} - \Delta REC_{it}) + b_{2i}PPE_{it}\,] \qquad (3)$$

where DA_{it} = discretionary or unexpected accruals for firm i in year t (1993),
TA_{it} = total accruals for firm i in year t as defined in equation (1),
a_i, b_{1i}, b_{2i} = estimated coefficients for expected accruals in equation (2) for firm i,
ΔREV_{it} = changes in revenues for firm i in year t,
ΔREC_{it} = changes in receivables for firm i in year t,
PPE_{it} = gross property, plant, and equipment for firm i in year t.

Cross-Sectional OLS Regression for Testing the Second Hypothesis

$$DA_{it} = a + b_1\, ROE_{it-1} + b_2\, SIZE_{it-1} + b_3\, DE_{it} \qquad (4)$$

where DA_{it} = Discretionary accruals for firm i in year t.
ROE_{it-1} = Year t-1 income before extraordinary/year t-1 stockholders' equity.
$SIZE_{it-1}$ = Natural log of beginning total assets.
DE_{it} = Long-term debt divided by total stockholders' equity.

This study uses the prior year's numbers to compute ROE because the current year's number may have already been managed in response to political pressure. The prior year's numbers are less likely to be managed because political pressure is not as apparent in the prior year as in the current year. The coefficients b_1 and b_2 are expected to be negative. The coefficient b_3 is expected to be positive. H2 will be supported if b_1 and b_2 are significantly negative. To assure that the earnings management is due to the political pressure in 1993, this study also conducts the regression analysis for the years 1992 and 1994. The coefficients b_1 and b_2 are expected to be insignificant in these two years. This study also performs a validity test by using profitability measures other than ROE. These measures are earnings per share and income before discretionary accruals. Earnings per share are based on year t-1. Income before discretionary accruals is computed as year t net income adjusted by the time-series estimate of discretionary accruals for year t.

NOTES

1. Some economists (e.g., Grabowski and Vernon 1994) seem to concur with the industry's argument.
2. See Griffin (1991) for more details on economics of the pharmaceutical industry.
3. The campaign also blamed the health insurance industry for the increase in health care costs. However, this study does not examine the health insurance industry for two reasons. First, several insurers that offer health insurance also offer other types of insurance that are not affected by the reform (e.g., accidental, life). Thus, the negative political impact of the reform on these insurers is likely to be less than the impact on pharmaceutical companies whose products (drugs) are all subject to the reform. Second, unlike the pharmaceutical industry, health care reform can positively affect some insurers and negatively affect others. According to the Value Line Investment Survey (March 12, 1993, page 2075), insurers with established managed care networks may be among the winners of reform whereas indemnity insurers may be among the losers.
4. See Conlan (1994) for more on Mrs. Clinton and Sen. Pryor's arguments.
5. See Watts and Zimmerman (1978 and 1986) among others.
6. Annual reports and 10K reports of firms with SIC code 2836 indicate that these firms are involved in biotechnology pharmaceutical products.
7. The other two groups of pharmaceutical firms which are not included in this study are 2833-Medicinals and Botanicals and 2835-Diagnostic Substances.
8. This eight-observation requirement is similar to Jones (1991).
9. Manegold and Karlinsky (1988) document a significantly negative stock price impact of TEFRA when the market was certain that this bill would pass.
10. Another potential control variable is the existence of earnings-based bonus plans. The study does not test this variable because the author does not have access to sample firms' proxy statements which contain bonus plan information. There are also another two justifications for not controlling for this variable. First, Holthausen, Larcker, and Sloan (1995), who use confidential data to examine bonus schemes and earnings management, find different results from and indicate several limitations of a bonus plan study (Gaver, Gaver, and Austin 1995) which relies on proxy statements. Second, because a successful health care reform would lead to price control which decreases future profits and, hence, future bonuses of managers, it is likely that the long-term benefit of managing earnings downward to alleviate political costs would outweigh the short-term benefit of managing earnings upward to increase the current year bonus.

11. One possibility is increasing LIFO cost of goods sold through year-end purchases. This study also examined research and development (R&D) expenses—pharmaceutical firms' major expenses—which concern operating decisions and are not likely to involve discretionary accruals. The examination did not reveal any significant increase in R&D expenses in 1993 relative to 1992 and 1994.

12. There is no change in inferences when the regression is estimated without excluding outliers.

13. The *Value Line Investment Survey* (February 4, 1994, p. 1259) noted that in 1993 drug stocks declined to the levels where yields approached ranges normally offered by electric utilities. This statement indicates the large increase in cost of capital of drug firms.

14. Twenty firms had discretionary non-cash write-offs in 1992 and 18 firms had discretionary write-offs in 1994. The percentage of write-offs (18.6%) is computed by dividing 38 by 204, which is the sum of number of sample firms in the two years (101 + 103).

15. These write-offs in the fourth quarter may help explain a report in the *Wall Street Journal* on February 22, 1994 that the pharmaceutical industry had the sixth worst net income of 59 listed industries—with a decrease of 46 percent when the fourth quarter of 1993 net income was compared to the same quarter one year earlier.

REFERENCES

Abbott, T.A. 1995. Regulating pharmaceutical prices. In *Health Care Policy and Regulation*, ed. T.A. Abbott, 105–134. Boston: Kluwer Academic Press.

Belsley, D.A., E. Kuh, and R.E. Welsch. 1980. *Regression Diagnostics: Identifying Influential Data and Sources of Collinearity*. New York: John Wiley & Sons.

Conlan, M.F. 1994. Winter of their discontent: Drug firms facing new storms. *Drug Topics* 138(March 7): 90–92.

DeAngelo, H., L. DeAngelo, and D.J. Skinner. 1994. Accounting choice in troubled companies. *Journal of Accounting and Economics* 17: 113–43.

Dechow, P.M., R.G. Sloan, and A.P. Sweeney. 1995. Detecting earnings management. *The Accounting Review* 70(April): 193–226.

Dietrich, J.R., and C. Olsen. 1985. Vertical information transfers: The association between retailers' sales announcements and suppliers' security returns. *Journal of Accounting Research* 23(Supplement): 144–166.

Gaver, J.J., K.M. Gaver, and J.R. Austin. 1995. Additional evidence on bonus plans and income management. *The Accounting Review* 70(January): 3–28.

Grabowski, H., and J. Vernon. 1994. Return to R&D on new drug introductions in the 1980s. *Journal of Health Economics* 13: 383–406.

Griffin, M.T. 1991. AIDS drugs and the pharmaceutical industry: A need for reform. *American Journal of Law and Medicine* 17: 363–410.

Hall, S.C. 1993. Political scrutiny and earnings management in the oil refining industry. *Journal of Accounting and Public Policy* 12: 325–351.

Holthausen, R.W., D.F. Larcker, and R.G. Sloan. 1995. Annual bonus schemes and the management of earnings. *Journal of Accounting and Economics* 19: 29–74.

Jacks, J.C., and L. Jacks. 1995. Chronology of the birth and death of a health bill. *Journal of Health Care Finance* 21(Spring): 59–67.

Jones, J.J. 1991. Earnings management during import relief investigation. *The Accounting Review* 29(Autumn): 193–228.

Larcker, D.F., and L. Revsine. 1983. The oil and gas accounting controversy: An analysis of economic consequences. *The Accounting Review* 58(October): 706–732.

Levitt, A. 1998. The "number game." www.sec.gov/news/speeches/spch220.txt (September 28): 1–8.

Luce, G.M., and T.E. Dutton. 1993. Health care reform: Models and implications. *Health care Financial Management* 47: 24–31.

Manegold, J.G., and S.S. Karlinsky. 1988. The security market impact of a tax law change: Possessions corporation revisions. *The Journal of American Taxation Association* 9: 65–83.

Mensah, Y.M., J.M. Considine, and L. Oakes. 1994. Statutory insolvency regulations and earnings management in the prepaid health-care industry. *The Accounting Review* 69(January): 70–95.

Schipper, K. 1989. Earnings management. *The Accounting Review* 3(December): 91–102.

Scholes, M., P. Wilson, and M. Wolfson. 1989. Tax planning, regulatory capital planning, and financial reporting strategy for commercial banks. Working paper, Stanford University.

Smith, C.W. 1993. A Perspective on accounting-based debt covenant violations. *The Accounting Review* 68(April): 289–303.

U.S. House Subcommittee on Technology, Environment, and Aviation of the Committee on Science, Space, and Technology. 1993a. *Health care reform and the role of medical technologies* hearing. 103rd Congress, First Session, June 16.

U.S. House Subcommittee on Health of the Committee on Ways and Means. 1993b. *Expansion of medicare benefits to include prescription drugs* hearing. 103rd Congress, First Session, June 22.

U.S. Senate Special Committee on Aging, Staff Report. 1993a. *Earning a failing grade: A report card on 1992 drug manufacturer price inflation*. February.

U.S. Senate Special Committee on Aging. 1993b. *Pharmaceutical marketplace reform: Is competition the right prescription?* hearing. 103rd Congress, First Session, November 16.

Watts, R., and J. Zimmerman. 1978. Toward a positive theory of determination of accounting standards. *The Accounting Review* 53(January): 112–134.

Watts, R., and J. Zimmerman. 1986. *Positive Accounting Theory*. Englewood Cliffs, NJ: Prentice-Hall.

White, H. 1980. A heteroskedasticity-consistent covariance matrix estimator and a direct test for heteroskedasticity. *Econometrics* 48(September): 817–838.

PART II

RESEARCH REPORTS

ASSESSING AUDITOR INDEPENDENCE:
AUDIT FEES AND ENFORCEMENT PATTERNS

John A. Pendley and Joseph Legoria

ABSTRACT

In this report, we examine the effect that fees earned from a client have on auditor independence. Recent comments by the Securities and Exchange Commission (SEC) and members and staff of the Independence Standards Board (ISB) continue to raise questions about the potentially adverse effects of auditor economic dependence on specific clients. We address this question by examining whether the chance of a poor quality audit increases if an auditor earns a greater proportion of fee revenue from a given client. For this study, poor quality audits are identified from the SEC's Accounting and Auditing Enforcement Releases (AAERs). We compare the audits identified in AAERs with audits with similar characteristics that are not cited in AAERs. Our findings show that even after controlling for other audit quality attributes (such as expertise), level of fee dependence is significantly related to the probability of being cited in an SEC enforcement action. Thus, our research findings lend support to concerns about the economic dependence of auditors as bearing an adverse influence on auditor independence and the perception of the quality of an audit.

Research in Accounting Regulation, Volume 13, pages 151-167.

ISBN: 0-7623-0520-7

INTRODUCTION

Practicing auditors have long treated independence as an individual attitude that is best fostered through education and training, internal firm practices and guidelines, and internal and external quality control mechanisms. Recently, however, the Securities and Exchange Commission (SEC) and the newly formed Independence Standards Board (ISB) have begun to ask questions concerning auditor independence that move beyond the traditional concept of independence as codified in professional pronouncements. For example, questions have recently arisen from regulators concerning auditor attitudes toward large clients (Wallman 1996), and the effect that fees earned from non-audit services have on auditor objectivity (Allen 1997, Rankin 1998). Although these questions are not new, their continual re-appearance in regulatory settings makes it clear that additional research is needed on the economics of the auditor-client relationship in relation to auditor independence.

In the current study, we examine a potential determinant of auditor independence that is based upon the level of fees earned from a given client.[1] Fee level is defined in three ways. First, fee level is defined as the percentage of estimated *audit* fees earned from a single client. Second, estimated *total* fees (audit plus consulting and tax fees) earned from a single client are used as a measure of fee level. Total fees are used to assess the effect that non-audit fees have on the analysis. Finally, a categorical variable is created (high fee level versus low fee level) that follows the view in the professional auditing standards that an auditor is either independent or not independent.

Observations of audit engagements cited in the SEC's Accounting and Auditing Enforcement Releases (AAERs) are used to examine the relationship between the fee level measures and audit quality. From the SEC's viewpoint, the engagements described in the auditing-related AAERs represent fact-specific descriptions of poor quality audits. If fee dependence induces less objective audit decisions, then there should be a positive relation between fee dependence and the probability of SEC censure.

To test this idea, a model is constructed that contains auditor-related variables representing other aspects of audit quality (e.g., auditor tenure and auditor industry expertise) plus the fee level measures. Audit engagements cited in AAERs are pair-matched with control engagements not cited in AAERs on the basis of size and industry. The results of the analysis provide convincing evidence that even after controlling for other quality-related attributes, the fee level measurement is predictably and significantly associated with the probability of SEC censure.

BACKGROUND[2]

Observations of poor quality audits are obtained from the SEC's Accounting and Auditing Enforcement Releases (AAERs). AAERs are official communications from the SEC to the accounting community at large concerning specific accounting and auditing issues.[3] Although they address specific issues, AAERs are carefully chosen by the SEC as vehicles for addressing perceived problems or potential problem areas. Auditors are often named in such releases either individually (if deemed necessary by the SEC's Enforcement Division) or together with the reporting company.[4] Concerning auditing issues, the SEC uses AAERs to "inform auditors about its views on the proper conduct of an audit practice" (Feroz, Park, and Pastena 1991).

Auditor sanctions contained in AAERs have proven useful to researchers in a number of contexts. Campbell and Parker (1992) provide a comprehensive analysis of AAERs as they relate to the audit function. They examine 307 Accounting Series Releases (the AAER's predecessor)[5] issued from 1972 through 1982 and 250 AAERs issued from inception through 1989. From these documents, Campbell and Parker (1992) identify those dealing with the independent audit function. A total of 132 enforcement actions are identified against independent auditors, 55 from Accounting Series Releases and 77 from AAERs.

A number of other studies have examined the relationship between auditor reputation and the SEC sanctions against auditors. These studies hypothesize that SEC enforcement actions against auditors will cause a loss of credibility which should be observable in the market for audits. Evidence generally supports this hypothesis. Wilson and Grimlund (1990) document declines in auditor market share subsequent to SEC enforcement actions, Davis and Simon (1992) report that sanctioned auditors tend to earn lower fees on new engagements, and Moreland (1995) finds an association between auditor sanction and lower earnings response coefficients of client companies. Finally, Rollins and Bremser (1997) also report reputation effects associated with sanctioned versus non-sanctioned auditors that are interpreted in terms of institutional theory.

DESIGN

AAERs will generally cite the GAAS violations encountered in the case. AAERs that cite independence problems usually involve violations of the AICPA's *Code of Professional Conduct*, such as a financial interest in the client or some other violation of the profession's rules of independence. In this study, however, auditor independence is considered a broader issue that depends in part upon the magnitude of fees accruing to an auditor from a particular client. With this broader interpretation, it may be that other GAAS violations, such as overreliance on client representations and lack of due care, are symptomatic of independence problems. For this reason, all GAAS violations in the sample AAERs are included in the analysis.

In the current study, all AAERs involving auditors through 1995 are identified. We use Campbell and Parker's (1992) list for AAERs through 1989. We then reviewed the AAERs from 1990 to September 1995 to identify those involving auditors for that time period. The AAER observations with complete data are pair-matched with control observations that are not named in AAERs.

Our purpose in the study is to examine whether there is a relationship between fee level, measured as the percentage of estimated fees earned from a single audit client, and the probability that an auditor is censured by the SEC. Three variations of fee level are tested. The first variation is based on estimated *audit* fees. With this measure, fee dependence is calculated as the percentage that a single client contributes to their auditor's total revenue from audit services.

The drawback to the audit fee measure is that accounting firms typically perform non-audit services (tax and consulting). Thus, the true impact of losing a client may not be assessed using only estimated audit fees. Therefore, a second variation of fee level is calculated using the ratio of estimated client audit fees to estimated *total* fees.

The findings concerning total fees may provide limited insight into the impact of non-audit services on auditor independence,[6] but only if there is a difference between the audit fee measure and the total fee measure on the probability of SEC censure. Specifically, if the audit fee measure has no effect *and* the total fee measure has the predicted significant effect, some support would be provided for the view that the provision of non-audit services may adversely affect auditor objectivity and independence. Similarly, if audit fees were found to be significant, and total fees were found to be insignificant, some support would be provided for enhancement of auditor objectivity through the provision of non-audit services.

Finally, the view of auditor independence embodied in the professional auditing standards suggests that auditor independence could be measured as a dichotomous condition (independent versus not independent). Thus, a third variation of fee level is constructed as an indicator variable.

VARIABLES USED IN THE STUDY

Table 1 contains a description of the variables, including relevant source citations and a brief description of our means of measuring the variables. The research variables of interest are the fee-level measurements. Other quality-related variables are included in the statistical models in order control for other aspects of audit quality that have been identified in prior academic research.

In other studies, the Big Six/non-Big Six variable and the auditor tenure variable have themselves been advocated as measures of independence. However, the Big Six/non-Big Six variable and the tenure variable may contain information that

Table 1. Description of Model Components

Model Component	*Quality Construct(s)*	*Variable Name*	*Measurement in the Current Study*	*Predicted Relation with Probability of AAER Citation*
Big 6 versus non-Big 6	Reputation (Dopuch and Simunic 1982; Simunic and Stein 1987; Francis and Simon 1987, Wilson and Grimlund 1990, Davis and Simon 1992, Moreland 1995, Rollins and Bremser 1997) Credibility (Tech and Wong 1993) Technical expertise and Independence (Feltham, Hughes, and Simunic 1991).	*BIG6*	A dummy variable coded "1" for a Big 6 or former Big 8 accounting firm; "0" otherwise.	Negative
Auditor tenure	Client-specific expertise (Stice 1991) Independence (Deis and Giroux 1992)	*TENURE*	Number of years contiguous service as a company's auditor.	Negative
Auditor industry expertise	Industry-specific expertise (Palmrose 1984, 1986; DeFond 1992)	*EXPER*	Percentage of an auditor's practice within a company's industry.	Negative
Fee level	Independence (DeAngelo 1981, Stice 1991, DeFond 1992; Krishman and Krishman 1996)	*(1) AFEELEV*	One minus the percentage of estimated audit fees earned from a specific client.	Negative
		(2) TFEELEV	One minus the percentage of estimated total fees earned from a specific client.	Negative
		(3) LOFEELEV	A dummy variable coded "1" for observations above the median value of AFEELEV, "0" otherwise.	Negative

is not related to independence. For instance, there may be other reasons that non-Big Six firms are more likely to named in an AAER, such as the extensive resources available to the Big Six firms to defend their positions during SEC investigations (DeFond and Smith 1991). In addition, the tenure variable has been described as a measure of expertise (Stice 1991). Therefore, we choose not to exclude these variables, because of the information content they may contain over and above their ability to measure independence.

Calculation of Fee Level

The fee level variables quantify the economic importance of a specific client to their auditor. Three fee-level variables are calculated: (1) One minus the ratio of estimated audit fees earned from a client to total audit fees earned by their auditor (variable name *AFEELEV*), (2) one minus the ratio of estimated audit fees to estimated total fees (consulting and tax revenues included, variable name *TFEELEV*), and (3) an indicator variable that equals one for low fee-level observations and zero for high fee-level observations (variable name *LOFEELEV*).

The fee-level ratios contained in the continuous variables *AFEELEV* and *TFEELEV* are subtracted from one. Thus, larger values of *AFEELEV* and *TFEELEV* represent smaller clients, and, conceptually, greater levels of independence. By subtracting from one, a negative association is hypothesized with respect to the probability of SEC censure.

Audit fees are estimated by the square root of client total assets. A square root transformation is used because the resulting variable exhibits a more realistic relationship to actual audit effort (Simunic 1980).

The fee level measures are calculated from summarized data obtained from a complete census of the Compustat database.[7] To accomplish the census, estimated audit fees for all observations on Compustat for the years 1980 through 1993 are calculated. Then the observations are summarized (aggregated) by year, auditor, and industry. Two-digit Standard Industrial Classification (SIC) is used for the industry categories.

To illustrate the calculation, assume that $AUDFEE_{y,a,i}$ represents the sum of the estimated fees for all clients of accounting firm a in two-digit SIC category i during year y. Further assume that $audfee_j$ represents the estimated audit fee earned from observed audit engagement j. This audit engagement is performed by accounting firm a in year y. Using this notation, the value of *AFEELEV* is given by:

$$1 - \left(\frac{audfee_j}{\sum_{i=1}^{27} AUDFEE_{y,a,i}} \right) \quad (1)$$

There are 27 two-digit SIC categories.[8] Thus, the denominator of the ratio within the parentheses in equation 1 represents total estimated audit fees earned by accounting firm a in year y (i.e., estimated fees are summed across industry groups).

The second fee-level variable incorporates an estimate of tax and consulting revenues. Total fees are estimated using the fee split data published in *Accounting Today*. In recent years, *Accounting Today* has published accounting firm fee data annually, including the percentage of fees earned from accounting and auditing, consulting, and tax. An estimate of total fees is calculated for each observation in the Compustat census. To derive the estimate, the auditor's accounting and auditing fee split percentage published in *Accounting Today* (1992)[9] is divided into their client's total assets. The square root transformation is then applied to the extrapolated number to derive a measure of estimated total fees. From this data, *TFEELEV* is calculated as follows:

$$1 - \left(\frac{audfee_j}{\sum_{i=1}^{27} TOTFEE_{y,a,i}} \right) \quad (2)$$

where $audfee_j$ represents the estimated audit fee earned from the audit engagement and $TOTFEE_{y,a,i}$ represents the aggregated estimated total fees earned by the auditor in the client's industry in the observed year.

A third fee-level measure is created as an indicator variable. This variable, *LOFEELEV*, takes the value of one if the observation is above the median value of *AFEELEV*, and zero if the observation is below the median value of *AFEELEV*. The process converts *AFEELEV*, which is a continuous variable, to an indicator variable, to accommodate the view in the professional auditing standards that an auditor is either independent or not independent.

Calculation of Auditor Industry Expertise

The industry expertise variable is also calculated from the Compustat census. The expertise variable is defined as the percentage market share held by an audit firm within a specific industry. Auditors that hold a higher market share within an industry have opportunities to develop industry-specific expertise due to relatively greater amount of audit work performed in the industry.

Using the notation introduced in the previous section, $AUDFEE_{y,a,i}$ represents the sum of the estimated fees for all clients of accounting firm a in two-digit SIC category i during year y. The calculation for the industry expertise variable (*EXPER*) is:

$$\frac{AUDFEE_{y,a,i}}{\sum_{a=1}^{10} AUDFEE_{y,a,i}} \qquad (3)$$

The numerator represents the industry-specific audit fees earned by accounting firm a in year y. There are ten accounting firm identifiers, one for each of the former Big Eight, a ninth identifier for national firms, and a tenth for all regional and local firms.[10] The denominator of equation 3 represents the total estimated fees earned within the industry by all accounting firms. Equation 3 thus results in accounting firm a's market share percentage within a specific industry.[11]

DATA SELECTION

Only AAERs that include independent auditor enforcement actions are included in the study. To identify potential observations, the list of AAERs involving auditors documented in Campbell and Parker (1992) is used to identify AAERs for the period 1982 (inception of AAERs) through 1989. Next, all AAERs issued from January 1990 through September 1995 (numbers 251 through 712) are examined to identify observations during that period. Finally, all observations are screened for data availability on Compustat. When an enforcement action covered multiple years, the most recent year cited is used. This process yielded a final set of 38 AAER enforcement actions.

Each of the 38 AAER observations is pair-matched to a non-AAER control observation on the basis of size (assets), industry, and time period. The industry pair-matching is performed on the firms' three-digit SIC.

RESULTS

Univariate Tests

Table 2 presents the descriptive statistics for the variables of interest. Included in Table 2 is a client size variable (*SIZE*), measured as the natural log of total assets. Total assets is one of the criteria used to pair-match AAER observations with non-AAER observations. As seen in Table 2, the pair-matching produced groups which are virtually identical with respect to *SIZE*. Mean *SIZE* for the AAER observations is 2.5057, compared to 2.4795 for the non-AAER group. The remaining variables, except for *LOFEELEV*, exhibit the hypothesized relationship with SEC censure. For example, it is hypothesized that a smaller proportion of AAER observations would have engaged a Big Six (or former Big Eight) auditor. From Table 2, the percentage of AAER observations engaging a Big Six auditor is 26.31 percent compared to 68.42 percent for the non-AAER observations. Other research variables, with the exception of *LOFEELEV*, which is not significant at conventional levels, are similarly consistent with the predicted relation contained in Table 1.

Table 3 presents the correlation matrix among the independent variables. Correlations among the three fee-level variables are all positive and highly significant, which would reasonably be expected, since the three variables are derived from the same data, and are constructed similarly. Further, *AFEELEV*, based on estimated audit fees, and *TFEELEV*, based on estimated total fees, are almost perfectly correlated (correlation coefficient of 0.998), indicating that the models separately estimated using these two variables will probably yield similar results. Among the other variables, the strongest correlation is 0.366 between *BIG6* and *EXPER*. The variables *AFEELEV* and *TFEELEV* are also significantly correlated with *EXPER*. The intercorrelations among these variables suggest that a multi-

Table 2. Univariate Statistics by AAER Grouping

	Auditor Sanctioned with AAER						
	1 = Yes (N = 39)			*0 = No (N = 38)*			*t-statistic*
Variables	*Mean*	*Median*	*Standard Deviation*	*Mean*	*Median*	*Standard Deviation*	*(one tailed probability)*
BIG6	0.2631	0.0000	0.4460	0.6842	1.0000	0.4710	0.001
TENURE	3.5526	3.0000	2.1140	5.2105	5.0000	3.3940	0.007
EXPER	0.1091	0.1019	0.0620	0.1305	0.1320	0.0680	0.078
AFEELEV	0.9993	0.9994	0.0006	0.9995	0.9996	0.0004	0.050
TFEELEV	0.9995	0.9996	0.0005	0.9996	0.9997	0.0003	0.042
LOFEELEV	0.4474	0.0000	0.5039	0.5526	1.0000	0.5039	0.183
SIZE	2.5057	2.4207	1.7583	2.4795	2.3898	1.6996	0.474

Note: See table 1 for variable names and definitions. SIZE is defined as the natural log of total assets.

Table 3. Pairwise Correlation Coefficients Among Dependent Variables

	BIG6	*TENURE*	*EXPER*	*AFEELEV*	*TFEELEV*	*LOFEELEV*
BIG6	1.000	–	–	–	–	–
TENURE	0.212	1.000	–	–	–	–
EXPER	0.366*	–0.037	1.000	–	–	–
AFEELEV	–0.029	–0.084	0.282*	1.000	–	–
TFEELEV	–0.016	–0.075	0.292*	0.998**	1.000	–
LOFEELEV	–0.158	–0.167	0.220	0.712**	0.702**	1.000

Notes: See table 1 for variable names and definitions.
*Significant at the 0.05 level
**Significant at the 0.01 level

variate approach is useful to assess the simultaneous effect of the variables on whether a firm is named in an AAER.

Multivariate Results

Table 4 shows the results of the three logistic regressions. The results are quite similar across the three models. Consistent with the univariate analysis, the coefficients on *BIG6* and *TENURE* are significant and have the predicted signs. These results provide evidence that auditors cited by the SEC in AAERs are smaller, consistent with Feroz, Park, and Pastena (1991), and have shorter tenure on their particular engagements than auditors who were not named in an AAER. The findings concerning auditor tenure suggest that greater tenure is associated with higher quality audits. This result counters the calls for mandatory auditor rotation that are often advocated by accounting regulators. For all three of the models, *EXPER* does not affect the probability of being named in an AAER citation. Further, the three regressions have similar correct classification rates.

The results show that there is a relationship between fee level and the probability of being censured by the SEC. The coefficients for *AFEELEV*, *TFEELEV*, and *LOFEELEV* are all significant (p values of 0.033, 0.032, and 0.061, respectively) and have the predicted sign. This finding suggests that the more economically dependent an auditor is on a particular client, the more likely it is that the auditor will be cited in an AAER.

CONCLUSION

In this study we examine the relationship between fee dependence and the probability that an auditor will be censured by the SEC. Fee dependence is only one of many factors that influence auditor independence. However, the importance of fee levels as a research topic is magnified by recent comments by regulators (e.g.,

Table 4. Results of the Logistic Regression Models Separately Estimated using the Three Fee Level Variants

Dependent Variable: = *1 if Auditor sanctioned with a AAER, N = 38*
= *0 if Auditor not sanctioned with a AAER, N = 38*

		Regression Using AFEELEV			*Regression Using TFEELEV*			*Regression Using LOFEELEV*		
Variable	*Expected Sign*	*Coefficient*	*Chi Square*	*p*	*Coefficient*	*Chi Square*	*p*	*Coefficient*	*Chi Square*	*p*
Intercept	?	1,353.60	4.59	0.032	1,910.60	4.63	0.031	1.12	1.93	0.165
BIG6	–	−2.00	9.95	0.002	−2.00	9.58	0.002	−2.03	9.82	0.002
TENURE	–	−0.22	4.36	0.037	−0.22	4.39	0.036	−0.21	4.32	0.038
EXPER	–	2.26	0.20	0.654	2.24	0.19	0.662	1.47	0.09	0.766
AFEELEV	–	−1,352.90	4.57	0.033	—	—	—	—	—	—
TFEELEV	–	—	—	—	−1,909.80	4.62	0.032	—	—	—
LOFEELEV	–	—	—	—	—	—	—	−1.15	3.52	0.061
Percent correctly classified			71.10%			71.10%			68.40%	
Chi-Square (*d.f.* = 4)			20.31			20.38			19.78	
p			0.0004			0.0004			0.0006	

Notes: See table 1 for variable names and definitions.
One tailed p-values are shown for the regression coefficients.

Wallman 1996) expressing concern about the potentially detrimental effect that economic dependence may have on auditor independence.

Auditor censure by the SEC is used as the indicator of a substandard audit. The hypothesis of the study is that relative fee levels will be higher for accounting firms cited by the SEC versus firms that are not cited. The sample used to create the model consists of 38 instances where auditors are specifically cited in the SEC's Accounting and Auditing Enforcement Releases (AAERs) and 38 pair-matched observations not cited in AAERs. The model used to test the fee level hypothesis also includes other quality attributes (i.e., Big Six/non-Big Six, auditor tenure, and auditor industry expertise).

A number of limitations arise through the use of SEC enforcement releases to study auditor fee dependence. First, the study implicitly assumes that observations of auditor censure obtained from AAERs are valid for making inferences about audit quality. Results are limited with respect to the degree that the SEC pursues policy agendas not related to audit quality (DeFond and Smith 1991). On the other hand, the SEC may specifically pursue audits where it believes economic dependence is an issue. In this case, our results simply reflect the SEC's enforcement action selection criteria. Thus, the study may suffer from self-selection problems driven by the SEC's process of selecting audits to pursue under their enforcement program. Finally, the small number of AAERs involving auditors (38 censure observations) may further limit the generalizability of results.

In the study, the dependent variable of interest is fee dependence, which is measured in three ways: (1) the percentage that a single client contributes to their auditor's revenue from *audit* services, (2) the percentage that a single client contributes to their auditor's *total* revenue (tax and consulting services included), and (3) an indicator variable measuring whether the auditor is "independent" or "not independent" based on relative fee level.

The results of the analysis show a predictable and significant relation between all three variations of fee level and the probability of an auditor being cited in an AAER. Thus, our research findings lend support to concerns about the economic dependence of auditors as bearing an adverse influence on auditor independence and the perception of the quality of an audit.

These findings suggest several important areas for future research. The current study does not specifically focus on the issue of non-audit services. Since the performance of non-audit services continues to be a controversial regulatory issue, an adaptation of the design of the current study to explicitly examine the role of non-audit services would be useful. In addition, an extension incorporating audit committee characteristics would also prove useful to regulators and professionals. Such a study would generate evidence about the relationship between specific audit committee characteristics and audit quality. The relationship between audit committee characteristics and audit quality would be especially relevant given the recent recommendations of a committee formed by the

New York Stock Exchange and the National Association of Securities Dealers (Blue Ribbon Committee on Improving the Effectiveness of Corporate Audit Committees 1999).

APPENDIX

Development of the Research Model

In the current study, audit quality factors are drawn from DeAngelo (1981). DeAngelo (1981) states that audit quality is a function of two aspects: Auditor technical expertise (the application of which means that the auditor would detect a material error) and auditor independence (leading the auditor to report material errors). Since audit quality and its determinants are unobservable, DeAngelo (1981) states that users must develop surrogates to serve as measures of the quality dimension. One readily observable characteristic of audit firms is size.

Auditor size serves as a surrogate for the independence component of audit quality, because the loss of a given client would have less of a detrimental economic impact on a large firm versus a small firm. Thus, smaller audit firms have greater incentives to retain clients, which in turn reduces audit quality. For example, a very large client may not pose any independence problems for a large accounting firm because the client, despite its large size, does not constitute a significant part of the accounting firm's audit practice. However, the same large client might induce compromises in independence if it were audited by a much smaller, regional firm. In the regional firm's case, the large client might constitute such a large proportion of the firm's practice as to make an independent attitude toward that client difficult or impossible.

Early empirical work in this area used a Big Six versus non-Big Six indicator variable to measure size. However, in the current study, we follow more recent work (Stice 1991; DeFond 1992; Krishnan and Krishnan 1996) that measures size as the percentage that a given client represents in their auditor's total base of audit work. Further, the size percentage is based on estimated fees, using the transformation suggested by Simunic (1980). Three different variations of the fee level measurement are tested in order to gauge the sensitivity of the model results to variations in constructing the variable.

The SEC's Accounting and Auditing Enforcement Releases (AAERs) are used to identify poor quality audits. The AAER observations with complete data are pair-matched (on the basis of size, industry, and time period) with control observations that are not named in AAERs. Then, models are constructed that contain control variables and the respective fee level measurements (see Table 1 for variable names and definitions). This design is used to test the following research hypothesis (stated in alternate form):

Ceteris paribus, fee level, measured as the percentage of total estimated fees earned from a single audit client, will be significantly associated with the probability that an auditor is censured by the SEC.

The hypothesis is tested using the following model:

$$P(AAER) = f\begin{bmatrix}\text{Big 6 versus non-Big 6}\\ \text{auditor tenure}\\ \text{auditor industry expertise}\\ \text{fee level}\end{bmatrix} \qquad \text{(A1)}$$

where *P*(*AAER*) represents the probability of an auditor being cited by the SEC. The research hypothesis is tested by examining the sign and significance of the fee-level measures.

We chose to model the probability of an auditor being censured by the SEC in terms of the cited auditor's characteristics. However, there are important *client*-related variables that may affect the question being addressed. Client size and degree of financial distress may affect the extent of audit work performed due to the degree of risk perceived by the auditor. Auditors of larger or more financially distressed clients may perceive greater risk of litigation or reputation loss should an inappropriate decision be made.

Control of these client-related factors is addressed via pair-matching and sensitivity analyses. Client size (as an indicator of differing levels of audit risk) is controlled by pair-matching. Each observation of an AAER auditor censure is pair-matched to a control observation (non-AAER) by total assets, industry and time period. Differing degrees of financial distress are addressed by testing the sensitivity of model results to the inclusion of a financial distress measure. Predicted values from Zmijewski's (1984) bankruptcy model are used as the measurement of financial distress.[12] However, the results shown in the "Results" section of this chapter are largely invariant to whether financial distress is included or excluded from the analysis.

NOTES

1. See the appendix for the academic theory justifying fee dependence as a component of independence.
2. Relevant background from the academic literature used in model development can be found in the appendix.
3. AAERs do not cover issues of financial reporting (these are handled via Financial Reporting Releases and Staff Accounting Bulletins).

4. See Feroz, Park, and Pastena (1991) and Pincus, Holder, and Mock (1988) for an in-depth description of the SEC's enforcement program, including the process culminating in the issuance of AAERs.

5. Accounting Series Releases (issued between 1937 and 1982) dealt with both financial reporting and accounting and auditing issues. In 1982, the SEC discontinued ASRs, replacing them with two new reports: Financial Reporting Releases (FRRs) which deal exclusively with reporting, and AAERs which deal with fact-specific violations of accounting and auditing rules.

6. Many in practice do not think that the provision of non-audit services impairs independence (see Elliott 1992). However, many regulators disagree and view the increase in the proportion of accounting firm revenues derived from non-audit services as having a negative impact on the appearance of independence (Rankin 1998).

7. We use the 1993 Standard and Poor's *PC Plus* CD-ROM version of the Compustat database. Both the current and research files are used.

8. Only industrial SIC classifications are considered. We do not consider financial companies (those with a two-digit SIC of 60–69) or utilities (those with the two-digit SIC 49) to improve the homogeneity of the final dataset.

9. Fee split data is not available for the entire period under study (observed audit engagements occur throughout the period 1980 to 1992). Since we could not obtain fee split data for the entire period, we used the fee split data corresponding to the most recent observations (occurring in 1992). See *Accounting Today Special Report: The Top 60 CPA Firms* (1992) for the fee split percentages used. Use of 1992 percentages for all observations limits the accuracy of the measurements, because the proportion of total revenues derived from non-audit services has steadily increased since 1985 (Wallman 1996). However, mitigating the measurement inaccuracy is the fact that the percentage of revenues from non-audit services increased similarly at all the large firms during the period under study (Antle, Griffin, Teece, and Williamson 1997).

10. A national firm group is formed from clients of Grant Thornton; McGladrey and Pullen; and Seidman and Seidman. The regional/local firm group includes all other non-Big Six accounting firms. These groupings are created because the non-Big Six firms individually hold a relatively small share of the market for audits of publicly-held companies.

11. To collect the market share data, the following procedures were employed. For every industrial company carried on the Compustat database for 1980–1993, the following data was extracted: year, accounting firm, SIC classification, client total assets, and client total sales. Then these data extracted from Compustat were condensed into a three-dimensional "matrix," with the dimensions defined by: (1) year (1980–1993), (2) accounting firm, and (3) industry. Within each cell of the "matrix," sum of client sales, sum of client assets, total fees (calculated as the sum of the square root of the individual client total asset numbers), and number of clients classifying in the cell are aggregated. The process of creating the *EXPER* or fee level ratios involved accessing or summing across the appropriate cells.

12. The unweighted probit parameters for the 40:800 (bankrupt to nonbankrupt ratio) estimation sample (Zmijewski 1984, table 3, p. 69) are used to produce the distress measure. The parameters of the model are:

$$DISTRESS = -4.336 + -4.513(ROA) + 5.679(FINL) + .004(LIQ)$$

where *DISTRESS* is estimated financial distress, *ROA* is net income to total assets (return on assets), *FINL* is total debt to total assets (financial leverage), and *LIQ* is current assets to current liabilities (liquidity).

REFERENCES

Accounting Today. 1992. Accounting Today special report: The top 60 firms. *Accounting Today* 1992: S11–S20.

Allen, W.T. 1997. Auditor independence and the promotion of the public interest. Second Annual Seymour Jones Distinguished Lecture. Delivered at the Ross Institute of Accounting, Department of Accounting, Leonard N. Stern School of Business, New York University, November 24. Available at http://www.cpaindependence.org/current/aippi.htm.

Antle, R., P.A. Griffin, D.J. Teece, and O.E. Williamson. 1997. An economic analysis of auditor independence for a multi-client, multi-service public accounting firm. In *Serving the Public Interest: A New Conceptual Framework for Auditor Independence*, Appendix B. New York: AICPA.

Blue Ribbon Committee on Improving the Effectiveness of Corporate Audit Committees. 1999. *Report and Recommendations of the Blue Ribbon Committee on Improving the Effectiveness of Corporate Audit Committees*. New York: New York Stock Exchange and the National Association of Securities Dealers.

Campbell, D.R., and L.M. Parker. 1992. SEC communications to the independent auditors: An analysis of enforcement actions. *Journal of Accounting and Public Policy* 11: 297–330.

Davis, L., and D. Simon. 1992. The impact of SEC disciplinary actions on audit fees. *Auditing: A Journal of Practice and Theory* (Spring): 58–68.

DeAngelo, L. 1981. Auditor size and audit quality. *Journal of Accounting and Economics* 3: 183–199.

DeFond, M. 1992. The association between changes in client firm agency costs and auditor switching. *Auditing: A Journal of Practice and Theory* 11(Spring): 16–31.

DeFond, M., and D. Smith. 1991. Discussion of the financial and market effects of the SEC Accounting and Auditing Enforcement Releases. *Journal of Accounting Research* 20(Supplement): 143–148.

Deis, D., and G. Giroux. 1992. Determinants of audit quality in the public sector. *The Accounting Review* 67: 462–479.

Dopuch, N., and D. Simunic. 1982. Competition in auditing: An assessment. In proceedings of *Fourth Symposium on Auditing Research*, 401–450. Urbana-Champaign, IL: University of Illinois.

Elliott, R. 1992. Audit independence: Concept and application. *The CPA Journal* March: 34–39.

Feltham, G., J. Hughes, and D. Simunic. 1991. Empirical assessment of the impact of auditor quality on the valuation of new issues. *Journal of Accounting and Economics* 14: 375–399.

Feroz, E.H., K. Park, and V. Pastena. 1991. The financial and market effects of the SEC's Accounting and Auditing Enforcement Releases. *Journal of Accounting Research* 20(Supplement): 107–142.

Francis, J., and D. Simon. 1987. A test of audit pricing in the small-client segment of the U.S. audit market. *The Accounting Review* 62(January): 145–157.

Krishnan, Jagen, and Jayanthi Krishnan. 1996. The role of economic tradeoffs in the auditor opinion decision: An empirical analysis. *Journal of Accounting, Auditing & Finance* 11: 565–586.

Moreland, K. 1995. Criticisms of auditors and the association between earnings and returns of client firms. *Auditing: A Journal of Practice and Theory* Spring: 94–103.

Palmrose, Z. 1984. The demand for quality differentiated audit services in an agency cost setting: An empirical investigation. In *Proceedings of the Sixth Symposium on Auditing Research*, eds. A.R. Abdel-Khalik and I. Solomon, 229–252. Urbana-Champaign, IL: University of Illinois.

Palmrose, Z. 1986. Audit fees and auditor size: Further evidence. *Journal of Accounting Research* 24(Spring): 97–110.

Pincus, K., W. Holder, and T. Mock. 1988. *Reducing the Incidence of Fraudulent Financial Reporting: The Role of the Securities and Exchange Commission*. Los Angeles, CA: SEC and Financial Reporting Institute of the University of Southern California.

Rankin, K. 1998. Auditor independence paper sparks AICPA, SEC clash. *Accounting Today* January 28: 5.

Rollins, T., and W. Bremser. 1997. The SEC's enforcement actions against auditors: An auditor reputation and institutional theory perspective. *Critical Perspectives on Accounting* 8: 191–206.

Simunic, D. 1980. The pricing of audit services: Theory and evidence. *Journal of Accounting Research* 18(Spring): 161–190.

Simunic, D., and M. Stein. 1987. *Product Differentiation in Auditing: Auditor Choice in the Market for Unseasoned New Issues*, Research Monograph No. 13. Vancouver, BC: The Canadian Certified General Accountants' Research Foundation.

Stice, J. 1991. Using financial and market information to identify pre-engagement factors associated with lawsuits against auditors. *The Accounting Review* 66(July): 516–533.

Teoh, S., and T. Wong. 1993. Perceived auditor quality and the earnings response coefficient. *The Accounting Review* 68(April): 346–367.

Wallman, S.M.H. 1996. The future of accounting, Part III: Reliability and auditor independence. *Accounting Horizons* December: 76–97.

Wilson, T., and R. Grimlund. 1990. An examination of the importance of an auditor's reputation. *Auditing: A Journal of Practice and Theory* Spring: 43–59.

Zmijewski, M. 1984. Methodological issues relating to the estimation of financial distress prediction models. *Journal of Accounting Research* Supplement: 59–82.

WHY DO BANKRUPT COMPANIES RECEIVE UNMODIFIED AUDIT OPINIONS?

Jeffrey R. Casterella, Barry L. Lewis, and Paul L. Walker

ABSTRACT

Regulators and the financial press often appear perplexed with the audit opinions issued to failing firms. The purpose of this paper is to offer some rather straightforward explanations for these opinions. The underlying argument of this study and the proposed model is that the auditor did not (or could not) anticipate the bankruptcy filing because there were not enough warning signs present to raise the auditor's suspicion. The approach taken in the paper is to build a model of the audit opinion that is simple, has face validity, and is consistent with both practitioners' explanation of their decision and with professional standards. Additionally, the paper explores the predictive accuracy of such opinions given various signs of trouble for each company. The results indicate that although auditors fail to modify the reports of many soon-to-be bankrupt companies, they are reasonably good at identifying and modifying the audit reports of companies with multiple signs of financial distress. Implications for future research, the profession, and regulators are discussed.

Research in Accounting Regulation, Volume 13, pages 169-177.

ISBN: 0-7623-0520-7

INTRODUCTION

The issuance of clean opinions to failing firms has been interpreted by both the financial press and Congress as evidence of serious problems in the auditing profession. An "audit failure" allegedly occurs when "an independent auditor approves the financial statements of a company that shortly thereafter goes bankrupt or develops major financial problems" (Ingersoll 1985). Critics of the audit profession believe that audit failures are caused by a lack of overall audit quality and/or problems related to independence. These concerns led Congressman Dingell to question the self-regulatory status of the public accounting profession (Dingell 1985). In response to this criticism, the AICPA issued Statement on Auditing Standard No. 59 (AICPA 1988), which required auditors to more actively evaluate the going concern status of the client on every audit. Subsequent research has shown that the effectiveness of SAS 59 has been unclear at best.[1] More recent cases have not helped to alleviate concerns about audit failures. For example, in 1994, Orange County, California accused its auditor of contributing to the largest municipal bankruptcy in U.S. history. The auditor allegedly failed "to detect about $150 million that was illegally shifted from the investment portfolio to other county accounts" (Berton 1999). The case was settled out of court early in 1999 for $75 million. The settlement ranked "among the highest liability settlements in accounting history" (Berton 1999).

Mutchler, Hopwood, and McKeown (1997), hereafter referred to as MHM, is the most recent addition to a substantial body of research devoted to finding an explanation for the audit opinions rendered to companies that subsequently file for bankruptcy protection. Bell (1991) has aided in the development of this research by suggesting that the audit opinion in these circumstances should be viewed from the multiple perspectives of (1) whether the data are reasonably predictive of failure, (2) whether the auditor has incentives not to issue a modified report, and (3) whether the auditor considers non-financial-ratio information that either is contrary to a going concern assumption or mitigates against a violation of the going concern assumption.

Responding to the suggestions by Bell, MHM extended prior research (Mutchler 1985; McKeown, Mutchler, and Hopwood 1991; Chen and Church 1992) by adding variables to indicate the existence of positive and negative coverage in *The Wall Street Journal* both before and after the issuance of an audit opinion. This extension of prior work was to account for the use of contrary and mitigating factors in the evaluation of the going concern status of the distressed firms. For their sample of 208 bankrupt firms, all of which exhibited some evidence of financial distress, MHM developed a model to distinguish the firms that received modified reports from the firms that received unmodified reports. Significant predictors were: probability of bankruptcy, the lag between fiscal year-end and the issuance of the audit report, the lag between the issuance of the audit report and the bankruptcy date, the size of the firm, the existence of debt violations, and the existence of negative news prior to issuance of the audit report (the last three variables were significant beyond their relationship to the probability of bankruptcy). The proxy for mitigating factors (positive news stories) was not significant. All but the negative news variable had been found to be significant in prior studies.[2]

The purpose of this paper is twofold. First, we provide additional insights into the opinion formulation process by presenting a model that is both simpler than models used in prior research and more consistent with what auditors say they actually do. Based on a sample of 311 bankrupt firms, our results indicate that our simple indicator model significantly outperforms prior models in distinguishing between modified and unmodified reports issued to bankrupt companies. Second, responding to Bell's suggestion, we evaluate the extent to which the data for these bankrupt firms are reasonably predictive of failure. Contrary to public perception, we find that auditors consistently modify the reports of those companies that are most distressed and issue unmodified reports to those companies that are least distressed. In fact, the auditors modified significantly more audit reports than they would have by using a well-accepted bankruptcy prediction model.

In summary, if we are interested in why auditors issue clean opinions to failing firms, the data puts forth a very simple reason: the firms did not appear to be in very bad shape. The results provide evidence that auditors are actually doing a reasonably *good* job in auditing soon-to-be bankrupt companies.

THE MODEL

Our goal here is to test a model of the opinion process that is both simple (that is, contains few variables) and that possesses a high degree of face validity. For that reason, we test a model that includes five financial distress indicator variables that are clear indicators of severe problems. They are: negative current earnings, negative retained earnings, negative working capital, extremely high levels of debt (debt > 90% of total assets), and debt violations, as measured by Chen and Church (1992). The use of variables that focus on earnings, liquidity, and leverage is based in part on the model put forth by Zmijewski (1984) and prior literature.[3] Similar variables can also be found in SAS No. 59, audit textbooks, and phrasing used in audit report modifications. The dependent variable is an indicator variable that is zero if the report was unmodified and one if the report was modified.

Several factors motivate consideration of the model. For some time now, auditors have been under increasing public pressure to function as an early warning provider about impending business failure. The profession responded with SAS No. 59 which made the going concern evaluation a necessary exercise for each and every audit.[4] Despite this change, auditors continue to argue that they are not in the business of predicting bankruptcy. Consistent with this, our conversations with numerous practice partners lead us to believe that the use of bankruptcy prediction models is not widespread in the going concern assessment. The data support this argument. Further, neither SAS 59 nor its predecessor, SAS 34 (AICPA 1981), equates substantial doubt about the firm's ability to continue as a going concern with filing for bankruptcy protection. On that point, Ellingsen, Pany, and Fagan (1989) specifically acknowledge that a firm that has filed for bankruptcy protection under Chapter 11, and that expects to maintain operations, may be considered a going concern. Others believe that Chapter 11 reorganization "preserves the entity as a going concern" (Schultz 1995). At the same time, audit manuals and SAS 59 stress the importance of key indicators of financial difficulty in raising doubt about the ability of a firm to continue as a going concern. Some of the items specifically mentioned in SAS 59 include recurring operating losses, working capital deficiencies, loan defaults, adverse key financial ratios, etc.[5] Not surprisingly, the audit report modifications in our sample frequently cite these same variables. In contrast, our review of the audit reports in our sample did not detect any phrases alluding to a probability of bankruptcy. For these reasons, we include distress indicator variables, but do not include a probability of bankruptcy per se.[6] If what auditors say is correct, we would expect these distress indicator variables to be highly significant as predictors of the opinions issued to soon to be bankrupt companies.

SAMPLE SELECTION AND DATA SOURCES

Using the *Wall Street Journal Index*, we identified 311 distressed companies that filed for bankruptcy during the periods 1974–1985 and 1990–1994.[7] The sample contained 143 modified reports and 168 unmodified reports. We obtained data on audit reports from the NAARS database and Compact Disclosure. We supplemented these sources with Q-Data microfiche files.

RESULTS

We begin with a tabulation of the five financial distress indicator variables inferred from SAS 59 and the wording used in many audit report modifications. We simply summed the number of warning signs that were present for each firm in the sample and looked at the relation of this number to the audit opinion. Table 1 provides a brief summary of this analysis.

As expected, the rate of audit report modification increases as the number of indicators of distress increases. Of the 94 bankrupt firms in the sample with no more than one indicator of financial difficulty, only eight (9%) received modified reports. Of the 81 firms with four or more indicators of distress, 71 (88%) received modified reports. These results are essentially the same if we analyze the two time period sub-samples, 1974–1985 and 1990–1994, separately. Clearly, the

Table 1. Financial Distress Warning Signs and Audit Report Modification Rates

Number of Warning Signs	*Number of Companies*	*Number of Companies with Modified Reports*	*Percentage of Companies with Modified Reports*
0	17	1	6%
1	77	7	9%
2	71	23	32%
3	65	41	63%
4	61	51	84%
5	20	20	100%
Totals	311	143	

number of financial distress signs is strongly correlated with the type of report issued.[8]

As an additional analysis, we performed a logistic regression to test our simplified audit decision indicator model on the aggregate sample.[9] As shown in Table 2, the model is highly significant and exhibits considerable explanatory power. With a pseudo R-square of 36 percent, our simple model provides better explanatory power than the more complex models in the prior literature.[10] Modified audit reports are associated with negative current earnings, negative retained earnings, negative working capital, debt violations, and high levels of debt. Each of the independent variables is significant at $p < 0.05$ and has the expected sign.[11]

Table 2. Logit Results for Audit Opinion Model (168 Unmodified Companies Versus 143 Modified Companies)

Variable	*Parameter Estimate*	*Standard Error*	*Chi-Square*	*p-value*
INTERCEPT	−2.262	0.627	13.020	0.000
NEGATIVE EARNINGS	1.096	0.486	5.087	0.012
NEGATIVE RETAINED EARNINGS	0.752	0.341	4.858	0.014
NEGATIVE WORKING CAPITAL	1.056	0.328	10.371	0.001
EXCESSIVE DEBT	1.803	0.706	6.518	0.005
DEBT VIOLATION	2.059	0.314	43.026	0.000
SIZE	−0.200	0.086	5.437	0.010

Notes: Model Chi-Square = 156.46 (df = 6), p = .000
Pseudo-R^2 = .364
Dependent variable definition:
Audit opinion = 1 if modified, 0 otherwise
Independent variable definitions:

NEGATIVE EARNINGS	=	1 if current net income is negative, 0 otherwise
NEGATIVE RETAINED EARNINGS	=	1 if retained earnings is negative, 0 otherwise
NEGATIVE WORKING CAPITAL	=	1 if current ratio is <1, 0 otherwise
EXCESSIVE DEBT	=	1 if total debt > 90% of total assets, 0 otherwise
DEBT VIOLATION	=	1 if debt default, 0 otherwise
SIZE	=	natural log of sales

Audit Judgment Quality

It is clear that the financial press and regulators view unmodified reports issued to bankrupt companies as audit mistakes. Following the suggestion of Bell (1991), our next test examines these audit reports from the perspective of whether the data are reasonably predictive of business failure. The question is whether or not the data for the bankrupt companies in our sample suggests severe financial distress and impending bankruptcy. To examine this issue we computed the probability of bankruptcy for the firms in the sample. Following Bamber, Bamber, and Schoderbek (1993), we computed the Zmijewski (1984) financial condition index for each firm in the sample, and then transformed this standard normal measure into a probability (of bankruptcy) measure. Surprisingly, only 102 firms in our sample of 311 bankrupt companies had a probability of bankruptcy in excess of .5. Auditors were very effective at identifying these truly distressed firms, issuing modified reports to 80 percent of them. For the firms with probabilities of bankruptcy below .5, auditors modified fewer than 30 percent of the audit reports.

DISCUSSION AND CONCLUSIONS

Regulators and the financial press often appear perplexed with the audit opinions issued to failing firms. The purpose of this paper is to offer some rather straightforward explanations for these opinions. The underlying argument of this study (and the proposed model) is that the auditors did not (or could not) anticipate the bankruptcy filing because there were not enough warning signs present to raise the auditors' suspicions. To this end, we test a simple, rather parsimonious, model of warning signs that are listed frequently in audit reports and that practitioners, standard setters, and researchers believe are important indicators of financial distress. The model incorporates four common financial condition variables, the existence of debt violations, and size. Our results suggest that more complex models may not be necessary to understand the opinions issued to failing firms. We tested this model on a sample of 311 firms from two time periods, 1974–1985 and 1990–1994, and find that it has more explanatory power than the 14-variable model employed by Mutchler, Hopwood, and McKeown (1997) to explain a sample covering the same time periods. Unlike MHM, our model consists of predictor variables, all of which are actually available to the auditor when making the opinion decision. While MHM found evidence that auditors use negative news stories and debt violations as factors, contrary to the going concern assumption, they failed to find evidence that auditors consider other factors that might mitigate the contrary indications. Our results suggest that auditors issue unmodified reports to failing firms because they are not faced with enough negative indicators to persuade them to do otherwise. In other words, it appears that a lack of sufficient negative indicators may act as a mitigating factor against a going concern modified report. Although it may be reasonable to describe the bankruptcy filings as business failures, it is not clear that they were all audit failures. We view this as good news for the audit profession and important information for critics of the audit profession.

It is not clear that the unmodified reports issued to the bankrupt firms in this sample were mistakes, although that seems to be the sentiment of the financial press. If auditors are expected to warn users of imminent bankruptcy, as implied by media coverage, they have clearly failed to do so in a majority of the 311 cases in our sample. Our analysis of the reasonableness of their decisions, however, demonstrates that they are actually reasonably good at identifying and modifying the audit reports of those firms that appear most distressed. In fact, auditors modified significantly more audit reports than they would have using a well-accepted bankruptcy prediction model. The vast majority of the firms in our sample, however, simply do not exhibit the characteristics we would expect of severely distressed firms. Further research should be directed at finding an explanation for the bankruptcy filings of the many firms in our sample that appear to have been in fairly good financial condition. In this regard, it would be helpful if auditors made users more aware of the various non-traditional reasons that encourage companies to file for bankruptcy; reasons that may be impossible for auditors to anticipate.[12] Auditors also need to educate users about the different forms of bankruptcy filings so that they understand that a company that is reorganizing under Ch. 11 of the bankruptcy code can still reasonably be considered a going concern.

Along with educating users about the intricacies of bankruptcy reorganizations, the profession should continue to find ways to improve its performance when auditing soon-to-be bankrupt companies. Although auditors manage to modify consistently the reports of companies that display many danger signs, they fail to modify the reports that have most, but not all, of the warning signs. When three to four warnings are present, roughly one-fourth (34 of 126) receive clean opinions.[13] What other information about this group of "marginal" companies would have helped auditors to know that bankruptcy filings were likely? Are there any readily available financial statement variables that can reliably identify those that ended up filing? Are there any financial statement footnote disclosures suggesting indirectly that a filing was possible or probable? Future research should focus on the companies that auditors seem to struggle with the most, rather than all bankrupt companies collectively. More carefully focused studies would go a long way towards satisfying the interest of regulators, users, and auditors on this important and seemingly timeless topic.

ACKNOWLEDGMENTS

We thank Denton Collins, David Frederick, Steve Henning, Gretchen Irwin, Duane Kennedy, Robert Lipe, Morris McInnes, Robert McNown, Wayne Shaw, and Jilnaught

Wong for their useful comments; and Lisa Bryant, Denise Jones, and Gavin Pacey for their research assistance. We appreciate the willingness of Jane Mutchler and James McKeown to share data with us. Our paper also benefited from comments of workshop participants at the University of Colorado, the University of Auckland, and the University of Miami.

NOTES

1. For instance, although Raghunandan and Rama (1995) and Johnson and Khurana (1995) report a significant increase in modified reporting after the issuance of SAS 59, Carcello, Hermanson, and Huss (1995) report no significant increase under SAS 59.

2. Johnson and Khurana (1995) and MHM provide a thorough review of prior literature that will not be repeated here.

3. Zmijewski's financial distress model is made up of three predictor variables: net income/total assets (earnings), current assets/current liabilities (liquidity), and total debt/total assets (leverage). He chose these variables "because of their performance, reported in the prior literature."

4. Prior to SAS No. 59, the going concern evaluation was required (under SAS No. 34) only when contrary information was discovered during the audit.

5. See section 341.06 of SAS No. 59.

6. Although we assert that the model proposed is consistent with what auditors say they do, we do not claim this is a model that describes the judgment process of the auditors. We merely use variables that auditors, the professional literature, and prior research suggest are useful.

7. To be consistent with prior research and for comparison purposes, we followed MHM's sample selection process. The period 1990–1994 was used to isolate instances that would have been under the professional guidance of SAS 59. The earlier period, 1974–1985, was prior to the issuance of SAS 59, and was primarily subject to SAS 34.

8. The Pearson correlation coefficient is .62, which is significant at $p = .0001$.

9. Consistent with prior research, size is included as a control variable and proxies for the incentive for auditors to please larger clients.

10. Specifically, MHM report that their logit model had a pseudo R-square of 30.55%.

11. Although the control variable *SIZE* is significant, it has little effect on the pseudo R-square. Removing it from the model reduces the pseudo R-square by only two percentage points.

12. For example, our sample includes AH Robins—a pharmaceutical corporation that received an unmodified report. Within one year of the report date, it allegedly filed for bankruptcy to stave off massive lawsuits related to its intrauterine device. Another example, although it is not part of our sample, is Continental Airlines, which allegedly filed to break labor union salary contracts, and Texaco which filed in an attempt to better its settlement with Pennzoil (Tavakolian 1994).

13. We thank the referee for clarifying this point.

REFERENCES

American Institute of Certified Public Accountants (AICPA). 1981. *The Auditor's Consideration When a Question Arises About an Entity's Continued Existence: Statement on Auditing Standards No. 34*. New York: AICPA.

American Institute of Certified Public Accountants (AICPA). 1988. *The Auditor's Consideration of an Entity's Ability to Continue as a Going Concern: Statement on Auditing Standards No. 59*. New York: AICPA.

Bamber, E.M., L.S. Bamber, and M. Schoderbek. 1993. Audit structure and other determinants of audit report lag: An empirical analysis. *Auditing: A Journal of Practice and Theory* (Spring): 1–23.

Bell, T.B. 1991. Discussion of "Towards an explanation of auditor failure to modify the audit opinions of bankrupt companies." *Auditing: A Journal of Practice and Theory* Supplement: 14–20.

Berton, L. 1999. Firms still coughing up the dough. *Accounting Today* February 8: 7.

Carcello, J.V., D.R. Hermanson, and H.F. Huss. 1995. Temporal changes in bankruptcy-related reporting, *Auditing: A Journal of Practice and Theory* (Fall): 133–143.

Chen, K.C.W., and B.K. Church. 1992. Default on debt obligations and the issuance of going-concern opinions. *Auditing: A Journal of Practice and Theory* Fall: 30–49.

Dingell, J. 1985. Who audits the auditors? Congress should be the watchdog. *The New York Times* (March 17): Section 3, 2F.

Ellingsen, J.E., K. Pany, and P. Fagan. 1989. SAS No. 59: How to evaluate going concern. *Journal of Accountancy* January: 51–57.

Ingersoll, B. 1985. House democrats question SEC's role in guarding against audit failures. *The Wall Street Journal* March 7: 46.

Johnson, V.E., and I.K. Khurana. 1995. Auditor reporting for bankrupt companies: Evidence on the impact of SAS No. 59. *Research in Accounting Regulation* 9: 3–22.

McKeown, J.C., J.F. Mutchler, and W. Hopwood. 1991. Towards an explanation of auditor failure to modify the audit opinions of bankrupt companies. *Auditing: A Journal of Practice and Theory* Supplement: 1–13.

Mutchler, J.F. 1985. A multivariate analysis of the auditor's going concern opinion decision. *Journal of Accounting Research* Autumn: 668–682.

Mutchler, J.F., W. Hopwood, and J.C. McKeown. 1997. The influence of contrary information and mitigating factors on audit opinion decisions on bankrupt companies. *Journal of Accounting Research* Autumn: 295–310.

Raghunandan, K., and D.V. Rama. 1995. Audit reports for companies in financial distress: Before and after SAS No. 59. *Auditing: A Journal of Practice and Theory* Spring: 50–63.

Tavakolian, H. 1994. Bankruptcy: An emerging strategy. *Management Research News* 17(5–6): 51–60.

Schultz, S.M. 1995. Financial reporting for firms in Chapter 11 reorganization. *National Public Accountant* January: 24–28.

Zmijewski, M.E. 1984. Methodological issues related to the estimation of financial distress prediction models. *Journal of Accounting Research* Supplement: 59–82.

UPDATE: THE STOCK INDEX AND MARKET SEASONALS (SIMS 2.0) DATABASE

Anthony J. Cataldo, II

ABSTRACT

A detailed description and descriptive statistics from the first version of the Stock Index and Market Seasonals (SIMS) database was published in the preceding volume of this series (Cataldo 1998). This article also contained a statistical test of the validity of Fosback's (1976) proposed three-day window for holiday effects, which was supported. A second version of SIMS is nearing completion.

SIMS 2.0 adds 4,098 trading days to the 27,568 (1897 through 1996) contained in the first version. First, 505 additional trading days are required to update SIMS for 1997 and 1998. Second, a backward extension of 3,593 additional trading days (February 16, 1885 through 1896) are included to encompass the years predating the Dow Jones Industrial Average (DJIA), per se. This brings the total continuous

Research in Accounting Regulation, Volume 13, pages 179-180.

ISBN: 0-7623-0520-7

daily observations of the DJIA (and its predecessor) to a total of 31,666 trading days, or slightly more than 115 years.

SIMS 2.0 also includes some additional data fields. First, the Russell 2000 index (*R2000*) and the daily close-to-close percentage change (*R2000CHG*) is included from the date of inception (December 31, 1986). The Russell 2000 represents a control variable for *small firm* stocks and their effects, which are stronger for most *seasonal anomalies*. Second, the 30-day rate of interest for commercial paper (*CP30*) and the daily close-to-close percentage change (*CP30CHG*) are included for more than 25 years (April 8, 1971–1998). The 30-day commercial paper rate provides for a relatively volatile measure in interest rates. Finally, *special closings* (of the New York Stock Exchange) event dates are included (*SCN2*, *SCN1*, *SCP1*, and *SCP2*). Their behavior is similar to that of *weekend* and *holiday* effects.

SIMS version 2.0 will be available in September 1999. SIMS 2.0 will be used in a forthcoming monograph (Cataldo and Savage 1999).

Those interested in receiving a copy of SIMS 2.0 should fax the registration form contained in Cataldo (1998, 218–219) to (616) 387-5710 or email the author at aj.cataldo@wmich.edu.

REFERENCES

Cataldo, A.J. 1998. The Stock Index and Market Seasonals (SIMS) Database. In Vol. 12: *Research in Accounting Regulation*, eds. G.J. Previts, T.R. Robinson, and N. Chandar, 201–221. Stamford, CT: JAI Press Inc.

Cataldo, A.J., and A.A. Savage. Forthcoming, 2000. *The January Effect and Other Seasonal Anomalies: A Common Theoretical Framework*, Vol. 9: *Studies in Managerial and Financial Accounting*, ed. Marc J. Epstein. Stamford, CT: JAI Press Inc.

Fosback, N.G. 1976. *Stock Market Logic*. Kingsport, TN: Institute for Econometric Research.

STATE ACCOUNTANT PRIVITY LAWS:
NARROWING THE SCOPE OF ACCOUNTANT LIABILITY TO THIRD PARTIES

Carl Pacini, David Sinason, and William Hillison

ABSTRACT

In the previous two decades, the accounting profession has confronted a litigation explosion. One of the accounting profession's responses to the litigation crisis has been to mount a campaign aimed at legislative reform. A key issue for state tort reform legislation is the extent to which someone other than the client is owed a professional duty and can sue an accountant for negligence. This article assesses the current status of accountant privity law reform. It also examines court decisions made under various state accountant privity statutes.

Policy implications of state accountant privity laws, including diminished litigation risk and reduced litigation costs, are also outlined. Several reasons are offered why more states have not enacted an accountant privity statute. A continuation of enactment of accountant privity laws may signal a change in state public policy toward limitations on the liability of accountants to nonclients.

Research in Accounting Regulation, Volume 13, pages 181-199.

ISBN: 0-7623-0520-7

Since the mid-1970s, the accounting profession has confronted a litigation crisis. The Big Five accounting firms' expenditures for settling and defending lawsuits has grown from near zero in the mid-1960s to an amount that represented almost 12 percent of their domestic auditing and accounting revenues by 1993 (Louis 1968; Dalton, Hill, and Ramsay 1994; Granelli 1995). The increase in litigation has led to: (1) a decrease in the availability and a rise in the cost of professional liability insurance;[1] and (2) accounting firms being more aggressive in refusing to render services to high-litigation-risk firms (MacDonald 1997; Jones and Raghunandan 1998). Moreover, a recent study by the International Federation of Accountants suggests that harsh legal liability weakens incentives for parties to monitor enterprises under their control, has a limited effect on reducing negligence by auditors, and may lead to increased litigation risk because of the availability of insurance money (*CMA Magazine* 1998).

One reaction of the accounting profession to the liability crisis has been to mount a campaign aimed at the adoption of legislation that would level the playing field upon which liability claims are resolved (Goldwasser 1995). In 1986, a model accountants' privity statute was proposed by the American Institute of Certified Public Accountants (AICPA). The model statute is now incorporated as section 20 of the Uniform Accountancy Act (UAA), a comprehensive model bill to regulate the practice of public accountancy released by the AICPA and the National Association of State Boards of Accountancy (NASBA).[2]

As we will discuss later in this paper, seven states have enacted statutes that have narrowed accountant liability. Also, accountant privity bills containing language similar to that in section 20 of the UAA were considered in 1998 as stand-alone legislation or as part of a comprehensive state accountancy bill in Maine, Massachussetts, Tennessee, and Washington (AICPA 1999). None of these states ultimately enacted an accountant privity law (AICPA 1999). The Texas legislature considered a near-privity accountancy law in 1997, but the bill was not passed (TSCPA 1999).

Although the net result at the state level for 1997 and 1998 was not positive, recent legislation indicates that the profession's efforts are producing results. In late 1995, the U.S. Congress passed the Private Securities Litigation Reform Act, which includes numerous amendments to the federal securities laws that either restrict the scope of accountants' liability or reduce the damages paid by accountants.[3] Loopholes in the original Act saw many plaintiffs file securities class action suits in state courts to circumvent the new restrictions. However, in 1998 Congress enacted the Securities Litigation Uniform Standards Act which will result in class-action securities lawsuits involving a nationally traded security and more than 50 parties being tried primarily in federal courts.

Despite the passage of this legislation, there has been no decline in the number of lawsuits filed against accountants (MacDonald 1997). One reason is that accountants have continued to confront the threat of lawsuits, based on state tort theories, both when nonclients incur financial losses due to negligent auditing and when nonclients seek a "deep pocket" (Daley and Gibson 1994). Negligence is one of the most significant state tort theories (Mednick and Peck 1994; Legal Liability Task Force 1994). Under this theory, nonclient plaintiffs argue that their reliance on accounting information served as the principal basis for their investments or loans, and that subsequent losses are due to the negligence of the accountant (Daley and Gibson 1994). Hence, the issue for state tort reform legislation is the extent to which someone other than the client is owed a professional duty and can sue an accountant over a negligent audit.

The purposes of this article are threefold. The first is to assess the current status of legal standards applied to determine an accountant's liability to third parties for negligence. The second purpose is to identify various state privity statutes and examine court decisions under those statutes. The third and overall purpose is to enhance and update the knowledge of accountants, attorneys, regulators, and educators about accountants' legal responsibilities to nonclients for negligence. The appendix provides an annotated literature review citing recent articles addressing the issues of auditor liability and privity laws.

LEGAL STANDARDS USED TO DETERMINE THE SCOPE OF AN ACCOUNTANT'S DUTY TO THIRD PARTIES FOR NEGLIGENCE

Four key legal standards have evolved to judge which nonclients have a legal right to sue accountants for negligent misrepresentation. The four legal standards are: (1) privity; (2) near privity; (3) the known users or Restatement standard; and (4) the reasonable foreseeability rule. These four standards are not discrete points, but lie on a continuum (see Figure 1). Application of one versus another to the same set of facts can lead to different outcomes regarding whether the third party has a right to sue.[4] Consideration of these four key standards is a starting point for analysis of accountant privity statutes.

Privity Standard

Privity requires a direct connection or contractual relationship between two parties. The accountant's liability to a third party is dependent on the establishment of this contractual relationship. The requirement of strict privity to establish an accountant's duty to nonclients is the most restrictive standard. Strict privity was first established as a legal standard by Pennsylvania in *Landell vs. Lybrand* (1919). Today, strict privity is the law in only two states (Pennsylvania and Virginia).

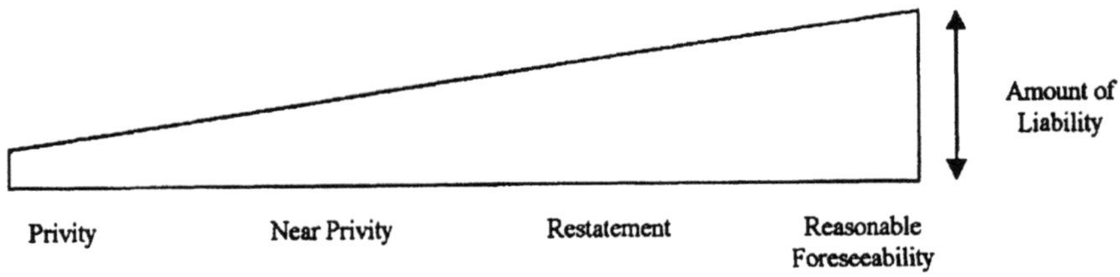

Figure 1. Continuum of Auditor Liability to Third Parties for Negligent Misrepresentation

Near Privity Standard

The near privity standard was first applied to determine the scope of an accountant's duty to third parties for negligence in *Ultramares Corporation vs. Touche* (1931). In that case, the New York Court of Appeals denied plaintiff Ultramares' negligence claim but fashioned an exception to strict privity that has become known as the primary benefit rule (i.e., the non-client must be an intended third-party beneficiary of the contract between the accountant and the client). The Court decided that although the auditor (Touche Niven & Co.) knew the audited balance sheet would be shown to various unidentified creditors and stockholders, Touche had not been hired by its client (Fred Stern and Co.) with the knowledge that Ultramares (the plaintiff) was an intended third-party beneficiary of Touche's work. In this case, the auditor's service was primarily for the benefit of the client and only collaterally for the use of third parties. Overly rigorous interpretations of *Ultramares* over the years have resulted in the case symbolizing a privity requirement for recovery under negligent misrepresentation (Daley and Gibson 1994).

In 1985, the New York Court of Appeals clarified the near privity standard articulated in *Ultramares* in *Credit Alliance vs. Arthur Andersen & Co.* (1985). The clarification consists of a three-prong test that a non-client must pass to fall within the ambit of an auditor's duty for the purposes of negligent misrepresentation: (1) the accountant must have known that financial reports were to be used for a particular purpose; (2) a known party was intended to rely on the reports; and (3) there must have been some conduct to link the accountant to that party, which indicates the accountant's understanding of the party's reliance. In *European American Bank vs. Strauhs & Kay* (1985), the New York Court of Appeals held that affirmative conduct linking the accountant to the relying party requires direct communications between the plaintiff and the accountant. The *Credit Alliance* standard gains significance because it serves as the basis for section 20 of the UAA and New Jersey's accountant privity statute. By court decision, Idaho,

Montana, Nebraska, and New York now follow the *Credit Alliance* rule or a variation thereof.[5]

The *Restatement* Standard

A federal district court in Rhode Island first expanded accountant liability for negligence to specifically foreseen or known users in *Rusch Factors, Inc. vs. Levin* (1968). Specifically, the District Court held that an accountant should be liable in negligent misrepresentation for financial misinformation relied upon by actually foreseen and limited classes of persons. The District Court actually applied §552 of the *Restatement (Second) of Torts*, a compendium of law drafted by the American Law Institute. Under the *Restatement* standard, an accountant who audits or prepares financial information for a client owes a duty not only to the client but to any other person or one of a group of persons whom the accountant or client intends the information to benefit, and may become liable if: (1) that person justifiably relies on the information in a transaction, or one substantially similar to it, that the accountant or his client intends the information to influence; and (2) that person suffers a pecuniary loss as a result of his or her reliance (Daley and Gibson 1994). No liability exists, however, for parties to whom the auditor had no reason to believe the information would be made available; or when the client's transaction, as represented to the auditor, changes so as to increase the audit risk materially (Daley and Gibson 1994).

The major difference between the primary benefit rule of *Ultramares* and the *Restatement* or known users rule is that the latter does not require the identity of specific parties be known to the auditor, only that they be members of a limited group known to the auditor, and thus it enlarges the class of persons to whom the accountant owes a duty to include both intended, identifiable beneficiaries and any unidentified members of the intended class of beneficiaries (Gossman 1988).

The Reasonable Foreseeability Standard

Auditor liability to non-clients was expanded in 1983 with the decision in *Rosenblum vs. Adler* (1983). The court viewed damages for physical injury as analogous to damages for economic loss, raising the query, "If recovery for defective products may include economic loss, why should such loss not be compensable if it is caused by negligent misrepresentation?" (Scherl 1994). The court concluded that an auditor has a duty to all those whom the auditor should reasonably foresee as receiving and relying on audited financial statements. However, the duty extends only to those users whose decision is influenced by audited statements obtained from the audited entity for a proper business purpose. The court's holding indicates that "the auditor owes a duty of care to all who obtain a firm's financial statement directly from the audited entity, but owes no such duty of care to those who obtain it from an annual report in a library or from a government file" (Causey 1987). Today, however, only Mississippi and Wisconsin follow the reasonable foreseeability standard.[6]

STATE ACCOUNTANT PRIVITY STATUTES

Significant activity promoting the limitation of accountant liability by the AICPA and state CPA societies has resulted in the consideration of liability issues by a number of state legislatures since the mid-1980s. The trend toward a narrower scope of liability due to legislative reform started when Illinois passed an accountant liability statute in 1986. Since that year, seven states have enacted statutes that narrow the scope of accountant liability to non-clients for negligence. These new statutes can be classified collectively in the near privity category, because they have a narrower scope of duty than Restatement §552 but a wider scope of duty than the *Credit Alliance* or *Ultramares* rule. The statutes do, however, exhibit some variation. Table 1 lists the seven states and the operative language of each state statute. The state statutes are discussed in the following sections.

Arkansas, Illinois, and Utah

The Arkansas, Illinois, and Utah statutes are considered together because they possess virtually identical language. However, despite common wording, the statutes enacted by these three states have been interpreted differently, creating uncertainty for accountants, lawyers, and regulators. In fact, distinct constructions have been placed on the statute by federal and state courts in Illinois.[7]

In *Robin vs. Falbo* (1992), a federal district court was the first to construe the Illinois accountant liability statute. The district court acknowledged that the operative language in subsection two of the Illinois statute may be reasonably interpreted in more than one way. First, the language may be construed as making liability to a non-client conditioned upon the auditor identifying in writing those who may rely on the auditor's work product. No liability attaches without such a writing from the accountant. Second, the statute may be read as simply providing the auditor with an exception to a general rule of liability (i.e., the primary benefit or *Ultramares* rule in Illinois's case) where the auditor prepares and sends a writing to specific persons who will rely on the services.

The *Robin* court noted that the first interpretation is unusual, but the legislative history of the law indicates that this was the statute's intended meaning. The first interpretation makes it effectively impossible for a non-client to sue an accountant for negligent misrepresentation. The accountant (rather than the client) must identify third parties who may rely on the accountant's work product and notify the client and third parties in order to be liable for negligent misrepresentation to third parties.

In 1993, the Northern District Court of Illinois again applied the same interpretation to the Illinois accountant liability statute in *Endo vs. Albertine* (1993). No Illinois state court had construed the accountant liability statute before the *Endo* ruling. In *Dougherty vs. Zimbler* (1996), the Illinois accountant liability statute was given the same meaning as it was in the *Endo* (1993) and *Robin* (1992) decisions.

The statutory interpretation adopted in three federal Illinois cases was followed by the Arkansas Supreme Court in *Swink vs. Ernst & Young* (1995). In that case, James Swink, Jr. individually sued Ernst & Young (E&Y) based on a 1985 audit and tax services contract between the auditor and the plaintiff's firm. The plaintiff was not named as a party to the contract, but argued that he suffered losses as a result of an inaccurate audit for fiscal year 1988. The Supreme Court found that the plaintiff was neither a third-party beneficiary to the contract, nor was he in privity with the auditor. Affirmative steps of written identification and notification were held to be a condition for liability to a third party for negligent misrepresentation. Under the Arkansas interpretation (which is the same as the one followed by the Illinois federal district court), a non-client must be in privity with the accountant to recover for negligent misrepresentation, unless the non-client has a writing from the accountant. The Arkansas approach is more strict than the most recent ruling by an Illinois state appellate court, discussed below.

In *Chestnut vs. Pestine Brinati et al.* (1996), the Illinois First District Appellate Court found that the language in subsection two of the statute (see Table 1) merely provides accountants with an exception to a general rule of liability when the accountant prepares and sends a writing to the specific persons who are intended to rely on the accountant's services. The defendant auditor argued for the statutory interpretation adopted by the Illinois federal district court in *Robin* (1992) and the Arkansas Supreme Court in *Swink vs. Ernst & Young* (1995). The First District Appellate Court rejected a reading of the statutory provision that makes written notice to a third party a condition of liability for negligent misrepresentation (Guerci 1997). Under the *Chestnut* court's reading of the statute, a non-client may state a cause of action under the statute without a writing. If no writing from the accountant exists, then the non-client must prove the intent of the client and the accountant's knowledge of that intent. The current Illinois interpretation is still a near privity standard, but it is not as narrow as the Arkansas standard.

In 1990, Utah enacted an accountant liability statute identical to the Arkansas and Illinois statutes. No reported court cases have been decided by Utah state courts, but the federal district court in Vermont applied the Utah statute in *Nordica USA, Inc. vs. Deloitte & Touche* (1993). The main point of contention in that case centered on *when* the defendant accountant knew that a primary intent of the client was for the services rendered to benefit or influence a particular third party. The Utah statute (as well as the Arkansas and Illinois statutes) is silent on when the accountant must possess the requisite knowledge of the client's intent. The district court decided that a defendant accountant must know of the client's intent

Table 1. Statutory Jurisdictions

State	*Arkansas*	*Illinois*	*Kansas*	*Michigan*
Statute Cite	ARK. CODE ANN. §16-114-302 1998). Took effect in 1987. In *Swink v. Ernst & Young*, 908 S. W. 2d 660 (Ark. 1995), the Arkansas Supreme Court construed the statute to shield an accountant from liability to a non-client unless the accountant has identified in writing those persons intended to rely on the services and sent a copy of that writing to those persons.	225 ILL. COMP. STAT. 450/30.1 (1998) formerly Ill. Rev. Stat. 1991, Ch. 111, ¶5535.1. Took effect in 1966. *Chestnut v. Pestine Brinati et al.*, 667 N. E. 2d 543 (Ill. App. 1996) held that a non-client may state a cause of action under the statute without a writing. The statutory language reely provides accountants with an exemption from liability where the accountant prepares and sends a writing to specified persons intended to rely on the accountant's services. The court did not address the question of the effect of a writing on the accountant's liability.	KAN. STAT. ANN. §1-402 (1998). Took effect in 1987. *Monarch Normandy v. Normandy Square,* 817 F. Supp. 899 (D. Kansas 1993) applied the statute in dismissing a negligent misrepresentation count against a CPA firm.	MICH. COMP. LAWS §600.2962 (1998). Took effect in January 1996.
Standard	Statutory modification of the primary benefit rule with a provision that allows the auditor to limit those nonclients who may rely on the services rendered. The statute reads as follows: No person shall be liable to persons not in privity of contract...for civil damages resulting from acts, omissions, decisions, or other conduct in connection with professional services, except for:	The statute's language is virtually identical to the wording of the Arkansas statute. The Illinois law has been interpreted differently than the Arkansas statute.	Statutory primary benefit rule similar to *Ultramares*. The statute reads as follows: No person...shall be liable to any person or entity for civil damages resulting from acts, omissions, decisions or other conduct amounting to negligence in the rendition of professional accounting services *unless:*	A certified public accountant may be liable for a negligent act, omission, decision, or other conduct if the "certified public accountant was informed in writing by the client at the time of the engagement that a primary

(2) Other acts, omissions, decisions, or conduct, if the person, partnership, or corporation was aware that a primary intent of the client was for the professional services to benefit or influence the person bringing the action...[I]f the person, partnership or corporation... (a) Identifies in writing to the client those persons who are intended to rely on the services, and (b) Sends a copy of the writing or similar statement to those persons identified in the writing or statement, then the person may be held liable only to the persons intended to rely, in addition to those persons in privity of contract...		(a) the plaintiff directly engaged such persons... or (b)(1) the defendent knew at the time of the engagement or the defendent and the client mutually agreed after the time of the engagement that the...accounting services rendered...would be made available to the plaintiff, who was identified in writing to the defendent; and (2) the defendent knew the plaintiff intended to rely upon the...accounting services rendered the client in connection with specified transactions described in writing.	intent of the client was for the...accounting services to benefit or influence the person bringing the action for civil damages... The certified public accountant may be held liable to each identified person, generic group, or class description."

(*continued*)

Table 1 (Continued)

State	*New Jersey*	*Utah*	*Wyoming*
Statute Cite	N.J. STAT. ANN. §2A:53A-25 (1998). Took effect in 1995.	UTAH CODE ANN. §58-26-12 (1998). Enacted in 1990. In *Nordica USA, Inc., v. Deloitte & Touche,* 839 F. Supp. 1082 (D. Vt. 1993), the federal district court in Vermont applied the same interpretation to Utah's statutory wording as the Arkansas Supreme Court did to virtually identical language (in Arkansas's statute). The federal court also held that the accountant must be aware of the client's intent to benefit or influence a third party at the time audit work is performed.	WYO. STAT. ANN. §33-3-201 (1998). Took effect in 1995.
Standard	Strict near-privity rule similar to *Credit Alliance*. The statute reads as follows: No accountant shall be liable for damage for negligence arising out of and in the course of rendering professional service unless…the accountant: (2)(a) knew at the time of the engagement by the client or agreed with the client after the time of the engagement, that the…service rendered to the client would be made available to the claimant, who was specifically identified to the accountant in connection with a specified transaction…;	Virtually identical to the Arkansas and Illinois statutes in wording	A strict near-privity statute that requires a positive action by the accountant. The statute reads as follows: No action may be brought under the section unless: (ii) the defendant accountant firm: (a) was aware at the time the engagement was undertaken…that the financial statements or other information were to be made available for use in connection with a specified transaction…and the transaction was specifically identified to the defendant; and

(b) knew that the claimant intended to rely upon the...service in connection with that specified transaction; and

(c) directly expressed to the claimant, by words or conduct that accountant's understanding of the claimant's intended reliance...

(3) In the case of a bank claimant, the accountant must acknowledge the bank's intended reliance on the...accounting service and the client's knowledge of that reliance in a written communication.

(b) was aware that the plaintiff intended to rely upon such financial statements or other information...

To be entitled to the limitation on liability the accountant shall:

(i) identify the purpose of the document and the persons or entities that are entitled to receive and rely upon the financial statement or other information...reported or opined on...in the document prepared by the accountant, and

(ii) include thereon a statement in a prominent place that advises users of the document that the liability of the accountant to third parties may be limited.

to benefit or influence a third party at the time the audit is performed. The court reasoned that a client could contract for audit services and forward the documents to third parties years later, creating the specter of indeterminate liability for auditors.

Kansas

In 1987, Kansas enacted a statute which does not require affirmative conduct by the accountant to restrict liability. Four conditions must be present for a non-client to have a legal right to sue. They are that: (1) the accountant knew that the third party intended to rely on the services; (2) the accountant knew that the services rendered to the client would be made available to the third party; (3) the non-client must have been identified in writing to the accountant; and (4) the third party's reliance must have been in connection with specific transactions identified in writing (*Gillespie vs. Seymour* 1994). Any writing that identifies the relying plaintiff and specific transaction(s) need not originate with the accountant, as it is required to under the Arkansas and Utah statutes. The Kansas statute clearly indicates that the accountant must have known of the third party's reliance during the engagement or assented to such reliance with the client after the engagement. Moreover, the Kansas statute explicitly identifies that liability extends only "to specific transactions described in writing" while the Arkansas, Illinois, and Utah statutes set forth no such requirement. In sum, the Kansas statute appears to be somewhat more restrictive than the Illinois statute, as it is presently construed, but not as narrow as the Arkansas statute.

New Jersey

In 1995, New Jersey passed a statute which limits accountant liability to non-clients. The enactment of a statute is particularly significant in New Jersey's case. Between 1983 and 1995, New Jersey adhered to the reasonable foreseeability rule set forth in *Rosenblum* (1983). Passage of an accountant liability statute moved New Jersey from one end of the liability continuum almost to the opposite end. The New Jersey statute is a virtual codification of the three-prong test of *Credit Alliance*. Despite the statute's restrictive scope, it does not require any of the three elements for an accountant's duty to non-clients to be in writing, except in the case of a bank claimant. In that case, the accountant must acknowledge in writing the bank's intended reliance and the client's knowledge of such reliance.

Many banks in New Jersey now require borrowers to obtain a "reliance letter." This is a letter from the borrower's accountant evidencing compliance with the New Jersey statute. It documents the accountant's knowledge of the creditor's intention to rely upon the accountant's work product. Most accountants have refused to provide such letters without a string of qualifications (Johnson 1995).

The New Jersey statute is different than the Arkansas, Illinois, and Utah statutes. The laws of the latter three states do not mandate that the accountant be aware of a specific transaction in which the non-client is benefitted or influenced, as required under the New Jersey statute. Also, the accountant's knowledge of the non-client's intended reliance must be expressed to the plaintiff under New Jersey's statute (the "linking conduct" requirement) but not under the statutes of Arkansas, Illinois, and Utah.

Wyoming

Wyoming's accountant liability statute was enacted in 1995. Three conditions must be present at the time an engagement was undertaken for a duty to non-clients to arise. They are that: (1) the accountant was aware that the services performed were to be made available in connection with a specific transaction; (2) the transaction was specifically identified to the accountant; and (3) the accountant was aware that the non-client intended to rely on the services. The Wyoming law bears some similarity to the Kansas statute, except that Wyoming requires the accountant to state in writing on any financial statement or other document those third parties who may rely, the document's purpose, and that the accountant's liability may be limited. The accountant's liability to non-clients is not restricted unless the writing requirements are met.

Michigan

In 1996, an accountant liability law took effect in Michigan. The liability limitation provided by the statute appears to be directed only at certified public accountants. A CPA cannot be liable for negligence to a third party unless the accountant was informed in writing by the client at the time of the engagement that it was the client's primary intent for the accounting services to benefit or influence the non-client. The statute allows the client to identify in writing not only specific persons but a generic group or class of persons who the client intends to benefit or influence. It is possible that the client could describe a class of users so large that a CPA could face potential liability to a significant number of non-clients.

POLICY IMPLICATIONS

All seven state statutes reduce the probability of a miscommunication or misunderstanding between the accountant, the client, and a third party. The various statutes provide more certainty, because the third party knows before relying on a financial statement whether recovery of a loss from the auditor is likely (Fencl 1989). Litigation risk for accountants is diminished by the near privity nature of each of the seven state statutes, because auditors generally need not be concerned about as many third-party claimants (except possibly in Michigan in some instances).

A significant policy implication of state accountant privity law reform is the potential reduction in litigation and liability insurance costs. A statute provides an accounting firm, in most cases, with more certainty and clarity, ex ante, concerning which third parties are owed a duty for negligent misrepresentation. Uncertainty may be increased, however, when a state adopts an accountant liability statute that may be interpreted in more than one way (e.g., Arkansas, Illinois, and Utah). Ideally, accountant privity laws should be written clearly to implement legislative intent.

CONCLUSION

Four legal standards have evolved to determine which third-party users are owed a duty by accountants for purposes of negligent misrepresentation. These four legal standards are known as privity, near privity, Restatement, and reasonable foreseeability. The expansion of accountant liability to non-clients from the 1960s through the mid-1980s has led to legislative reform efforts by the accounting profession during the last decade. The enactment of state accountant privity laws reflects legislative reaction to judicial efforts that expanded the scope of accountant liability to non-clients for negligence. Recent experience in several state legislatures, however, points out the difficulty in achieving legislative reform.

It can be argued that state legislatures are better suited than courts to weighing the competing policy issues and to defining the rights and responsibilities of both the accountant and third parties. By the time a case reaches the courts, a party has been injured and a court must decide who will bear the loss. A legislature, however, can design a statute that defines rights and duties before the harm has occurred, thus making results more predictable.

Since 1985, seven states have enacted accountant liability statutes which collectively are near privity in nature. Four potential reasons can be offered why more states have not passed into law an accountant privity statute. First, state efforts may be diluted because the profession's resources are being directed toward federal securities laws, joint and several liability, and limited liability partnerships and corporations. Second, two states, Mississippi and Georgia, currently have statutes that expressly strip accountants of the privity defense in negligence actions for economic loss. Third, state legislatures may not place a high priority on the enactment of an accountant privity law because a judicial trend has emerged at the state level toward a narrower scope of accountant liability to non-clients for negligence. During the last ten years, 14 states rejected the reasonable foreseeability rule in favor of the Restatement standard, four states adopted or reaffirmed some form of the *Credit Alliance* or *Ultramares* rule, and one state adopted the strict privity rule (Pacini and Sinason 1998). Only one state (Alabama) has expanded the scope of an accountant's duty to non-clients for negligence.[8] Fourth, New York and Pennsylvania judicially adopted a privity or near privity standard prior to 1986.

This judicial trend and enactment of state accountant privity statutes may signal a change in state public policy decisions away from the transfer of risk from financial statement users to accountants. State legislatures, however, are uniquely qualified to weigh the competing policy issues in defining the scope of accountant liability to non-clients. Judge Cardozo stated more than sixty years ago in *Ultramares* (1931) that any change in an accountant's duty of care should be wrought by legislation.

APPENDIX

Recent Articles Relating to Auditor Legal Liability and Privity Laws

Fencl, E. 1989. Rebuilding the citadel: State legislative responses to accountant non-privity statutes. *Washington University Law Quarterly* 89(Fall): 863–888.

This article provides an overview of the different standards of liability used to gauge the scope of an auditor's duty to third parties and an analysis of three state accountant privity statutes. The three statutes examined are Illinois, Arkansas, and Kansas. The author provides a somewhat detailed comparison of the requirements and conditions of the three statutes based on their wording. The article is intended for a legal audience.

Bonham-Yeaman, D., and J.J. Jurinski. 1994. Auditors' liability to third parties: Can the states adopt a unified approach? *Western State University Law Review* 22: 37–59.

In defining the scope of an auditor's duty to third parties for negligence, state legislatures and the courts consider both practical considerations and public policy. This article examines the statutes of Arkansas, Illinois, Kansas, and Utah in the context of a discussion of the various legal standards applied by the states to determine the scope of an auditor's duty to third parties. Statutes are surfacing to better define responsibilities in this area. The authors note that all three legal standards are flawed, but legislation is preferable to court decisions because it provides more clarity and uniformity.

Faussie, J. 1994. Limiting liability in public accounting suits: A desperate appeal from a beleaguered profession. *Valparaiso University Law Review* 28: 1041–1109.

This article takes the viewpoint that the reasonable foreseeability standard and the *Restatement* standard place a disproportionate burden of liability on CPAs by ignoring pre-contractual relations between the client and the CPAs, and expanding the classes of third parties who may recover. The "deep pocket" theory is cited as one reason for so many lawsuits against accountants. The article notes that a few states have proposed legislation that will help end the third-party liability problem in accounting cases. The statutes of Illinois and Kansas are both discussed, along with the *Gillespie* case in Kansas and the *Robin* case in Illinois.

Siliciano, J.A. 1997. Trends in independent auditor liability: The emergence of a sane consensus. *Journal of Accounting and Public Policy* 16(Winter): 339–353.

This paper retraces the development of auditor legal liability by describing significant court cases. This paper notes several recent cases, and also notes that the *Restatement of Torts* provides some expectations that the environment might be changing. The article does not document changes among the states. The paper's intended audience is accountants.

Pacini, C., and D. Sinason. 1998. State legislative responses to the call for reform of accountant's liability to nonclients for negligence. *Journal of Legal Studies in Business* 6(Summer): 45–66.

This article provides an in-depth legal analysis of various state accountant privity statutes. A model accountant privity statute is presented. The Private Litigation Securities Reform Act of 1995 is also discussed. Those with a legal background are the intended audience.

Pacini, C., and D. Sinason. 1998. Gaining a new balance in accountants' liability to nonclients for negligence: Recent developments and emerging trends. *Commercial Law Journal* 103(Spring): 15–66.

This article reviews the state court decisions and statutes that have reversed or slowed the expansion of accountant liability to third parties for negligence. This trend is examined in light of the different legal standards used by the states in deciding which third parties have a right to sue accountants for negligent misrepresentation. The primary focus of the article is on case law decisions and analysis. The article is not written for accountants or accounting educators, but for a legal audience.

Pacini, C., W. Hillison, and D. Sinason. 1999. Executive briefing: Accountants' liability. *Business Horizons* 42(2): 3–7.

This executive overview suggests that recent changes in the legal environment for accountants signals a trend toward a more narrow scope of liability for accountants to third parties. The intended audience is the business community.

ACKNOWLEDGMENT

We would like to thank two anonymous reviewers for their suggestions.

NOTES

1. The market for accountant liability insurance is segmented into three markets: large firms, medium-size firms, and small firms (Goldwasser and Arnold 1998). Large firms are now able to buy only a portion of the coverage they could buy prior to 1985 and only for much higher premiums. Reports indicate that the Big Five firms are spending more than 15 percent of their audit and accounting revenue on liability insurance (MacDonald 1997). Also, virtually all mid-size firms tend to be highly underinsured. Liability insurance for small firms is expensive, and almost 50 percent of small firms carry no insurance at all (Goldwasser and Arnold 1998).

2. Section 20 of the Uniform Accountancy Act is a near privity standard that reflects the holding of the New York Court of Appeals in *Credit Alliance vs. Arthur Andersen & Co.* (1985). The operative language of the model law is:

> Sec. 20–Privity of Contract
>
> (b) This section governs any action based on negligence brought against any accountant or firm...by any person or entity claiming to have been injured as a result of financial statements or other information...reported or opined on...by the defendant accountant....
>
> (c) No action covered by this section may be brought unless:
>
> (1) The plaintiff (1) is issuer...of the financial statements or other information...reported or opined on...and (2) engaged the defendant licensee...; or
>
> (2) The defendant...:(1)was aware at the time the engagement was undertaken that the financial statements or other information were to be made available for use in connection with a specified transaction by the plaintiff who was specifically identified to the...accountant, (2) was aware that the plaintiff intended to rely upon such...information in connection with the specified transaction, and (3) had direct contact and communication with the plaintiff...and expressed...understanding of the reliance....

3. Some of the more important provisions of the Private Secunties Litigation Reform Act for accountants include:

> (a) The Securities Exchange Act of 1934 was amended to limit the use of joint and several liability. Defendants, such as accountants, who do not intentionally violate the securities laws are responsible only for their share of the judgment with two exceptions: (1) for those plaintiffs who demonstrate they are entitled to damages greater than 10 percent of their net worth (which may not exceed $200,000); and (2) when a defendant is insolvent each of the remaining defendants must pay up to 50 percent of their own liability as damages;
>
> (b) A limitation on the damages an accountant can be held liable for under §10(b) of the Securities Exchange Act of 1934. The traditional manner of computing damages has the potential to overestimate substantially the plaintiff's actual damages (Lev and deVilliers 1994); and
>
> (c) Any plaintiff bringing a §10(b) suit must prove that the accountant's material misstatement or omission actually caused the loss. For more discussion on provisions of the Private Securities Litigation Reform Act of 1995 applicable to accountants see King and Schwartz (1997), Seligman (1996), Schneider and Dubow (1996), and Thompson (1996).

4. One example of such a scenario occurred in *Performance Motorcars vs. Peat Marwick* (1994). Performance Motorcars, Inc., a New York business, sued Peat Marwick in a New Jersey court,

alleging that it suffered losses after one of its customers, Coated Sales, Inc., went bankrupt. Performance claimed it had relied on audited financial statements negligently prepared by Peat Marwick. Performance conceded that if New York law applied, it would not be able to sue Peat Marwick. Ultimately, an appeals court held that New Jersey law applied, giving Performance a legal right to sue under the New Jersey law applicable at the time of the suit.

5. The relevant court decisions are: Idaho (*Idaho Bank & Trust Co. vs. First Bancorp* 1989), Montana (*Thayer vs. Hicks* 1990), and Nebraska (*Citizens National Bank of Wisner vs. Kennedy and Coe* 1989). New York upheld the *Credit Alliance* rule in *Security Pacific vs. Peat Marwick Main* (1992).

6. Mississippi (*Touche Ross vs. Commercial Union Insurance Co.* 1987) and Wisconsin (*Citizens State Bank vs. Timm, Schmidt & Co.* 1983).

7. Several federal district court decisions addressed the Illinois accountant liability statute before any state appellate court rendered a statutory interpretation. Under the *Erie* doctrine, these federal court decisions interpreted the statute based on statutory rules of construction, legislative history, and the plain meaning of the operative language (Moore 1996).

8. In 1989, the Supreme Court of Alabama adopted the *Credit Alliance* rule in *Colonial Bank of Alabama vs. Ridley & Schweigert* (1989). In a stunning reversal five years later, the same court retreated from the *Credit Alliance* near-privity standard to the *Restatement* standard in *Boykin vs. Arthur Andersen & Co.* (1994). Interestingly, Alabama is one of three states cited by a 1994 study conducted by the American Tort Reform Association that had massive amounts of political campaign contributions made by plaintiffs' trial lawyers to candidates for state offices (Torry 1994).

REFERENCES

American Institute of Certified Public Accountants (AICPA). 1999. *Interview of Virgil Webb, Assistant General Counsel of the AICPA*, April 9. New York: AICPA.

Causey, D. 1987. Accountants' liability in an indeterminate amount for an indeterminate class?: An analysis of *Touche Ross & Co. vs. Commercial Union Ins. Co. Mississippi Law Journal* 57: 379–416.

Chestnut vs. *Pestine Brinati et al.*, 667 N.E. 2d 543 (Ill. App. 1996), appeal denied 671 N.E. 2d 727 (1996).

Citizens Nat. Bank vs. *Kennedy and Coe,* 441 N.W. 2d 189 (Neb 1989).

Citizens State Bank vs. *Timm, Schmidt & Co.*, 335 N.W. 2d 361 (Wisc. 1983).

CMA Magazine. 1998. Auditor liability evokes wider concerns. *CMA Magazine* 72(July/August): 31.

Colonial Bank of Alabama vs. Ridley & Schweigert, 551 So. 2d 390 (Ala. 1989).

Credit Alliance vs. *Arthur Andersen & Co.*, 483 N.E. 2d 110 (N.Y. 1985).

Daley, B., and J. Gibson. 1994. The delineation of accountants' legal liability to third parties: *Bily* and beyond. *St. John's Law Review* 68(Summer): 609–641.

Dalton, D., J. Hill, and R. Ramsay. 1994. The big chill. *Journal of Accountancy* 178(November): 53–56.

Dougherty vs. *Zimbler*, 922 F. Supp. 110 (N.D. Ill. 1996).

Endo vs. *Albertine*, 812 F. Supp. 1479 (N.D. Ill. 1993).

European American Bank vs. *Strauhs & Kay*, 483 N.E. 2d 110 (N.Y. 1985).

Fencl, E. R. 1989. Rebuilding the citadel: State legislative responses to accountant non-privity suits. *Washington University Law Quarterly* 67(3): 863–888.

Gillespie vs. *Seymour*, 876 P. 2d 193 (Kan. App. 1994), revs'd in part, 877 P. 2d 40 (Kan. 1994).

Goldwasser, D. 1995. Is the storm ending? *The CPA Journal* 65(October): 16–21.

Goldwasser, D., and M. Thomas Arnold. 1998. *Accountants' Liability*. New York: Practicing Law Institute.

Gossman, T. 1988. The fallacy of expanding accountants' liability. *Columbia Business Law Review* 1988: 213–241.

Granelli, J. 1995. Jumping ship. *Los Angeles Times* 22 October: D1.

Guerci, C. 1997. Liability of independent accountant to investors or shareholders. In *American Law Reports*, 5th Vol. 5: 48, 389–420.

Idaho Bank & Trust vs. *First Bancorp.*, 772 P 2d 720 (Idaho 1989).

Johnson, C. 1995. Impact of accountants' liability law on lenders. *New Jersey Lawyer* June 5: 17.

Jones, F., and K. Raghunandan. 1998. Client risk and recent changes in the market for audit services. *Journal of Accounting and Public Policy* 17: 169–181.

King, R., and R. Schwartz. 1997. The Private Securities Litigation Reform Act of 1995: A discussion of three provisions. *Accounting Horizons* 11(March): 92–106.

Landell vs. *Lybrand*, 107 A. 783 (Pa. 1919).

Legal Liability Task Force of the National Association of State Boards of Accountancy. 1994. *Current Legal Liability Issues of Concern to State Boards of Accountancy*.

Lev, B., and M. deVilliers. 1994. Stock price crashes and 10b-5: A legal, economic, and policy analysis. *Stanford Law Review* 47: 7–37.

Louis, A. 1968. The accountants are changing the rules. *Fortune* 81: 177–179.

MacDonald, E. 1997. More accounting firms are dumping risky clients. *Wall Street Journal* 25 April: A2.

Mednick, R., and J. Peck. 1994. Proportionality: A much-needed solution to the accountants' legal liability crisis. *Valparaiso University Law Review* 23(3): 867–918.

Mich. Comp Laws § 600. 2962 (1998).

Miss. Code Ann. § 11-7-20 (1997).

Moore, J.W. 1996. *Moore's Federal Practice*, Vol. 1a, 2nd ed., Part 2. New York: Matthew Bender.

N.J. Stat. Ann. § 2A: 53A-25 (1998).

Nordica USA, Inc. vs. *Deloitte & Touche*, 839 O.C.G.A. 351-1-11 (1998). F. Supp. 1982 (D. V4. 1993).

Pacini, C., and D. Sinason. 1998. Gaining a new balance in accountants' liability to non-clients for negligence: Recent developments and emerging trends. *Commercial Law Journal* 53(Spring): 15–66.

Performance Motorcars vs. *Peat Marwick*, 643 A. 2d 39 (N.J. Super. 1994).

Private Securities Litigation Reform Act of 1995; Pub. L. No. 104-67, 109 stat. 737 (1995).

Restatement (Second) of Torts § 552. 1977. New York: American Law Institute.

Robin vs. *Falbo*, No. 91C-2894, U.S. Dist. LEXIS 11075 (N.D. Ill. 1992).

Rosenblum vs. Adler, 461 A. 2d 138 (N.J. 1983).

Rusch Factors, Inc. vs. Levin, 294 F. Supp. 85 (D.R.I. 1968).

Scherl, J. 1994. Evolution of auditor liability to noncontractual third parties: Balancing the equities and weighing the consequences. *American University Law Review* 44(Fall): 255–289.

Schneider, C., and J. Dubow. 1996. Forward-looking information: Navigating the safe harbor. *Business Lawyer* 51: 1071–1125.

Security Pacific vs. *Peat Marwick Main*, 597 N.E. 2d 1080 (N.Y. 1992).

Seligman, J. 1996. The Private Securities Reform Act of 1995. *Arizona Law Review* 38(Summer): 717–737.

Swink vs. *Ernst & Young*, 908 S.W. 2d 660 (Ark. 1995).

Texas Society of CPAs (TSCPA). 1999. *Interview of Robert Owen, Legislative Director*, April 12. Austin, TX: TSCPA.

Thayer vs. *Hicks*, 793 P. 2d 784 (Mont. 1990).

Thompson, R. 1996. "Simplicity and certainty" in the measure of recovery under rule 10b-5. *Business Lawyer* 51: 1177–1227.

Torry, S. 1994. Study cites lawyers' campaign donations: $17.3 million went to candidates in three states weighing suit award limits. *Washington Post*, 13 September: D3.

Touche Ross vs. *Commerical Union Ins. Co.*, 514 So. 2d 315 (Miss. 1987).

Ultramares Corp. vs. *Touche*, 174 N.E. 441 (N.Y. 1931).

Utah Code Ann. & 58-26-12 (1998).

Wyo. Stat. Ann. & 33-3-201 (1998).

A SURVEY OF AUDIT SERVICE PRICING IN SOUTH KOREA

Mark H. Taylor, Daniel T. Simon, and F. Greg Burton

ABSTRACT

This paper studies the audit services market in South Korea. Compared to the audit services market in other countries, the market for audit services in South Korea is unique because it is heavily regulated. The findings indicate significant differences in the market for audit services in South Korea and countries previously studied. For example, the results suggest that the large audit-firm fee premium observed in many countries does not exist in South Korea, and that variables other than firm size that are typically related to client characteristics, such as complexity and risk, are not significant. The differences between the results for Korea and the results for other countries is likely due to the very different regulatory environment in Korea, especially the regulation of the fee setting process.

INTRODUCTION

Previous research on the market for audit services has found a high degree of consistency in terms of the variables that explain audit fees. This is especially true for

Research in Accounting Regulation, Volume 13, pages 201-207.

ISBN: 0-7623-0520-7

those variables related to auditee size, audit risk and audit complexity, and the use of a "Big Six," all of which have been found to be associated with higher audit fees. However, most of the audit markets in the countries that were previously analyzed are not subject to government-imposed price-setting and market-share regulation. In contrast, the market for audit services in South Korea is subject to extensive regulation. The imposed price-setting rules are very detailed, and focus primarily on the audit client's size. Consequently, we expected to observe significant differences in a model of audit fees for the South Korean market as compared to the typical models from other countries. The results of our analysis show that this is the case. Few of the determinants of audit fees, aside from audit size, which have typically explained the variance in audit fees in previous studies, are significantly related to audit fees in South Korea, suggesting that regulation distorts the fee setting process from what would be found in an unregulated market.

The remainder of this research report is organized as follows. The results of previous research on the market for audit services in other countries is reviewed briefly. This is followed by a discussion of the institutional background of accounting and auditing in South Korea. Next, the data and the empirical tests are described. And finally, the empirical results are presented and discussed.

PREVIOUS RESEARCH

Beginning with the work of Simunic (1980), many studies have analyzed the market for audit services in several countries. The majority of these studies have focused on a few highly developed countries—the United States, the United Kingdom, and Australia. Recently, more attention has been given to the market for audit services in other countries, especially non-highly developed nations. The major results of these studies have established the responsiveness of audit fees to variables related to auditee size, audit risk, and audit complexity. In general, these papers have found that these variables explain a large proportion of audit fees. In addition, these studies have generally found that "Big Six" audit firms receive premium fees.

INSTITUTIONAL BACKGROUND

The accounting and auditing environment in South Korea is influenced by elements of continental European civil law, Anglo-American law, and Chinese classical thought (Roden 1996). It is also heavily regulated. The auditing standard-setting body in South Korea, the Korean Institute of Certified Public Accountants, is attempting to adopt and integrate international auditing standards into its body of standards. However, financial accounting rules are promulgated by the Securities and Exchange Commission (SECK), a government agency (CIFAR 1993,

267). A study of financial disclosure regulation classifies South Korea as "highly regulated" (Cooke and Wallace 1990). A study relating legal system and accounting practices (Salter and Doupnik 1992) indicates that South Korea differs significantly from most of the countries previously examined in audit market research. It can thus be considered "unique" compared to the countries that have been studied in prior audit services market research.

Foreign accounting firms have been reluctant to enter the South Korean market because of the control the government exerts over the profession. For example, the fees an audit firm can charge to its clients are heavily regulated. Audit engagement fee guidelines imposed by the government model are based primarily on the auditee's size as measured by total assets. The fee is allowed to be adjusted slightly if the audit is a first-time audit, or if the auditee is publicly traded or registered. The model also allows adjustment depending on the number of divisions the auditee operates and for certain other "abnormal" expenses. Annual audit fee increases are also capped, not exceeding 6.5 percent over the past several years (Roden 1996). Additionally, the number of statutory audits that an accounting firm is allowed to conduct is calculated according to the number of qualified accountants employed by the firm (Moliterno 1990). These regulations have likely suppressed or virtually eliminated the typical price competition that is prevalent in most other countries. Price setting by the government also acts as a barrier to entry for new and smaller audit firms.

While all of the Big Six (now Big Five) firms have a presence in South Korea (through affiliate offices), two of the firms have significantly more clients than the others. In 1995, Deloitte Touche Tohmatsu International conducted 1006 statutory audits, while Coopers & Lybrand performed nearly 900. The remaining four firms audited between 300 and 500 companies each. However, Coopers & Lybrand appears to be the leading firm in South Korea and had country-leading revenues in 1995 of 39.5 billion won. All of the Big Six firms have multiple offices in the country.

Although the accounting profession in South Korea is similar to other countries in terms of the importance of the largest international accounting firms, the market for auditing is quite different. Governmental control and intense regulation of the audit fee setting process (which emphasizes auditee size) suggests that many of the determinants of audit fees observed in studies of the market for audit services in other countries will not be observed in the market for audit services in South Korea.

DATA AND METHODOLOGY

Because audit fees are not required disclosure in South Korean financial reports as in some countries,[1] audit fee data were collected directly from 40 South Korean companies by questionnaire. Respondents were requested to provide fee charges from the company's independent audit firm for the two-year period 1994–1995. Upon receipt of the responses, financial statement and other information used in the data analysis was collected from the company's annual reports.[2]

The basic research approach is to develop a regression model of audit fees similar to those used in most prior studies of audit fees. Typically, as in this paper, audit fee has been a dependent variable to be explained by various characteristics of the client. Among client characteristics found most important in explaining audit fees in previous studies are size and variables related to the complexity of the audit, such as the number of subsidiary firms and the relative proportion of assets that require more auditor effort to verify (e.g., inventory and receivables). These models have consistently explained a considerable proportion of audit fees in studies of Canada, the United States, the United Kingdom, Australia, New Zealand, South Africa, Hong Kong, Malaysia, Singapore, Bangladesh, Pakistan, Japan, and India. This basic regression model will therefore serve as a useful benchmark for assessing the similarities and differences in the audit services market in these countries as compared to South Korea.

The basic regression model to explain audit fees is:

$$AUDITFEE = b_1 + b_2 ASSETS + b_3 SUBS + b_4 INVREC + b_5 BIG6$$

where

AUDITFEE	=	audit fee paid to the independent auditor
ASSETS	=	total assets of the client
SUBS	=	the number of consolidated subsidiaries
INVREC	=	the proportion of total assets represented by inventories and receivables
BIG6	=	a variable which has a value of one if the company is audited by a Big Six audit firm

The first explanatory variable (*ASSETS*) represents the size of the audit client. Auditee size is clearly an important determinant of audit fees, because larger clients will require more audit effort; further, as already noted, the regulatory guidelines imposed on the market in South Korea emphasize auditee size.[3] The next two variables (*SUBS* and *INVREC*) relate to audit risk and audit complexity, which have been found in prior research to affect fees significantly. *ASSETS*, *SUBS*, and *INVREC* have been positively related to audit fees in other countries. Prior studies (for a summary, see Simon, Teo, and Trompeter 1992) also find that Big Six (now Big Five) auditors receive premium fees in most countries, and the *BIG6* variable has been positively related to audit fees in other countries.

This basic model will allow an assessment of the extent to which the results of previous studies apply to the determination of audit fees in South Korea, where the fee-setting process is highly regulated relative to other countries that have been studied.

EMPIRICAL RESULTS

Table 1 presents descriptive statistics for the sample. Considerable differences in the explanatory variables exist, allowing for enough variation to test the hypotheses. The firms have a considerable size range and come from a variety of industries. Thus, the sample, while it is relatively small, seems to represent a fairly wide range of South Korean firms. Table 2 presents the results of the basic regression equation. The overall results suggest a very good fit in which a large proportion of the variation in audit fees is explained. The value of the F-statistic is significant at better than the .0001 level. The value of adjusted R^2 is 0.84, indicating that the model explains more than four-fifths of the variation in audit fees. This value of the R^2 statistic is higher in magnitude than those found in studies of other countries.[4]

An examination of the t-statistics for the individual explanatory variable indicates close correspondence to the emphasis on audit size in the government-imposed fee-setting rules and little other similarity between the determinants of audit fees in South Korea and the countries studied in previous research. The client size variable (*ASSETS*) is statistically significant at better than the 0.001 level while the audit complexity variables (*INVREC* and *SUBS*) are not significant at conventional levels. Thus, the results for the auditee risk and audit complexity variables indicate considerable dissimilarity between the determinants of audit fees in South Korea and the countries studied in previous research. Moreover, the auditor-size variable, *BIG6*, which has generally been found to be significant in most other countries, is not statistically significant.

Table 1. Descriptive Statistics (n = 79)

Variable	*Mean (Std. Dev.)*
Audit Fee (thousands of South Korean won)	5306
	(2368)
Assets (millions of South Korean Won)	3681
	(6858)
Range of Assets (minimum to maximum)	
(in millions of South Korean won)	1.7 - 10.5
Subsidiaries	6.20
	(5.33)
Proportion of Assets in Inventory and	0.37
receivables	(0.15)
Percentage of Firms by industry	
Construction	9%
Financial Services	16%
Manufacturing	62%
Other	13%
Percentage of Firms Audited by Big Six Firms	77%

Table 2. Regression Results for Basic Model ($n = 79$)

Variable	*Coefficient (t-statistic)*
INTERCEPT	6.71 (59.95)**
ASSETS	0.23 (14.49)**
INVREC	0.25 (1.41)
SUBS	0.03 (1.31)
BIG6	−.05 (−.96)
Adjusted R^2	0.84
F-Statistic	97.15**

Note: **Significant at the .0001 level.

Overall, the results suggest that government regulation of audit fees eliminates what might be considered the "normal" relationships that have been shown to exist between several variables and audit prices in previous research.

SUMMARY AND CONCLUSIONS

The results demonstrate that aside from auditee size, most of the audit complexity and auditor identity variables found to be important in studies of other countries are *not* important in explaining audit fees in South Korea. Thus, most of the major client-specific factors which determine audit fees in other countries have virtually no importance in determining audit fees in South Korea. For example, the inventory-receivables variable, which has been important in almost every other study of audit fees, is not significant in Korea. In addition, unlike the vast majority of the countries previously studied, there appears to be no fee premium accruing to large international accounting firms. This is a result that is very different from most of the countries previously studied. Government regulation appears to eliminate the Big Six fee premium that (based on studies of other countries) we would usually expect to find. Overall, the results suggest that the regulatory environment can significantly alter the audit services market, potentially distorting what might be deemed a "normal," market-based fee determination process. Possible directions for future research include investigating the effects of regulation, not only on audit fees as we did in this study, but also on related questions such as audit quality, market share, auditor changes, and other issues related to auditor-client relationships. Even without future research, however, the results provide clear evidence that government regulation causes considerable differences in audit pricing from what would be expected in markets that are not encumbered by similar regulatory practices.

NOTES

1. In general, only countries that are current or former members of the British Commonwealth require audit fees as standard disclosures in firm's annual reports.
2. One of the responding firms provided audit fee information for only one of the years (1995). For a second firm, complete information on its financial statement variables was unavailable for both years, and hence this firm could not be included in the sample.
3. Logarithmic transformations of audit fees and client assets, and square root transformations of subsidiaries are employed because previous research (e.g., Francis and Simon 1987) indicates that these specifications provide a good linear fit in which the assumptions of ordinary least squares regression are satisfied.
4. Values of R^2 for previous studies of audit fees are typically in the range of .50 to .70.

REFERENCES

Center for International Financial Analysis and Research (CIFAR). 1993. *International Accounting and Auditing Trends*, third edition. Princeton, NJ: CIFAR.

Cooke, T., and R. Wallace. 1990. Financial disclosure regulation and its environment: A review and further analysis. *Journal of Accounting and Public Policy* (Summer): 79–110.

Francis, J., and D. Simon. 1987. A test of audit pricing in the small-client segment of the U.S. audit market. *The Accounting Review* (January): 145–157.

Moliterno, S.F. 1990. *The Accounting Profession in South Korea*. New York: AICPA.

Roden, S. 1996. Unruffled by change. *The Accountant* (May): 12–15.

Salter, S., and T. Doupnik. 1992. The relationship between legal systems and accounting practices. *Advances in International Accounting* 5: 3–22.

Simon, D., S. Teo, and G. Trompeter. 1992. A comparative study of the market for audit services in Hong Kong, Malaysia, and Singapore. *International Journal of Accounting Education and Research* 27: 234–240.

Simunic, D. 1980. The pricing of audit services: Theory and evidence. *Journal of Accounting Research* (Spring): 161–190.

PART III

PERSPECTIVES

CLAIMING THE RIGHT TO KNOW:
AN INFORMATION PERSPECTIVE FOR BUSINESS REPORTING

Robert James Bricker and Gary John Previts

ABSTRACT

Traditionally, business reporting has been oriented towards investors and creditors. This paper studies business reporting from a property rights perspective. Our paper begins by developing historical and philosophical links between property rights, rights of use, information rights, and reporting. We argue that contemporary reporting tends not to fully reflect the changes in information rights because of technological limitations, transaction costs of changing, and habit. Consequently, reporting remains traditionally oriented towards investors and creditors. We introduce a broader perspective of accountability that addresses the information rights of all business organization claimholders. The resulting model theoretically describes the relationship between a company's resources, claims, and related information rights, but does not address how the information rights of claimholders are to be met. While the traditional reporting model is adequate to meet some information rights, alternate reporting methods may be necessary when accounting technologies are inadequate. The paper concludes by asserting a need to re-examine business reporting and expressions of the traditional reporting model as it is currently understood and

Research in Accounting Regulation, Volume 13, pages 211-230.

ISBN: 0-7623-0520-7

concludes by asserting a need to re-examine business reporting and expressions of the traditional reporting model as it is currently understood and taught. We argue for research to reorient business reporting to bring it more into consonance with the global operations of current capital markets institutions, and the property rights and information rights of a broader community of user constituencies.

THE ORIENTATION OF BUSINESS REPORTING

Underlying accounting and business reporting[1] concepts and principles are postulates about the orientation of financial reports. Zeff (1978), who apparently originated the phrase "orientation postulate," distinguishes between the subject subpostulate, which describes the reporting entity, and the beneficiary subpostulate, which describes the intended beneficiaries of business reporting.

In this paper, we explore the orientation of business reporting in terms of its intended beneficiaries. A beneficiary orientation is critical in any model of business reporting, because the set of information beneficiaries largely determines the content and form of financial reports, and consequently the arenas for possible regulation. The orientation of business reporting towards traditional debt and equity holders has been implicitly or explicitly recognized in academic and practice publications.

We develop an information rights perspective as a basis for orienting business reporting. This perspective focuses on the rights of individuals to be informed about business organizations.[2] It is broader than the widely employed explicit contracting perspective, which uses business reporting to design formal,[3] optimal contracts, or the market-based perspective, which uses the demand for business reporting as the basis for its supply. In comparison to contracting models of business reporting, which are based upon explicit contracting, the property rights perspective is based on the premise that a social system establishes implicit agreements among parties even when no formal arrangements exist. This social contract[4] is the basis for the establishment of property rights and obligations among parties. These implicit contracts and resulting property rights can emerge when uncontracted costs are borne by a party. The development of product liability law illustrates this, and is particularly applicable to accounting and business reporting because of the linkage between liability and information disclosure. The establishment of property rights through implicit contractual arrangements has also received increasing recognition by legislatures and courts (Tinker and Ghicas 1992; Arthur Andersen and Co. 1989). From this perspective, property rights are implicit contracts that are in force in the absence of any binding, explicit contract.

Property rights include a right to use property, and this in turn implies a right to information—a right to be informed about the property status and use. This is particularly cogent for business reporting because of the separation between corporate control and claimholders, including the largely nominal role that most corporate shareholders have in ownership activities. Accounting and business reporting are important in providing information to claimholders, subject to cost/benefit considerations, whether their information rights are derived from explicit contracting or from implicit contracting.

Several important developments have changed the scope and nature of implicit property rights, including manufacturing scale, the effects of human activity on ecological resources and social welfare, and changes in product liability. These changes have generally broadened property rights, correspondingly broadening both parties having information rights in business organizations and broadening the nature of those information rights.

However, accounting and business reporting have not evolved correspondingly. They continue to be oriented principally towards traditional claimholders, with firm equity-holders considered to be the principal set of information beneficiaries. This orientation is incongruent with society's contemporary understanding of property and information rights holders. The remainder of this paper is organized in the following way. The next section reviews the nature of property rights. The third section links property rights to information rights, particularly using product liability arguments. The fourth section models accounting and business reporting from this property-and-information rights perspective. The fifth section reviews social reporting generally. The sixth section introduces a claimholder model of business reporting, which has a social reporting orientation based on property and information rights. The paper concludes in the seventh section.

PROPERTY RIGHTS

The Nature of Property Rights

A society's property rights evolve historically out of a complex interplay of factors such as culture, economics, technology, resources, and demographics. Property rights may be exclusive or non-exclusive, restricted or unrestricted. Property right exclusivity is defined by the holder's ability to exclude others from the use of a good. Exclusivity implies transferability of interest. Non-exclusive property rights imply a communal, or first-come, first-use basis of property utilization. Property rights are restricted when society places limitations on "owners'" actions over resources. In this sense, the degree to which property rights are attenuated is a measure of the restrictions placed on liberty by a society. Thus liberty and the private ownership of productive property are close relatives, because liberty implies non-interference over an individual's acts. Furthermore, the rights of action for a resource are divisible, so that many individuals can be said to have ownership interests in it. This divisibility of property rights among individuals is a precept of modern capitalism.

Private ownership is a form of property rights that has been important in both free enterprise and mixed economies. Ownership is an individual's "socially recognized right of action" to use a resource without interference from those not holding rights. Ownership implies (1) right of use, (2) the right to appropriate returns, and (3) the right to change the form or substance of the thing owned (Furobotn and Pejovich 1974, 4). The first of these is important in establishing a right of information over owned resources, which will be discussed later in this paper.

In some historical periods, western social contracts have permitted individuals a wide scope of action rights over both owned and common resources in terms of decision making about their use. However, harmful social welfare effects of individual decisions, particularly for common resources such as water and air (the public-good problem), have become increasingly problematic.

This public-good problem occurs when resources are such that either their physical control or the monitoring of their use by individuals is impractical, and social costs are generated (Coase 1960). The property rights for such non-exclusive resources are often allocated on a first-come, first-served basis. However, the costs of the use of these resources may not be allocated in proportion to their use. Thus, users may consume a larger share of the resource than they bear of its costs. This may encourage over-consumption of such resources. Even when private property rights are specified, the technological problems of control or monitoring make a "market" solution for the efficient allocation of these resources difficult to achieve, potentially resulting in a situation characterized as a "market failure." In such a setting, there is a divergence of social and private welfare. One solution to this condition is to alter the property rights over the resource in favor of identifiable constituent groups. A second solution is to have the government, for whom scale economies make control and monitoring of these resources practical, act as a social welfare agent.

When a resource is not perceptibly scarce, its consumption may matter little to society. For instance, if natural resources such as water or air are abundant, their use by one party does not appreciably affect another, and there is no need to define property rights over them. The technological problems with the physical control and monitoring of such resources have made this historically convenient for societies. The realization of the scarcity of such resources has led to greater appreciation of their intrinsic value, and corresponding needs for a conception of property rights as well as an accounting interpretation of such property rights. However, as Owens (1992, 10) observes: "Much critical natural capital is not owned and is therefore treated as a free good by traditional accounting systems."

The Evolution of Property Rights

Global political, technological, and demographic changes have substantially altered the conception of property rights during the past two centuries. John

Locke's *Two Treatises on Government* (circa 1688), provided a powerful philosophical basis for natural rights. This and other works profoundly influenced the American republic, whose economic and political systems were founded upon beliefs of humans' natural rights, as reflected in documents such as the Declaration of Independence, the Constitution, and the Bill of Rights. Natural rights, God-given to humans in common, were reflected in the affirmation of "life, liberty, and the pursuit of happiness."

As thinking moved gradually towards a more utilitarian basis, a shift towards social welfare considerations also occurred. John Stuart Mill, for instance, viewed property rights as a creation of law, and thus held that government could re-arrange property rights so as to maximize social welfare.

While the Social Darwinism of William Graham Sumner provided an important utilitarian logic for the maintenance of strong private property rights, American constitutionalists such as John Burgess recognized a shift away from laissez faire economics and private property rights, and towards public welfare regulation of property. Particularly beginning in the 1930s, there developed in the United States a perception that unrestricted, self-interested action was often costly to society as a whole, as reflected by writers such as Berle and Means (1932). Social philosophers such as Bellamy, Veblen, Croly and Dewey argued that:

> ...individual control over production and unregulated enterprise necessarily led to exploitive and acquisitive behavior.... Only by eliminating or radically curtailing tradition property rights could the United States expect to establish a better society (Scott 1977, 159–160).

Dewey, in particular, believed in a need for a new socially oriented nationalism and believed that competitive, profit-oriented capitalism was inadequate to maximize social welfare. The evolution towards a social welfare perspective became a revolution in social thought during the 1960s. In 1963 McGuire wrote:

> The idea of social responsibilities supposes that the corporation has not only economic and legal obligations, but also certain responsibilities to society which extend beyond these obligations.

Throughout that decade and into the 1970s, property rights laws and attitudes continued to evolve towards a more social orientation. In *Accounting and Corporate Social Responsibility*, the Reverend Homer Henderson (1978, 11) asserted corporate social welfare and stewardship functions when he wrote:

> ...a corporation should concern itself with moral and social issues...both in terms of the needs of dominion (power, profit, progress) as well as the needs of garden keeping (the stewardship of social responsibility)...

Similarly, Goodpaster and Atkinson (1992) stated:

> ...the efficiency of the free-market system and its respect for individual economic freedoms cannot justify a blank check in the pursuit of wealth. Business operates as a legitimate component of the common good and as a promoter of individual economic freedoms only on the condition that it meets the just claims and reasonable expectations of all the different stakeholders.

As the twentieth century closes, it can be said that much of the social reconstruction of property rights relations has been accomplished through social legislation and court decisions which have given government, citizen groups, employees, and consumers greater property rights in business organizations. Powell (1977, 494) observed:

> As one looks back along the historic road traversed by the law of land in England and in America, one sees a change from the viewpoint that he who owns may do as he pleases with what he owns, to a position which hesitatingly embodies an ingredient of stewardship; which grudgingly, but steadily, broadens the recognized scope of social interests in the utilization of things...

PROPERTY RIGHTS AND THE RIGHT TO KNOW

There are two sources for a right to information. There is, first, an information right that occurs when parties explicitly and formally contract over information rights: for example when an agreement with a creditor or investor specifies the receipt of periodic financial reports. This information right basis has been addressed extensively in the accounting literature, and we will not consider it further here. The right to information also emanates from an underlying property right relation in which there exists an implicit contract that is derived from the social contract.

As discussed above, an important feature of a property right is the corresponding right to use the resource, not simply hold title to it. This is a simple matter in instances in which a party has physical possession or control of a resource, but is more difficult otherwise. For example, with ownership of corporate equity securities (among other property right claims in a corporation), the owner may not physically observe or use the property. To make use of the property, the owner must be informed about its condition, and therefore has a derived right of information which protects access to timely reports so as to be fully informed about the property.

A right to be informed includes the right to information about the characteristics of an item that are not immediately apparent, such as characteristics that are covered by product liability laws. While product liability has historically been a relatively unimportant part of tort law, it has emerged since the 1960s into a place of prominence, to the point of creating controversy. It has been suggested that the warning "caveat emptor" has today been replaced with "caveat venditor." Below, we consider the evolution of U.S. product liability and the right to information, and we apply the resulting observations to accounting and business reporting.

During early American business history, product liability existed principally in cases of privity, and was a part of contract law. Manufacturers, therefore, were rarely liable to consumers, as evidenced by cases such as Winterbottom vs. Wright in 1842, in which a coach manufacturer was not held liable for a defective wheel. Exceptions to this rule developed out of tort law in the late nineteenth and early twentieth century, particularly in dealing with products with potentially hazardous properties such as explosives and food. This was extended to automobiles in the 1916 case of MacPherson vs. Buick Motor Co., effectively ending privity, and moving product liability into the area of tort law.

Following MacPherson, product liability claims were pursued under negligence rules. Manufacturers were still able to defend themselves using risk assumption and product misuse arguments. However, in the 1960s, product liability evolved towards strict liability (and then towards absolute liability), and was applied progressively to a broader and broader set of goods. This was reflected in the American Law Institute's 1965 Second Statement of Torts (Section 402A) which was revised to state:

> One who sells any product in a defective condition unreasonably dangerous to the user or consumer or to his property is subject to liability for physical harm (even though)...(a) the seller has exercised all possible care in the preparation and sale of his product, and (b) the user or consumer has not bought the product from or entered into any contractual relation with the seller.

It has been established that a defective condition includes a defect in manufacture, a defect in design, or a failure to warn of product dangers (Cooter and Ulen 1988, 434). As to the latter, manufacturer liability has been held even in cases in which the danger of a product was not known or reasonably knowable by the manufacturer at the time.[5]

Failure to warn implies the user's right to information about a product's dangers. Obvious dangers, such as the danger of being cut by an axe, need no disclosure. However, dangers that are not obvious must be disclosed, or the manufacturer will be liable to any user for resulting damage or injury.[6]

Cooter and Ulen (1988) express the surplus value of a product to a consumer or user in terms of: willingness to pay, price, precaution, and risk of uncompensated harm. The risk of uncompensated harm arises when the manufacturer warns the user about the risks of use. The manufacturer's warning transfers the corresponding risk of the product to the consumer, and reduces the consumer's surplus value by increasing the expected amount of uncompensated harm, and presumably affecting the price that the consumer is willing to pay for the product. Thus, by not informing consumers of the dangers of the product, the manufacturer may induce consumers to buy products that they would not buy if they were fully informed of the dangers. At the same time, such a lack of disclosure means that the consumer has not contracted over such product risks, and leaves the manufacturer liable for damages.

Cooter and Ulen further argue that when a weak warning is made by a manufacturer, then the company's profits are: *revenue* less *production cost* less *damages*. Cooter and Ulen referred specifically to eventual tort damages. From a reporting perspective, the corresponding liability occurs when the consumer buys a product with an inadequate warning, and it is at the point of sale that a consumer can gain a property right and corresponding information right in a company.

This reasoning also has a far more fundamental implication for accounting and business reporting. As early as the 1920s, J.M. Clark asserted that economic values fail to capture all "social costs." He argued for "social cost keeping" to reveal the full costs of products (Clark 1923). Similarly, Ing (1992) wrote:

> An organization or operation will have impacts on people and society in general. We can see effects arising from the particular product or process, both effects on the local community and other effects on special interest groups.

The presence of the business in the community may be thought of as a product to the community (apart from the product that the business actually offers). This is accompanied by explicit and implicit contracts about the community's acceptance of certain kinds of cost-bearing related to the company's presence. However, it is also possible that the company may impose uncontracted costs on the community. For example, unknown to the community, the company may discharge its waste products in the river or air instead of adopting more costly treatments and disposal approaches. As a result, the community that uses the river and breathes the air bears uncontracted costs, which may be incurred in a number of ways. There may be an increased cost for medical care or medical insurance. Special treatment facilities may be required to treat the water or air before it will be fit for human use. The recreational use of the waterway may also be affected.

The product liability reasoning outlined above implies that, to the extent that the company fails to operate in the manner implicitly or explicitly agreed upon (or contracted) with its community, and imposes uncontracted costs on that community, then the community gains a corresponding property and information right in the business. This relationship has received legal recognition in various ways, including the Emergency Planning and Community Right-To-Know Act, adopted 1986, which gave communities extensive information rights in the activities of local businesses, the Toxics Release Inventory (Smith 1991), and provisions of the Clean Air Act of 1990 and the Consumer Confidence Report Rule of the 1996 Safe Drinking Water Act. Furthermore, the AICPA Accounting Standards Committee's SOP No. 96-1, *Environmental Remediation Liabilities* (1996), while it retained the basic liability approach to recording environmental liabilities, suggested the disclosure of circumstances which might trigger liability.

It may be objected that the social benefit a company provides a community may far outweigh the costs it imposes. That is, the net social benefit provided by the company eliminates the net cost borne by the community and, correspondingly, its corresponding property or information rights. Two responses are in order. First, the provision of a benefit by the company to parties does not relieve the company of its other obligations with respect to them. For instance, the payment of dividends to a shareholder in excess of the shareholder's original investment does not eliminate the shareholder's claim in the corporation. Similarly, the provision of salary and benefits by the company to employees does not relieve the company of other obligations to employees.

Second, the fact that a party provides a benefit to another does not relieve that party of a liability should it subsequently harm the other. Society does not net such effects. A company's liability should it injure an employee is not erased because, overall, that employee was treated well, given a bonus, a raise, and a favorable working environment.

In summary, uncontracted cost bearing gives rise to a claim, and this property right in turn implies a corresponding information right that may not be captured in the accounting equation or otherwise addressed under existing financial reporting rules. Thus, from a stewardship view, subject to reasonable constraints, the claims and information rights of cost bearing communities and other nontraditional claimholders should be contained in business reports. This implies that business reporting should be oriented towards the full set of claimholders. Below, we discuss how business reporting is oriented and how it addresses the information rights of claimholders.

ACCOUNTING: AN INFORMATION RIGHTS PERSPECTIVE

Property Rights and the Orientation of Business Reporting

Writers such as Yamey (1950) have asserted the importance of accounting to economic systems of ownership such as capitalism. Others have asserted the importance of a notion of ownership to the development of accounting. Littleton (1933), for example, stated that a precondition for the existence of bookkeeping was "Private Property, since bookkeeping is concerned...with recording the facts about property and property rights." From either perspective, there are clear relationships between accounting, conceptions of ownership, and information. It is therefore most useful to think of business reporting as important, because it provides a way of identifying resources and claims, and expressing the information to which claimholders have rights in a formal, comparable, and consistent manner over multiple periods of economic activity.

In general, as illustrated above, property rights can be acquired through certain cost-bearing activities.[7] If a party exchanges something of value for the sole "ownership" of a firm, then that party has acquired a property right in that firm's resources. In this case, the party has obtained this property right in an explicit contractual transaction. A similar case could be made for creditors. In both instances, a cost is incurred in a contractual arrangement to obtain the property right. The cost incurred and the contractual arrangement are used as the justification for including the property rights of these parties as owners' equity or a liability in the accounting model. But nontraditional holders of claims against the resources of a business organization may also exist, specifically in settings in which parties bear uncontracted costs, as we illustrated earlier.

Some might argue that the community claim in the business described above is not an accounting claim when no contractual liability exists. However, although an explicit contract between the company and the community may not exist, both operate within society's broader social contract whereby property rights relations are established. Others might concede that while an accounting claim does exist, it is covered by rules related to contingent liabilities (FASB 1975).

This latter argument illustrates the orientation of contemporary business reporting, which provides traditional claimholders with information about potential future obligations. This orientation effectively ignores the claims of nontraditional claimholders in the resources of a company, even though their property rights entitle them to relevant information about their claim. Such information might have nothing to do with the traditional contingency disclosures, whether in financial statements, notes, or other media. This also illustrates the disclosure paradigm of accounting which attempts to capture as much information as possible in the form of a single, money valuation base. Transactional accounting, which teaches and depicts accountants' recognition of property and information rights, remains calibrated both to this sort of measurement and reporting, and to the interests of traditional claimholders.

These thoughts suggest an importance for reassessing the orientation of business reporting. Business reporting is valuable to society because it facilitates the information rights-holders' decision making about the use of the business's resources. Business reporting fails in this social role if its orientation about rights-holders is incongruent with society's definition of them.

The Case of Accounting and the Environment

The development of thought, law, and regulation regarding environmental resources provides a useful case for considering the role of business reporting in providing information about the environmental effects of businesses. While there has been ongoing concern about pollution and the use of natural resources in many countries, factors such as increased population in urban areas and growing recognition of the effects of pollutants have dramatically increased society's attention to environmental issues. This trend also reflects changes in social values that emerged in the 1960s which stressed the interdependence of individuals and a shared sense of responsibility for social welfare. These attitudes led to restrictions on the use of property, and recognition of the rights of individuals as embodied in government and society to natural resources in which particular individuals did not have well-defined property rights.

The 1972 U.S. Supreme Court decision in Sierra Club vs. Morton, concerning a proposed development of an area of the Sierra Nevada Mountains, reflects the growth of public interest and activism in environmental issues.[8] Although the U.S. Supreme Court refused to accept the Sierra Club's standing in the case, it nonetheless reaffirmed a public interest. Justice Stewart wrote:

> Aesthetic and environmental well-being, like economic well-being, are important ingredients of the quality of life in our society, and the fact that particular environmental interests are shared by the many rather than the few does not make them less deserving of legal protection....

Three dissenting justices argued for the Sierra Club's standing in the case. Justice Blackmun wrote:

> I would permit an imaginative expansion of our traditional concepts of standing in order to enable an organization such as the Sierra Club...to litigate environment issues.

Justice Douglas went further, arguing that natural objects should have judicial standing to sue. He stated:

> Contemporary public concern for protecting nature's ecological equilibrium should lead to the conferral of standing upon environmental objects.... The ordinary corporation is a "person" for purposes of the adjudicatory processes.... So it should be as respects valleys, alpine meadows, beaches, ridges, groves of trees, or even air that feels the destructive pressures of modern technology and modern life.

While property rights in the environment have changed dramatically, reporting has not. Business reports are not designed to accommodate the legitimate information rights of many classes of claimholders. Indeed, in *Blueprint for a Green Economy* (Pearce, Markandya, and Barbier 1989), the authors argue that the failure of traditional accounting and reporting models in the matter has contributed to the exploitation and damage of the environment, particularly in the omission of the environmental effect of business operations. Similarly, the Chartered Association of Certified Accountants' *The Greening of Accounting: The Profession After Pearce* (Gray 1990) discusses the need for accounting for resource depletion and social responsibility in business reporting. Hines (1991), argues that the technology of accounting is used inappropriately to attempt to reduce environmental effects to monetary values. Growing accounting research interest in "green accounting" is evidenced by: the recent special "environmental" issues in leading accounting journals, the establishment of the Centre for Social and Environmental Accounting Research at the University of Dundee, conferences CAAA Education Committee on the integration of environmental issues in accounting, and the attention paid to environmental accounting and auditing. Also, from industry, the

British Institute of Management has considered a 12-point policy for management and the environment (Lester 1992). Finally, British Trade Unions have campaigned for "a statutory right of access to information for employees and the community on matters related to a workplace and the environment" and "full public access to information on the environment" (Benn 1992).

In short, a line of reasoning has been developed about a "right to know," either because other parties are affected, or because firms are accountable to society. However, these issues have been addressed at a policy level within accounting practice from a more traditional perspective. While Senge, writing in *The Ohio CPA Journal,* asserts "to account for environmental concerns...the audience focus must shift to the concept of stakeholders. This is a much broader orientation...." (1993, 35), the AICPA, FASB, and SEC have reflected a traditional investor orientation (for example, see FASB 1978). To date, the profession has continued to view environmental reporting in traditional terms, and the AICPA Accounting Standards Committee's SOP No. 96-1, *Environmental Remediation Liabilities*, focuses on environmental liabilities. Similarly, SEC registrants need to comply with SAB 92, *Accounting and Disclosures Relating to Loss Contingencies*, again dealing with liabilities related to environmental remediation.

"Green accounting" is only one of a number of areas in which the expanded scope of property rights needs to be considered. Roberts (1992) suggested the following possible areas of disclosure: the environment, affirmative action, equal opportunity employment, community involvement, product safety, policies towards South Africa, energy, and social responsibility disclosure. Other, more specific areas include, for example, employee claims in matters such as underfunded defined benefit pension plans, or even, as suggested by recent court decisions and proposed bills of the U.S. Congress, in the event of the termination of a pension plan. Some, but not all of these areas, are justifiable under the information rights model presented here.

SOCIAL REPORTING

Attention to corporate social responsibility and accountability predates the 1970s. In the 1920s, accountants such as Stuart Chase argued for an accounting role in assessing corporate social stewardship (Bloom 1981). D.R. Scott (1976) envisioned a continued drift away from a laissez faire economy toward increasing government involvement. He saw accounting as an important social instrument whose goal was the protection of economic interests in society.

However, since the rise of the modern corporation, accounting and business reporting practices have persistently reflected a debt and equity holder orientation in business reporting. From a historical perspective, the industrial revolution's impact on accounting and reporting, and the need to specify the factors of economic activity related thereto in a manner consistent with the property and information rights of claimholders fostered debates during the eighteenth and nineteenth centuries about both the form and the content of business reporting (Previts and Merino 1998). A result of these early debates was an algebraic notation consistent with the industrial property rights relationships, as articulated by Charles Sprague in a series of essays in 1880 as "*Assets = Liabilities + Proprietorship*." This proprietary-entity model made the object of interest the business and the beneficiary of information the proprietor. Although Paton (1922) later redefined the object of interest as the business entity, the information beneficiary orientation inherent in "The Accounting Equation" has remained fundamentally unaltered in educational exhibition since the second decade of this century. Accounting and business reporting have since been rooted in this orientation and are presently inadequate to address the information rights of nontraditional claimholders.

Despite this, thought about company obligations has evolved in line with general property rights thinking towards a social welfare perspective. In the 1960s, the term "stakeholder" appeared, to refer to a broad set of parties who have legitimate interests in a company (Ansoff 1965). Bruyn (1987, 55) writes:

> [Our concern with corporations] is with their capacity to govern themselves socially so as to avoid government intervention. One way to accomplish this end is to promote systems of accountability [for] the stakeholders of the corporation. Stakeholders...are people who are affected by corporate policy. They are the direct competitors, buyers, sellers, employees, consumers, stockholders, and the community at large.[8]

Writers such as Cornell and Shapiro (1987), in finance, argue for reflecting the claims of all corporate stakeholders in financial reports, and many writers note the narrow claimholder focus of extant business reporting. Adams (1992) writes:

> The traditional view is that a company is accountable to its shareholders but these, by any measure, are a tiny, unrepresentative group. By contrast, the "stakeholder" concept of corporate responsibility is increasingly being recognized as valid by our major companies.

A stakeholder orientation received limited recognition in accounting, for example, by the U.K. Accounting Standards Steering Committee (1975), and (at least indirectly) by the FASB's conceptual framework via its reference to "other users" and by FAS 106 (FASB 1990) in which non-contractual obligations are identified for inclusion within the traditional accounting model.

An AICPA interest in social reporting became evident in the late 1960s at its annual meetings, culminating in the "Charleston Roundtable." A resulting AICPA committee led to the 1977 publication of Social Measurement (AICPA 1977). In 1974 management accountants also considered a social reporting basis for business organizations in its "Accounting for Corporate Social Performance" (NAA 1974). In academia, in the early 1970s, the American Accounting Association sponsored several committees charged with studying (1) corporate social performance; (2) the environmental effects of organizational behavior; and (3) the measurement of social costs. Writers such as Tinker and Lowe (1980) and Ramanathan (1978, 1976), suggested extending the accounting model to capture social effects. More recently, a University of Southern California Study Group (USC 1990) recommended rethinking financial accounting standards to incorporate, among other ideas, a social welfare perspective. Generally, however, practice-oriented studies have continued to reflect an orientation towards traditional investors, including the AICPA "Jenkins Committee's" report (1994) entitled "Improving Business Reporting: A Customer Focus: Meeting the Information Needs of Investors and Creditors" and the Financial Accounting Standards Board's Recent "Business Reporting Research Project."

The accounting community's interest in the issue of social responsibility and accountability temporarily peaked in the late 1970s, but has re-emerged during the past few years, particularly in terms of the environmental and social impact of companies. Roberts (1992), for instance, specifically explored the application of stakeholder theory to business social responsibility disclosure. This multi-threaded issue has now also been addressed in terms of corporate governance. Lorsch has spoken in terms of the responsibilities of company directors (Grant 1992), prescribing that directors should be "stewards of important national assets" for a broad set of parties. Corporations also now demonstrate some sensitivity to social responsibility reporting, as illustrated by the results of one recent study (Patten 1992), which showed increased disclosure of petroleum company environmental disclosure following the Exxon Valdez disaster.

TOWARD A CLAIMHOLDER ORIENTATION IN REPORTING

One of the difficulties for social reporting is the specification of parties with legitimate information interests, to assist in reorienting business reporting. We propose addressing this issue by applying the property rights/information rights model introduced in this paper. A second difficulty of social reporting is disclosure specification. We propose a conceptual accounting model reflecting the dominant socioeconomic view of resources and claims (property rights) from which business reporting principles can be derived. Together, these comprise our claimholder model of business reporting, which asserts, at a conceptual level, that:

RESOURCES = RESOURCE CLAIMS

It subsumes Paton's (1922) model by transcending its technical basis and its orientation toward traditional claimholders. Our model is similar in some ways to Hendriksen's (1982) Enterprise Theory, which views the corporation as a socioeconomic organization having reporting responsibilities to all claimholders in society. It broadens the set of recognized parties with information rights in companies, as a stakeholder model does, but it does not necessarily include all stakeholders as claimholders. It is sufficiently broad to capture the now-established claims of owners, lenders, government, employees, and community. The claims and information interests of these parties are both dynamic and varied. Consequently, multiple flexible approaches to business reporting are important.

While it is not conceptually difficult to reflect upon a reoriented reporting model that incorporates a broader set of resource claims, the practical implementation of such a model is far more challenging. For example, technological limitations make it impractical to fully capture property rights relations in an "equational model," although even for "green accounting," new technologies are developing (Milne 1991).

Yet arguments that such claims are difficult to measure or include in the equational model do not obviate the conceptual basis for their inclusion. Claimholders retain their information rights even if they cannot be captured in some particular, applied way because of technological limitations. Technological or other limitations or model specification issues need not deter the profession from studying the reorientation of business reporting. Furthermore, if our traditional equational model is to be oriented to reflect contemporary property rights, then it should be respecified to include the attributes and claims of the growing community of claimholders.

In this context, the equational model retains a role, though a somewhat diminished one, as an algebraically based and technologically constrained partial interpretation of the broader conceptual accounting and reporting model. As reporting technologies improve, better specifications of the equational model can be expected.

The inability to capture all claims[10] in the equational model because of limitations in accounting technologies does not diminish the underlying rights of nontraditional claimholders. Nor does it free us from the need to develop new and innovative methods of presenting information. It implies instead that we must begin to move away from a single valuation and transaction base as a dominant business reporting paradigm. Both the complexity of information rights and the sophistication of users argue in favor of reporting more than numbers that purport to represent a single type of value. While attempts to capture social costs and benefits (e.g., Rubenstein 1992) should not be dismissed, it is more important for accounting to develop alternate approaches to disclosure, as suggested by Gray (1992).

The orientation of business reports, then, should ultimately reflect the claims recognized in the conceptual business reporting model, whether or not they are included in the equational model. This orientation should reflect the property rights of all claimholders. Business reporting should have, in short, a claimholder orientation, where claimholder is understood to mean the broad set of information rights holders in a business.

Our claimholder model does not imply that all claimholders have equal status; some will have priority over others. Also, the information rights of claimholders need to be tempered by social welfare and cost/benefit considerations. The simple existence of information rights may not justify reporting when the social cost of doing so is larger than the resulting social benefit. It is similarly important not to misconstrue the claimholder orientation as an assertion of the rights of all in the activities of every business enterprise. Such a view is intrusive and incompatible with individual rights in a capitalist economy. Finally, the claimholder model does not protect parties from poor judgment when dealing with business organizations. Losses because of such judgment need to be distinguished from the sort of cost bearing and implicit contracting that we have described here as the basis for the claimholder orientation.

CONCLUDING REMARKS

In this paper, we have presented the issues for considering the orientation of business reporting from a property and information rights perspective. "Orientation" is important because it determines the information beneficiaries, the content, and the form of financial reports. When resources were historically more narrowly defined in our society (there were more "free goods," and fewer recognized scarce resources), and the presumption of the optimality of individual decisions on social welfare was dominant, it was acceptable for business reporting to be oriented solely towards creditors and owners. However economic and social developments have fundamentally expanded the set of parties bearing uncontracted costs of companies' activities. This has resulted in an expanded set of information rights holders. We finally present a claimholder orientation for business reporting, based on the view that cost-bearing parties have information rights in companies. This is a more fundamental right to information than is asserted by the stakeholder model, which only posits an "interest" by affected parties.

The issue to be addressed is whether the orientation of business reporting is consistent with a socially responsible disclosure of information to claimholders. Information rights, broadly conceived, have grown to include many disparate groups whose interests are not clearly reflected in contemporary business reporting. As claimholders' ability to exercise control and influence over business organization resources becomes increasingly nominal, their information rights become increasingly vital.

We invite accounting academics and practitioners to consider the adequacy of the traditional equational model against the claimholder model presented here. Decision usefulness has been labeled the objective of business reporting. But useful to whom? Business reporting and the accounting equation must be more than an expression of an outdated conception of information beneficiaries. The best interests of society will be served by considering the changing nature of information rights with innovative approaches to business reporting. Failure in this regard carries the potential of reducing traditional financial reports to increasing irrelevance. The activities in the 1990s of the AICPA, FASB, and FEI in studying expanded roles of business reporting augur well for broader perspectives on the parties having legitimate information right in companies. And yet this broadening remains as a next step in the development of business reporting.

Our conclusions have important research implications. Specifically, there is a need to: (1) formally identify parties who are information rights holders; (2) model the relations between resources and claimholders from an information rights perspective at both conceptual and applied levels; (3) develop multiple methods for presenting information; (4) establish cost/benefit disclosure criteria for consideration by regulatory authorities in addressing the information rights of all claimholders; and (5) correspondingly broaden the scope of financial reports. Such efforts will enhance the business reporting process and product by facilitating a reorientation that acknowledges all of a business organization's claimholders, and that will establish a dynamic and flexible basis for the profession to address the changing set of claimholders in the twenty-first century.

ACKNOWLEDGMENTS

We gratefully acknowledge helpful comments from Tony Tinker, Barbara Merino, Lee Parker, Jesse Dillard, and Wai Fong Chua. An earlier version of this paper was presented at a national meeting of the American Accounting Association.

NOTES

1. By "business reporting" we mean the broader notion of corporation communications with investors and other parties, as developed by the AICPA Special Committee on Financial Reporting (AICPA 1994).

2. Since the issue of accounting and explicit, formal contracting has been addressed extensively in other research, this study focuses on information rights even when such contracts do not exist.

3. By formal, we simply mean contracts that are explicitly or implicitly negotiated and agreed to by the contracting parties. These contracts may be written or oral.

4. Rousseau writes extensively about the idea of a social contract. Generally, a social contract may be thought of as a social welfare association comprised of a set of laws, traditions, common practices, and ethics which bind some group of individuals together.

5. In public accounting, this occured as a result of the Ultramares case.

6. For example in Beshada vs. Johns-Manville Prods. Corp., 90 NJ 191, 447 A.2d 539 (1982).

7. There are, obviously, many other ways that property rights can be acquired or transferred, including by gift.

8. The Sierra Club's suit claimed standing in the case based on "a special interest in the conservation and sound maintenance of the national parks, game refuges, and forests," and further invoked

certain judicial review provisions applicable when parties are injured by action of a government agency (in this case the Forest Service and the Department of the Interior). The District Court accepted the Sierra Club's standing, but standing was rejected on appeal by the Ninth Circuit Court of Appeals.

9. The author's omission of bondholders or other creditors is presumably a mere oversight.
10. Or for that matter resources.

REFERENCES

Accounting Standards Steering Committee. 1975. *The Corporate Report*. London: ICAEW.

Adams, R. 1992. Green reporting and the consumer movement. In *Green Reporting*, ed. D. Owen. London: Chapman & Hall.

American Institute of Certified Public Accountants (AICPA). 1994. *Report of the Special Committee on Financial Reporting; "Jenkins Committee Report."* New York: AICPA.

American Institute of Certified Public Accountants (AICPA). 1996. *Accounting Standards Committee's SOP No. 96-1: Environmental Remediation Liabilities*. New York: AICPA.

American Institute of Certified Public Accountants (AICPA). 1977. *Social Measurement*. New York: AICPA.

Ansoff, I. 1965. *Corporate Strategy*. New York: McGraw Hill.

Arthur Andersen & Co. 1989. Postretirement benefits other than pensions: Business and social issues and the FASB exposure draft. *Arthur Andersen Newsletter* 15(1), March.

Benn, H. 1992. Green negotiating: The MSF approach. In *Green Reporting*, ed. D. Owen. London: Chapman & Hall.

Berle, A., and G. Means. 1932. *The Modern Corporation and Private Property*. New York: MacMillan.

Bloom, R., 1981. The ideas of Stuart Chase: Pioneer social accountant and economist. Working Paper No. 52, Academy of Accounting Historians.

Bruyn, S.T. 1987. *The Field of Social Investment*. New York: Cambridge University Press.

Clark, J.M. 1923. *Studies in the Economics of Overhead Costs*. Chicago: University of Chicago Press.

Coase, R.H. 1960. The problem of social cost. *The Journal of Law & Economics* October: 1–44.

Cooter, R., and T. Ulen. 1988. *Law and Economics*. Glenview IL: Scott, Foresman & Co.

Cornell, B., and A.C. Shapiro. 1987. Corporate stakeholders and corporate finance. *Financial Management* Spring: 5–14.

Financial Accounting Standards Board (FASB). 1990. *Financial Accounting Statement 106: Employers' Accounting for Postretirement Beneftis Other Than Pensions*. Stamford, CT: FASB.

Financial Accounting Standards Board (FASB). 1978. *Statement of Financial Accounting Concepts 1*. Stamford, CT: FASB.

Financial Accounting Standards Board (FASB). 1975. *Financial Accounting Statement 5: Accounting For Contingencies*. Stamford, CT: FASB.

Furobotn, E.G., and S. Pejovich. 1974. Property rights and economic theory: Some basic issues. In *The Economics of Property Rights*, eds. E.G. Furobotn and S. Pejovich, 1–10. Cambridge, MA: Ballinger Publishing Co.

Goodpaster, K.E., and G. Atkinson. 1992. Shareholders, individual rights, and the common good. *Phi Kappa Phi Journal* Winter: 14–17.

Grant, L. 1992. Activists hope to redesign corporate structure. *The Cleveland Plain Dealer* November 3: 8F.

Gray, R.H. 1990. *The Greening of Accounting: The Profession After Pearce*. London: Chartered Association of Certified Accountants.

Gray, R.H. 1992. Accounting and environmentalism: An exploration of the challenge of gently accounting for accountability, transparency, and sustainability. *Accounting Organizations and Society* July: 399–425.

Henderson, H.D. 1978. Do corporations have a responsibility to society? In *Accounting and Corporate Social Responsibility*, ed. L.A. Gordon, 9-16. Lawrence, KS: University of Kansas.

Hendriksen, E. 1982. *Accounting Theory*. Homewood, IL: Irwin.

Hines, R. 1991. On valuing nature. *Accounting, Auditing, and Accountability* 4(3).

Ing, B. 1992. Developing green reporting systems: Some practical implications. In *Green Reporting*, ed. D. Owen. London: Chapman and Hall.

Lester, K. 1992. Protecting the environment: A new managerial responsibility. In *Green Reporting*, ed. D. Owen. London: Chapman and Hall.

Littleton, A.C. 1933. *Accounting Evolution to 1900*. New York: American Institute Publishing Company.

Locke, J. 1998 [1688]. *Two Treatises on Government*. Cambridge: Cambridge University Press.

Maunders, K.T., and R.L. Burritt. 1991. Accounting and ecological crisis. *Accounting, Auditing, and Accountability* 4(3).

McGuire, J.W. 1963. *Business and Society*. New York: McGraw Hill.

Milne, M.J. 1991. Accounting, environmental resource values, and non-market valuation techniques for environmental resources: A review. *Accounting, Auditing, and Accountability* 4(3).

National Association of Accountants' (NAA) Committee on Accounting for Corporate Social Performance. 1974. Accounting for corporate social performance. Management Accounting February: 39–41.

Owens, D. 1992. The implications of current trends in green awareness for the accounting function: An introductory analysis. In *Green Reporting*, ed. D. Owen. London: Chapman and Hall.

Paton, W. 1922. *Accounting Theory*. New York: Ronald Press.

Patten, D M. 1992. Intra-industry environmental disclosure in response to the Alaskan oil spill: A note on legitimacy theory. *Accounting Organizations and Society* July: 471–475.

Pearce, D., A. Markandya, and E.B. Barbier. 1989. *Blueprint for a Green Economy*. London: Earthscan Publications Ltd.

Powell, R. 1977. *The Law of Real Property*. New York: Matthew Bender & Co.

Power, M. 1991. Auditing and environmental expertise: Between protest and professionalisation. *Accounting, Auditing, and Accountability* 4(3).

Previts, G.J., and B. Merino. 1998. *A History of Accountancy in The United States*. Columbus, OH: The Ohio State University.

Ramanathan, K.V. 1978. Accounting for the social costs of business: An entry market-based approach. In *Accounting and Corporate Social Responsibility*, ed. L.A. Gordon, 17–34. Lawrence, KS: University of Kansas.

Ramanathan, K.V. 1976. Toward a theory of corporate social accounting. *The Accounting Review* July: 516–528.

Roberts, R.W. 1992. Determinants of corporate social responsibility disclosure: An application of stakeholder theory. *Accounting Organizations and Society* July: 595–612.

Rubenstein, P.B. 1992. Bridging the gap between green accounting and black ink. *Accounting Organizations and Society* July: 501–508.

Scott, DR. 1976. [1931]. *The Cultural Significance of Accounts* Lawrence KS: Scholars Book Co.

Scott, W.B. 1977. In pursuit of happiness: American conceptions of property from the seventeenth to the twentieth century. Bloomington, IN: Indiana University Press.

Senge, S.V. 1993. Accounting for the environment. *The Ohio CPA Journal* February: 33–40.

Smith, R.B. 1991. Right to know. *The Wall Street Journal* January 2: 1, 8.

Sprague, C.E. 1880. The algebra of accounts. *The Book-Keeper* July: 2–4.

Tinker, A.M., and E.A. Lowe. 1980. A rationale for corporate social reporting theory and evidence from organizational research. *Journal of Business, Finance, and Accounting* 7(1): 1–16.

Tinker, A.M., and D. Ghicas. 1992. Dishonored contracts: Accounting and the expropriation of employee pension wealth. Working paper, Baruch College.

USC Study Group. 1990. *Setting Financial Accounting Standards for the Twenty-First Century.* Working paper, University of Southern California.

Yamey, B.S. 1950. Scientific bookkeeping and the rise of capitalism. *In Studies in Accounting,* ed W.T. Baxter, 13–30. London: Sweet and Maxwell.

Zeff, S. 1978. [1961]. *A Critical Examination of the Orientation Postulate in Accounting*. New York: Arno Press.

IMPROVING AUDIT COMMITTEE EFFECTIVENESS

Gregory J. Jonas and Stephen J. Young

ABSTRACT

Concepts such as board accountability and audit committee effectiveness are increasingly becoming topics of discussion and the subject of corporate governance studies and surveys. In 1998, Arthur Andersen commissioned a study of audit committee best practices. In this paper, we share the results of that study by identifying the ten key areas of audit committee responsibility and the best practices associated with each.

In today's corporate environment, concepts such as board accountability and effectiveness are increasingly topics of discussion and the subject of corporate governance studies and surveys. The highly publicized Caremark International case has, in the minds of many, expanded the role of directors in the area of corporate compliance with regulatory matters. We dwell here on one crucial party in the governance process—audit committees—and how audit committees can be made more effective.

Research in Accounting Regulation, Volume 13, pages 231-240.

ISBN: 0-7623-0520-7

Recently, Arthur Levitt, Chairman of the SEC, announced the formation of a "blue ribbon" task force to study audit committee effectiveness. That task force has just issued its report. Its recommendations, if they are implemented, will require many corporations to rethink the nature and responsibilities of their audit committees.

Arthur Andersen has long advocated improving the effectiveness of audit committees. In early 1998, we commissioned a study involving personal interviews with more than 20 seasoned audit committee members and some senior Andersen partners with extensive public-company audit experience. What we found was a surprising consensus on the ten key areas of responsibility that make an effective audit committee. The findings of our study are broadly consistent with the recommendations of the blue ribbon task force.

In the remainder of this article, we share the ten key areas of responsibility we identified, and the "best practices" associated with each. We hope that members of the financial reporting community will find our research helpful as they consider the recommendations of the blue ribbon task force.

BEST PRACTICES FOR AUDIT COMMITTEES

Developing an Effective Audit Committee Charter/Mandate

The audit committee has a written charter, tailored to the company environment, clearly indicating committee duties and responsibilities. This charter is reviewed and approved carefully by the board of directors and challenged and updated periodically by the committee/board.

Best Practices

- Define the background and experience requirements for committee members.
- Define the committee's authority and *specific* responsibilities, particularly those relative to business and financial risk identification and related controls, compliance with laws and regulations, and oversight of internal and external audit activities.
- Set guidelines for the committee's relationships and meetings with members of the management team, internal and external auditors, and others, as appropriate.
- Set the frequency and general timing of meetings, allowing adequate time for preparation of substantive reporting to the full board.
- Define the committee's accountability and reporting requirements to the board and to the shareholders.

- Provide the authority for access to internal and external resources as the committee may require.
- Review the charter with, and obtain input from, appropriate members of management, auditors, and counsel.

Selecting, Orienting, and Updating Audit Committee Members

The size of the audit committee is typically between three and five independent directors. Members and the committee chairman are appointed by the board or nominating committee. The committee's knowledge and effectiveness are enhanced by a strong orientation program for new members, timely access to focused, relevant information, and adequate meeting time for discussion and sharing of views.

Best Practices—Selection of Members

- Maintain committee continuity but also provide fresh perspective through the selection process.
- Look for certain key qualities in candidates, including:
  - knowledge of the company's industry segment;
  - good listener, inquisitive, and tough-minded;
  - financial reporting or auditing background (in at least one member);
  - experience in business and financial risk management;
  - international background and experience, if applicable; and
  - available time to serve.
- The committee chairman meets with potential candidates to discuss roles, responsibilities, levels of interest, and qualifications.
- Select a chairman who is knowledgeable of the duties and responsibilities of the position; has the requisite industry, business, financial, and leadership skills; and is a good builder of relationships.

Best Practices—Orienting and Updating Members

New members. Meet with committee chairman and jointly agree on specific orientation and education needs.

  - Receive tailored information about the company's:
  - business and industry;
  - key business and financial risks and risk control processes;
  - important legal and regulatory requirements; and
  - code of ethical conduct.
- Meet with CEO/CFO and, as necessary, internal and external auditors, to get the background on key business and financial risks, accounting principles, and other relevant matters.

All members. Routinely receive highly focused information about:

- important, relevant industry issues, developments, and trends;
- key financial and other performance indicators;
- significant and relevant proposed changes in financial reporting and regulatory requirements; and
- other ongoing business risk matters as determined by the committee.

- Participate, over time, in in-depth discussions of business processes to manage risk, such as:
  - risk management;
  - regulatory compliance; and
  - company-specific "vital few" key processes.
- Selectively have committee members make periodic visits to new or troubled locations, meet with local management, and then report to the full committee.
- Attend relevant outside seminars and share information at subsequent committee meetings.

Influencing the Overall Corporate "Tone" for Quality Financial Reporting, Sound Business Risk Controls, and Ethical Behavior

The committee strongly influences the overall company financial reporting and regulatory compliance environment. This influence is apparent in the committee charter. More importantly, relationships and communications between management and the full board reflect, beyond the "form," to the committee members the attitudes toward and substance of their role.

Best Practices

- Be visible—communicate the committee's role and expectations in a positive, constructive light to relevant groups within the company and in relevant internal publications.
- Meet periodically with key management, internal and external auditors, and compliance staff to understand the company control environment and important regulatory issues.
- Assess management's attitude toward the internal audit function. Consider input from operating management.
- Review, approve, and continuously assess the code of ethical conduct.
- Review and assess the company's processes for administering a code of ethical conduct, disseminating and explaining it to all employees, providing relevant employee training, monitoring compliance, and enforcing disciplinary actions.

- Maintain ongoing interaction with management. Encourage senior management to involve other management team members in committee meetings to more fully understand committee *values*.
- Report to shareholders annually on committee responsibilities and activities.

Planning and Conduct of Committee Meetings/Agenda

The audit committee effectively uses valuable meeting time through solid planning by the chairman, advance distribution of relevant materials/information, and a highly focused agenda. The relevance, value, and overall quality of each meeting is benefited by a proactive chairman, and pre-meeting discussions with management and other meeting participants to assure proper focus, meeting time allocation, and necessary actions.

Best Practices

- Chairman meets annually, outside normal meeting times, with management and internal/external auditors to:
  - clearly agree on mutual expectations;
  - agree on an annual detailed plan of committee activities; and
  - agree on the nature, extent, and timing of committee information needs.
- Chairman reviews and agrees upon meeting agenda in advance of its distribution to committee members and others.
- Distribute meeting agenda and selective and focused pre-read materials at least one week in advance of meetings.
- Manage meeting agenda to assure:
  - significant time for committee member questions and open dialogue;
  - a focus on discussion of important business and financial risks and related controls, qualitative aspects of financial reporting, and potential future issues;
  - adequate time for regular, private, committee-only discussions with internal and external auditors; and
  - substantive discussion of "required" external auditor communications.

Reviewing the Internal and External Auditors' Risk Assessments and Overall Audit Plans

The audit committee reaches a common understanding with management and auditors about the company's business risk management process, key business and financial risks, and related controls. The committee understands the focus of the internal and external audit plans, the logic behind such planning, and provides appropriate input based on committee member insight and experience.

Best Practices

General. Review and assess the company's business risk management process with management and internal/external auditors.

- Review and assess internal/external auditors' responsibility for detecting accounting and financial reporting errors, fraud and defalcations, illegal acts, and non-compliance with the corporate code of conduct and regulatory requirements.
- Monitor the *coordination* of internal/external audit efforts, focusing on solid audit coverage of key business and financial risk areas and related risk controls, without duplication of effort.

External audit. Review the overall scope and focus of the annual audit. Consider input from management and the internal audit. Request expansions, as appropriate.

- Review and assess audit scope and level of auditor responsibility regarding unaudited quarterly or other interim-period information.
- Review and understand the auditors' assessment of financial statement materiality.

Internal audit. Review and approve the internal auditors' charter and relate it to committee expectations.

- Review the process for establishing the annual internal audit plan and the focus on risk.
- Review and assess the annual audit plan with management and internal auditors, recognizing the need to balance financial and operational auditing. Ask for input from external auditors.

Risk Controls—Monitoring Company Processes for Management's Identification and Control of Key Business, Financial, and Regulatory Risk

The committee thoroughly understands the company's key business and financial reporting risks, and focuses on the reasonableness of control processes to manage such risks.

Best Practices

- Periodically review the adequacy of the company's overall control environment. Consider views of management, auditors, and others, as appropriate, with particular emphasis on:
  - management's attitudes about controls;
  - key policy matters, documentation, and internal communication;

  - adequacy of key management and audit committee information, particularly key performance indicators;
  - focus and timeliness of financial and other information for management and the board; and
  - timeliness and substance of management response to important internal/external auditor control recommendations.
- Meet with management and internal/external auditors to fully understand and assess management's response (and auditors' views) to controlling important key risk situations.
- Focus very specifically on the adequacy of key controls over those *vital few* risks considered to be, currently or in the future, more significant and more likely to occur.
- Inquire of management and auditors about the "root causes" of any significant year-end financial adjustments with a focus on the need to improve financial controls and the reliability of interim reporting.

Financial Reporting—Monitoring the Integrity and Quality of Annual and Interim Financial Reporting to Stakeholders

The committee reviews all annual and interim financial reports to stakeholders with particular emphasis on the accuracy and completeness of information and key disclosures, changes from prior reporting periods, and important judgment questions that will have an impact on the overall integrity of the information.

Best Practices

- Establish appropriate processes and protocols for the timing and extent of the committee's review of financial information, including the quality of disclosures (i.e., press releases, broker and institutional investor briefings, interim reports, statutory filings, annual report). Each company is unique; however, committee members generally review the annual and quarterly reports before release. Consider:
  - the current and prospective financial health of the company;
  - the depth and quality of the company's processes for management review of this information;
  - the degree of involvement of the internal and external auditors before financial information is released;
  - the nature, and perceived magnitude, of risks involved in disclosure issues; and
  - the company's history and experience regarding accuracy and completeness of financial reports.

- Review and approve important company accounting principles, and changes therein, and their method of application to both annual and interim financial reports.
- Assess alternative accounting principles that are proposed or considered.
- Meet with management and external auditors to fully understand and assess all key financial statement issues and risks, the impact or potential future impact on reported financial information, the processes used by management to address such matters, and the basis for auditors' conclusions. Consider, in particular:
  - important management judgments and accounting estimates;
  - unusual transactions, including matters that involve related parties;
  - asserted and unasserted litigation and claims; and
  - instances of noncompliance or possible noncompliance with laws and regulations.
- Review and assess the results of governmental or other regulatory audits.
- Discuss auditors' views on the overall quality of the company's internal and external financial reporting, including:
  - the "appropriateness" of important accounting principles, particularly revenue recognition and asset valuation;
  - comparison with industry or other peer company practices; and
  - annual report—"management discussion and analysis."
- Understand and assess company processes and policies for communication with institutional investors, analysts, and brokers.
- Review quarterly teleconference communications between management and the investor community (audio tapes are made available to committee members as a common practice).
- Meet periodically with the company officer responsible for investor relations. Understand the investor community's overall views and concerns about the company.

Compliance—Monitoring Compliance with the Corporate Code of Conduct and Regulatory Requirements, and Reviewing and Assessing Conflicts of Interest and Related-Party Transactions

The audit committee understands the overall environment, relevant laws, and regulations of particular significance to the company, and the company program to provide reasonable assurance of compliance. The audit committee acts, as designated in the charter, on illegal acts, reported conflicts of interest, and related-party transactions.

Best Practices

- Interact with the CEO, CFO, compliance officer, and others, as appropriate, to review and understand the laws and regulations having the most significant impact on the company.
- Meet periodically with counsel to understand changing regulations, the potential impact on the company, and management's control response.
- Review and assess the compliance monitoring programs that are in place within the company. Consider the input of auditors, counsel, and compliance officer, as appropriate.
- Review and assess auditors' responsibility for detecting noncompliance with the code of conduct and regulatory requirements, and for detection of illegal acts.
- Noncompliance—Obtain periodic updates from counsel and other parties responsible for monitoring compliance with laws, regulations, and code of conduct, and review management disposition of *all* instances of noncompliance.
- Review, assess, and approve significant conflict-of-interest and related-party transactions, as well as current violations and issues, if any.
- Taxes—Meet periodically with those responsible for income tax and other significant tax-related compliance. Periodically meet with external tax advisors to review, understand, and assess important tax issues and related judgments.
- Monitor audits/examinations by governmental or other regulatory agencies.

Assessing Internal and External Auditor Performance

The audit committee periodically focuses on the performance of internal and external auditors and their responsiveness to committee needs and expectations. The committee recommends external auditor selection or reappointment to the board of directors/shareholders.

The external auditor's role, in a publicly held company, is to serve the shareholders through the board of directors and audit committee. In most situations, the internal auditor's role also includes some level of reporting and assistance to the audit committee.

Best Practices

- Maintain a direct line of communication with internal and external auditors, including periodic informal contact by the committee chairman.
- Understand the role of other partners (tax, concurring, advisory) involved in the external audit, and request their periodic involvement at audit committee meetings.

- Committee chairman meets periodically with management and internal and external auditors to review and agree on mutual expectations.
- Annually request management and committee member views on internal and external audit performance against committee criteria and expectations.
- Set aside time, at least annually, to discuss and assess overall auditor effectiveness, objectivity, and independence. Review committee assessment with management.
- Review the nature of all services performed by external auditors and the potential impact, if any, on the independence of the external auditors. Consider the relative magnitude of fees and the engagement personnel involved.
- The committee chairman should meet annually with internal and external auditors and review the committee overall performance assessment.
- Review and approve any personnel change in the director of internal audit position.
- Recommend the external auditor selection or reappointment to the board of directors/shareholders.
- Concur with the external audit fee arrangements, while gaining reasonable assurance of a complete audit.

Assessing Audit Committee Performance

The committee periodically assesses its own performance, considering the effective use of committee time, responsiveness to the board-approved charter, and the effectiveness of relationships and communications with management, auditors, and the full board.

Best Practices

- Solicit informal feedback from the board, CEO, CFO, and external auditors on specific opportunities to improve overall committee effectiveness.
- Complete a self-assessment process at least every two years and review the results with the board of directors, top management, and auditors.
- Assess the contribution and performance of individual committee members (this should be done periodically by the committee chairman) for review with the chairman of the board and the CEO.
- Consult with external auditors and others on how audit committee best practices relate to committee practices, and institute appropriate change.

ACKNOWLEDGMENT

This work is reprinted by permission from Arthur Andersen LLP. No material from this chapter may be reproduced without the prior written permission of Arthur Andersen LLP.

REGULATION OF HEDGE FUNDS: THE BAILOUT OF LONG-TERM CAPITAL MANAGEMENT

Roman M. Fatkhiyev and Kyle M. Hannaford

ABSTRACT

The expanding presence of hedge funds in the global capital markets has raised concerns over the virtually unregulated condition of these funds. This has become even more apparent after the near-collapse and subsequent rescue of one of the most successful hedge funds, Long-Term Capital Management, in September 1998. However, as a result of the government-initiated bailout, American investors are left with unanswered questions regarding the government's role in the marketplace and the future direction of federal regulatory authority. While some market participants, especially lenders, have already begun to impose restrictions voluntarily on the activities of hedge funds in the wake of the LTCM crisis, greater government involvement in this area is still likely.

Research in Accounting Regulation, Volume 13, pages 241-246.

ISBN: 0-7623-0520-7

BACKGROUND

Hedge funds have become major participants in the global economy recently, investing trillions of dollars in the market each year. As with similar large institutional investors, hedge funds add depth to the capital markets by increasing liquidity and linking the markets together. Yet, accurate information about hedge funds is difficult to obtain, because they are only partially regulated. This scarcity of information regarding their financial conditions and operations, along with the risky and aggressive actions taken by some larger funds lately, has raised concerns about the impact these funds could have on the stability of the U.S. financial market. The recent crisis involving Long-Term Capital Management LP (LTCM) has only intensified these concerns (Lindsay 1998).

LONG-TERM CAPITAL MANAGEMENT

Begun in 1994 as an investment partnership, LTCM exhibits many of the characteristics of a typical hedge fund. The company attracts capital from wealthy investors, and then borrows money to leverage the capital. LTCM's investment strategy involves the use of complex mathematical formulas—developed in part by the two Nobel laureates, Myron S. Scholes and Robert C. Merton, who co-founded the fund—to identify temporary price discrepancies between financial instruments. For example, the firm might determine that the current yield on corporate bonds relative to Treasury bonds is higher than the range observed in recent years. If LTCM managers believe the former relationship will reassert itself, the fund will purchase corporate bonds and sell short Treasury bonds. If the spread between yields narrows as expected, the firm will profit. If the spread continues to widen, however, the company will incur losses. LTCM uses this basic strategy and several variations of it on numerous interest rate products in the U.S. market and abroad. Plus, the company trades actively in both traditional securities and, more importantly, in derivative products such as futures, swaps, and options. This strategy of diversification across product lines and geographic markets allows the firm to absorb the losses incurred when some positions move against the fund, with the gains realized when other positions move in its favor. As a result, in both 1995 and 1996, LTCM was able to generate substantial returns in excess of 40 percent.

THE BAILOUT

Although the company enjoyed initial success, LTCM soon realized how quickly the market turns. By 1998, the firm had assumed riskier positions by leveraging the fund's investments at even higher levels. While the company was able to return capital to its investors, it was unable to reduce its risk exposure. This became even more apparent as the firm took on dangerous positions in both swaps and options contracts. The reputation of LTCM's partners as accomplished traders and economists, bolstered by their initial success, no doubt contributed to the willingness of lenders to continue dealing with the company despite its uncertain standing.

Then, on August 17, 1998, the Russian government announced a devaluation of the ruble and declared a debt moratorium—an event that shook investor confidence throughout the world. The global markets began moving sharply against LTCM's positions. In a letter issued to investors on September 2, the partners acknowledged a 52 percent loss on the year through August 31, with $4.4 billion of losses occurring in just six weeks, and stated that they were seeking an injection of capital to sustain the fund. Management's efforts proved unsuccessful, so on September 18, the Federal Reserve Bank of New York, along with the Federal Reserve Chairman and Secretary, announced their decision to intervene in the LTCM crisis. The failure of the fund itself would be unpleasant, but of even greater concern to the Federal Reserve was the effect it could have on the global capital markets. LTCM was highly leveraged at that time, with a debt to equity ratio of 50:1 (McDonough 1998). Plus, several funds had made the same investments as LTCM. In the view of federal regulators, the company's inability to pay its debts could have caused a chain reaction in the markets with potentially catastrophic results. The Federal Reserve Bank organized a bailout by securing $3.5 billion of additional private investments in the fund by a consortium of 14 leading banks and securities houses, including Chase Manhattan, J.P. Morgan, Goldman Sachs, and Merrill Lynch (Anonymous 1998a).

Prior to the LTCM bailout, the U.S. monetary authorities had never resorted to the use of this "convoy system" to protect financial institutions. In fact, the Federal Reserve had been critical of bailouts by its counterpart institutions in nations like Japan (Yomiuri 1998a). The bailout of LTCM therefore raises several questions. If the U.S. is a free market economy, how can a bailout of this nature be explained? If the federal government organized a bailout for LTCM, can American investors expect similar actions for other funds? If public companies and mutual funds are required to make certain disclosures to investors, why are hedge funds exempt from such requirements?

DISCUSSION OF ISSUES

An inherent activity of hedge funds is betting on future currency exchange rates. While intricate formulas can be applied to support a certain position, ultimately, there is always a winner and a loser. In the case of these interest rate bets, LTCM was betting against the governments of other countries (Yomiuri 1998b). When LTCM lost its bets, the firm used the argument that it was "too big to fail" to justify the government-organized rescue. The Federal Reserve's action sends a clear message to the very foreign governments it has denounced for subsidizing their own nations' financial institutions—namely, that the U.S. government is not opposed to sustaining domestic financial institutions in the event of a possible collapse. As a result, the bailout of LTCM has prompted a backlash of criticism in certain countries. The Malaysian Prime Minister, Dr. Mahathir Mohammad, for example, asserted that the bailout of LTCM amounted to nothing less than governmental corruption, and the "...worst form of cronyism." He continued, "By using the banks' money to rescue LTCM, they were using the banks' money to rescue their own investments" (Yomiuri 1998c).

However, there is no question that the U.S. government should protect the interests of American investors as its primary responsibility. The Federal Reserve Chairman, Alan Greenspan, indicated that the bailout was intended to protect the U.S. capital market rather than LTCM (Greenspan 1998). But the fairness of that action from the perspective of other investors remains in doubt. Some important officials at the banks and investment companies that contributed to the bailout held extensive personal investments in LTCM. This apparent conflict of interest is clearly evident in the case of Merrill Lynch, which contributed $300 million for the bailout. Merrill Lynch CEO David Komansky had $800,000 invested in LTCM through a fund of funds in his deferred compensation plan. All together, Merrill Lynch executives at the time of the bailout had $22 million invested in LTCM through the same plan (Spiro and Woolley 1998).

The bailout of LTCM raises an important question. Generally, federal regulatory bodies such as the SEC favor policies that protect investors who hold long positions in securities, and reject policies that would protect investors who hold short positions. While this practice is based on the rationale of promoting stability within the capital market for the benefit of the investing public, it conflicts with the efficient market theory view that investors should be free to exercise their own discretion in holding securities. The LTCM bailout, therefore, represents an interesting change in the government's traditional policy. It is the first time that the federal government rescued a fund that held short positions in securities. Whether this is an indication of what the government's future approach toward the market will be remains to be seen. At least in this instance, however, it appears to be a complete departure from the widely-accepted belief that the government should protect the public interest by discouraging short securities.

The recent developments concerning the deregulation of the financial industry highlight another important issue. During the chaotic period of the early 1930s, one of the most important factors in stabilizing the U.S. economy was the Glass–Steagal Act. This act separated banking functions from the activities of investment houses by prohibiting banks from investing in securities. Lately, however, the increased merger activity between banks and investment companies indicates the government's relaxed commitment to federal regulation of banking activities. As a result, several banks were able to hold substantial investments in LTCM prior to its near collapse, and banks have since played a major role in its bailout. This fact has important implications for the future health of the financial market. The public tends to hold unreasonably high expectations for the growth and stability of the capital markets, and relies on the government to ensure this stability. While the Glass-Steagal Act was at one time instrumental in preventing significant crashes in the U.S. financial system, the current state of deregulation suggests that the public's expectations for the financial markets may be unfounded.

Finally, the LTCM crisis presents certain ethical problems. In the midst of the market slaughter that sent LTCM and its creditors to the brink of catastrophe, a principal partner and founder of LTCM, John Meriwether, was still able to arrange matters to protect his personal assets. On August 27, just prior to the company's announcement of its financial trouble, Meriwether signed an "interpersonal transfer grant deed" to transfer a 20-acre vacant lot in the exclusive residential community of Pebble Beach, California, to his wife. This was the only property still remaining in his name by that date. A *Business Week* examination of public records indicates that to protect his property from creditors, Meriwether had shielded his own assets, as the other partners had, in the event that LTCM ever collapsed. In a similar vein, four LTCM principals had borrowed money to finance their investments in the fund, so they had little personal investment at stake (Weiss, Silverbush, and Stevens 1998; Day 1999). Clearly, although the bailout has left the partners with a large, though undisclosed amount of losses, their personal liability had been kept to a minimum. With the limited personal exposure these individuals had, then, the likelihood for moral hazard in the management of LTCM was high.

AFTERMATH

As a consequence of the LTCM crisis, the U.S. Congress in late 1998 ordered the President's Working Group (made up of the Treasury, Federal Reserve, SEC, and Commodity Futures Trading Commission), to investigate the need for additional regulation in the hedge funds industry. The SEC's Office of Compliance, Inspections, and Examinations began a comprehensive study of several major brokerage firms to analyze their exposure to hedge funds (Anonymous 1998b). In addition, the House banking committee took action in early 1999 to study the hedge fund issue from the lending side, with the likelihood for new legislation on the matter (Wolffe and Corrigan 1999). Since many hedge funds are located offshore, the federal government recognizes the difficulty in asserting direct regulatory authority. As a result, regulating the banks that lend to hedge funds appears to be the most feasible method for indirectly regulating the activities of the funds. Although the Federal Reserve has issued several recommendations for banks dealing with hedge funds, it has failed to institute any specific rules yet (Pacelle 1999). Still, many creditors have deliberately begun demanding greater disclosure from the hedge funds they lend to, and imposing limits on the amount of leverage a hedge fund is permitted. In light of a possible move toward expanded government regulation of banks' lending practices, these institutions will undoubtedly continue to assume a role of private oversight within the hedge fund industry.

REFERENCES

Anonymous. 1998a. A $3.5 billion tranquilizer. *Business Week* (October 5): 42.

Anonymous. 1998b. SEC to examine some firms over hedge-fund dealings. *The Wall Street Journal* (November 19): B12.

Day, K. 1999. Two at long-term capital retire as active partners. *The WashingtonPost* (February 3): E3.

Greenspan, A. 1998. Hedge fund activities in the U.S. financial markets. In *House of Representatives: Testimony before the House Committee on Banking and Financial Services*, Washington, DC, October 1. Available at www.hedgefunds.net.

Lindsey, R.R. 1998. Hedge fund activities in the U.S. financial markets. In *House of Representatives: Testimony before the House Committee on Banking and Financial Services*, Washington, DC, October 1. Available at www.hedgefunds.net.

McDonough, W.J. 1998. Hedge fund activities in the U.S. financial markets. In *House of Representatives: Testimony before the House Committee on Banking and Financial Services*, Washington, DC, October 1. Available at www.hedgefunds.net

Pacelle, M. 1999. Hedge funds face tougher times: As Ellington's Vranos discovers, less leverage and more scrutiny pose new challenges for managers. *The Wall Street Journal* (February 12): C1.

Spiro, L.N., and S. Woolley. 1998. The rescue: What you need to know. *Wall Street* (October 12): 38.

Weiss, G., B. Silverbush, and K. Stevens. 1998. Meriwether's Curious Deed. *Business Week* (October 19): 145.

Wolffe, R., and T. Corrigan. 1999. U.S. Congress Plans Moves to Limit Risks from Hedge Funds. *Financial Times* (March 2): 16.

Yomiuri, J. 1998a. Crisis clarifies risky operations of hedge funds. *The Daily Yomiuri* (October): 1.

Yomiuri, J. 1998b. August raid on HK dollar and stocks. *The Straits Times* (October 27): 48.

Yomiuri, J. 1998c. Dr. M.: LTCM bailout is worst form of cronyism. *New Straits Times* (October 31): 2.

PART IV

BOOK REVIEWS

ACCOUNTING SERVICES AND GROWTH IN SMALL ECONOMIES: EVIDENCE FROM THE CARIBBEAN BASIN

by David L. McKee, Don E. Garner, and Yosra AbuAmara McKee

(Westport, CT: Quorum Books, 1998, $59.95, 184 pp.)

Reviewed by **Oscar Holzmann**

Accounting Services and Growth in Small Economies: Evidence from the Caribbean Basin is divided into four major sections (or Parts), each of which includes three chapters. Part I, entitled, "The General Frame of Reference," provides the broad context for the rest of the book. Its first chapter, "International Services as Facilitators," discloses the importance of externally provided services as components of a nation's GNP and in the international economy in general. Large and effective service providers in many areas of business have favorably affected the movement towards increased outsourcing ("externalization") by firms seeking cost efficiencies and access to specialized knowledge and expertise. Various published points of view about the causes of service providers' growth are reviewed,

Research in Accounting Regulation, Volume 13, pages 249-253.

ISBN: 0-7623-0520-7

ranging from direct changes in the service-providing sector (e.g., the substitution of capital for labor along with increases in technology and sophistication), to the view that the size and geographic growth of today's "service chains" is an effect of serving as facilitators for growing clients. These causes for growth have affected all sorts of service providers, including accounting firms.

The second chapter, "Services, External Linkages, and Growth," reviews the contribution of services to the external linkages and growth of nations. The specific geographical setting contemplated is the Caribbean basin (including the Gulf of Mexico), other than the United States. Foreign trade (one would assume tourism is included as a component of trade), direct investments, and technology transfers are critical for the economic development of this area. However, many of the countries in the region lack natural resources, capital, trained manpower, and a significant agricultural or industrial base. Many of their supplies come from the outside world. In addition, given their relatively small populations and low per capita income, it is difficult for businesses to enjoy economies of scale and, accordingly, it is unlikely that they will earn foreign exchange by becoming competitive exporters. Accordingly, it appears that the road to economic progress lies with the development of service-providing businesses and other economic activities that are not subject to increasing returns to scale. Examples of service-providing opportunities being exploited by the Caribbean countries are revealed, for example: offshore offices in Barbados and other areas; container transshipment in Jamaica; and financial centers in the Cayman Islands, Bahamas, Aruba, Barbados, and the British Virgin Islands. The provision of services is an important revenue and employment source for the Caribbean economies, but the demand for these services is external and, therefore, efforts must be made to identify and capture that demand.

"Some Specifics on Accounting Services," the third chapter, completes Part I of the book. The chapter consists of a review of accounting services provided by large accounting firms, which is followed by a discussion of some operating aspects of selected accounting firms. The information presented in these two sections should be familiar to readers who are at least somewhat knowledgeable about the operations of the large, international firms. The chapter closes with the following conclusions about these firms:

- They are very important service providers.
- They have helped to develop a truly global economy by serving as international linkages and facilitating the operations of their clients, both foreign and local, in many locations around the world.
- They contribute to the harmonization of accounting standards and procedures (thereby benefiting the local economies).
- Their operations may also provide training and demonstration effects, thereby further impacting the local businesses culture.

The second major section of the book, Part II, is entitled, "The Role of Accounting Services in the Caribbean Basin." The authors wisely distinguish four major cultural/economic areas in this region of the world: the area more closely influenced by the British, the areas influenced by the French and the Dutch and, finally, the Spanish-speaking nations. The firms operating in the region obviously have to adjust their operations to the mores and various other requirements of the different cultural/economic areas. Part II opens with Chapter 4, "The Accounting Firms In The Commonwealth Caribbean," which is followed by Chapter 5, "The Firms in Selected French and Dutch Jurisdictions," and Chapter 6, "The Firms in the Spanish Caribbean," which include similar reviews of the activities of accounting firms in Dutch, French, and Hispanic jurisdictions. The firms whose activities are primarily described are Arthur Andersen, Deloitte Touche Tohmatsu, and Price Waterhouse. The firms are significantly represented everywhere in the region except in the French Caribbean, where the nature of the small local economies appears not to offer the business opportunities found in the other, more growth-oriented, modern, and generally larger economies. The services they provide run the gamut of their usual consulting services, auditing, and tax; and, as one may expect, their relative magnitudes are affected by the relative importance of the various industries in the local economies.

The main sources of information about the large firms for the chapters in Part II are these firms' own publications. The chapters are well written and interesting, but the discourse remains at a rather general level of description, which is consistent with the authors' speculation that what these firms are doing must have positive effects on the local economies. It's understandable that it is probably impossible to obtain juicier information about these firms' successes and failures, but if it were included, it would enhance the value of these chapters for the accountant reader. As they are, the reader that is generally knowledgeable about accounting firms will find little new information in these chapters. Nonetheless, they represent a valuable integrative description of the work of these firms in the Caribbean region.

Part III is entitled, "Legal and Institutional Parameters for Accounting Practices." It is structured somewhat differently than Part II in that, while it covers the same jurisdictions, the size of the respective economies becomes a relatively important classification criterion. Accordingly, its chapters are: Chapter 7, "Selected Accounting Environments in the Commonwealth Caribbean," Chapter 8, "Accounting Environments in Small Caribbean Economies," and Chpater 9, "Accounting and Reporting in Selected Spanish-Speaking Jurisdictions." On the other hand, the content of these chapters is no longer information about the large accounting firms operations but, rather, an overview of the legal and political climates facing business firms and accounting practices in the various lands of the region. The chapters briefly cover business regulations, forms of organization and operations, as well as financial reporting, auditing and tax requirements, and generally accepted accounting principles for each of a number of countries and territories (including Puerto Rico). In summary, the information in these chapters is very similar to the information that is available in the country-specific booklets provided on demand by the large accounting firms.

The last major section of the book, Part IV, is entitled, "Implications for Growth and Change in the Caribbean Basin." It commences with Chapter 10, "A Summary of Institutional Specifics," the objectives of which are (1) "to examine how effectively existing legal and institutional frameworks serve the jurisdictions concerned," for the purpose of (2) establishing "a better basis for understanding the real and potential impacts that the major accounting firms may be expected to impose." This is hardly accomplished. The major portion of the chapter is mostly an abbreviated recapitulation of the contents of the three preceding chapters (those included in Part III). The conclusion section mainly points out that the various Caribbean jurisdictions have legal systems which provide the parameters within which businesses, including professional services providers, must operate. Naturally, some differences exist among these jurisdictions on these matters, and the wise firms will adjust accordingly. It's hard to see how the chapter's contents and the rather weak and overly general conclusion work to accomplish the stated objectives. Actual examples, war stories, even news-based speculation, etc., might have helped greatly to make this chapter more than just a summary of the previous three chapters.

Chapter 11, "An Overview of Services in the Process of Growth and Change," draws on the findings of many authors to convey the message that economic growth and the development of the service economy go hand-in-hand. Information is an increasing component of the services provided in the international economy. The provision of information-based services represents an opportunity for developing countries who acquire the new communication technologies, and there is evidence that Caribbean countries are exploiting this opportunity. The accounting firms are helping their clients and the local economies by promoting linkages with the world economy, and by providing support to local operations, training, and demonstration effects. Part IV and the book end with Chapter 12, "Economic Impacts from Accounting Services in the Caribbean Region." This chapter once again, but with greater brevity, provides a rundown of the activities in the region of some of the major international accounting firms. The firms receiving most coverage are Deloitte Touche Tohmatsu and Price Waterhouse; followed by Arthur Andersen and, much further behind, KPMG Peat Marwick. There is no mention of Coopers or Ernst & Young, and no explanation is given for the variation in the degree of attention given to the various firms.

This book has some limitations. It does not discuss the availability, growth, or evolution of local (native) firms. This book is not a source of original information, but rather a marriage of information published in academic as well as non-academic outlets. The information about the specific firms may also be found, in greater detail, in the various promotional pamphlets distributed by these firms. The information about the broader impact of such firms and the provision of services is based on a multiplicity of published sources. The book seems at times very detached and full of generalities; it often reads like an academic term paper. Although it is well written, it would likely have a much greater punch if it included a more personally involved approach, one that would include views of practitioners and other significant individuals, as well as anecdotal or other first-hand evidence about the peculiarities of operating and growing in these areas.

On the other hand, the book would be useful to anyone looking for one source of general knowledge about the provision of accounting and related services in the Caribbean region by large international accounting firms and the setting in which these firms operate. A major strength is its geographical counterclockwise organization of contents along the major cultural spheres of influence in the area (British, French, Dutch, and Spanish). This highlights major differences and, therefore, provides valuable information to the reader.

SIGNIFICANT CURRENT ISSUES IN INTERNATIONAL TAXATION

by Ahmed Riahi-Belkaoui

(Westport, CT: Quorum Books, 1998, $59.95, 183 pp.)

Reviewed by **Timothy J. Fogarty**

Ahmed Riahi-Belkaoui is the author of an impressively long list of monographs on selected topics in accounting. His latest title for Quorum Books tackles international tax. To my knowledge, this is his first in the tax area.

The book is divided into five general topics, which form its five chapters. The first attempts to discern the fundamental principles of international taxation. The second gives special treatment to the U.S. tax system as it pertains to foreign income. The nature and mechanisms of transfer pricing structures form the author's third major topic. The system of tax incentives for exporting activities is the next concern. The book concludes with an overview of value added taxation, including the prospects for its adoption in the United States. By not focusing on entity structure, types of income, and particular legislative differences, the book purposefully departs in several ways from other materials on international tax.

International taxation has been an area of significant growth in the practice community for the past decade. Unfortunately, the academy has not kept up with

Research in Accounting Regulation, Volume 13, pages 255-257.

ISBN: 0-7623-0520-7

this development. There remains a critical shortage of quality materials that exist to support the limited foray of higher education into this area. Therefore, Belkaoui's book joins a thin market of similar titles.

The book is designed to provide an introduction to some fairly complex topics. However, because it does not see itself as a textbook, it provides only limited numerical illustrations of these concepts. The book also attempts to provide reportage of the current state of affairs through the provision of statistical information. This also proves somewhat problematic, because this objective is only occasionally serviced. The amount of "facts and numbers" that one takes away from reading this book is modest.

To a large extent, the book (either as textbook or treatise) provides decent information about the U.S. perspective only. On more than one occasion, there is a nod to Canada and the United Kingdom. This remains well short of the type of coverage we would have expected. The pivotal role of the Continental European nation-states is rather absent.

The book makes good use of the academic literature, integrating some of the better insights of the empirical tax work. Accordingly, it could be thought of as one of the very few bridging works in the area. Each chapter contains a summary, ample footnotes, and further readings.

The ideal reader of this book would be a person with a tax background that wanted to extend their expertise towards international transactions. The book does not work as a primer on tax for the completely uninitiated. It also is not a very technical effort, and therefore would not be valuable to practitioners who are already immersed in this practice segment. I suspect that the readership will be composed of doctoral students and accounting faculty who are looking for breadth. It would also be appropriate for masters of accountancy students.

Those who are familiar with tax textbooks will find this book rather atypical. For the most part, the analysis does not delve deeper than the guiding statutes. In other words, the dense thicket of regulations and case law is not penetrated. The calculations provided resemble those that would be used in a classroom, that is, purposefully deceptive simplifications. The tax forms that are included in the appendices to three chapters are not well integrated into the analysis. The author does not use them for pedagogical gain. For that matter, a full 32 percent of the text is given over to appendices, including the full text of a 1996 *Journal of Accounting Literature* article.

My reading of this book left me with an curiously empty feeling. First, despite the book's title, I failed to get a clear fix on what the issues in international tax are. This is not to say that there is not considerable and useful clarification of many tax distinctions and concepts. However, the author has failed to stamp sufficient priorities upon the area. Second, there is an unusually high amount of "cut and paste" in the construction of each chapter. Large chunks of the text are abstracted from the academic and practitioner literature. This, together with the liberal use of quotations, substitutes for a more individual and unique analysis. Several lists of advantages and disadvantages, for example, are presented (and cited) in an undigested manner. The book tends to rely rather heavily upon the West Publishing Company's tax texts for technical detail, and upon the 1992 Scholes and Wolfson monograph for its better theoretical insights. The statistics and trends that are documented either already have been, or soon will be, eclipsed by the march of time. Unlike the author's other works, the lack of a distinctive critical edge was also disconcerting.

Notwithstanding its limitations, Belkaoui should be applauded for contributing in a sorely needed area. The book provides a decent introduction to an important, challenging, and often controversial area. Belkaoui has produced a much-needed monograph that services the middle market for international tax information. The book is recommended for those who want a quick way to get on top of the area.

CRITICAL FINANCIAL ACCOUNTING PROBLEMS: ISSUES AND SOLUTIONS

by Ahmed Riahi-Belkaoui

(Westport, CT: Quorum Books, 1998, $65.00, 183 pp.)

Reviewed by **Dwight M. Owsen**

Ahmed Riahi-Belkaoui's new book, "Critical Financial Accounting Problems" promises to aid our students' understanding of the contentious gray areas that send us to the original SFASs to mull over the sometimes contradictory phrases of the growing standards explosion. This almost malevolent expansion of accounting standards has been steadily reducing our class time for teaching the essentials, such as multi-year integrative problems, that mark real practice. Thus, we should welcome Belkaoui's new book which provides a series of simplified illustrations in crucial areas such as leases, income tax allocation, and pensions. These areas have become so complex that we often settle for a mere summary of them, muttering to ourselves that practitioners spend years specializing in these areas. Moreover, unless we have spent years teaching these ideas or have worked with them in our consulting practices, it is very likely that the subtleties concerning these areas will escape us. Finally, his book assists us in deciding which aspects

Research in Accounting Regulation, Volume 13, pages 259-261.

ISBN: 0-7623-0520-7

of important topics are crucial for students to learn and thus need our particular attention when we lecture.

Belkaoui, a prolific author and co-author with at least 42 books published by the Greenwich group, organizes his 185 pages into eight chapters covering long-term liabilities, stockholders' equity including contributed capital and retained earnings, investments, income taxes, pensions, leases, segmental reporting, and foreign currency transactions and futures contracts. It also includes a brief but very useful index, with topics chosen to reflect how students and practitioners conceive of and label topics.

The book focuses on procedures, and there is little of the profusion of research or theory that characterizes many of Belkaoui's other books. His approach here is to use a variety of levels of titles and subtitles, short paragraphs, and tables. In this he mimics CPA preparation manuals, which trade space for emphasis. Ultimately, it is the brevity and quality of these titles, short explanations, and tables that is much of the value of this book. But it is also the depth with which he selectively delves into the complexities of these problems that makes this book more than a simple CPA examination preparation manual.

It is noteworthy to discuss how the analysis and writing form changes throughout this book. Certainly, the eight chapters vary in the nature of the discourse and the profusion of references. For example, chapter three, "Investments," is in the form of primarily journal entry illustrations and directly supporting text. APB 18 is the only reference cited at the end of the chapter. Moreover, Belkaoui explains the recording of investment in debt securities held to maturity with two tables of bond amortization using the effective interest method in the case of a premium and a discount. He then shows the journal entries for investments available for sale and trade debt securities. However, Belkaoui attends to the controversy concerning management intention in a very subtle manner. For example, in recording equity securities here, probably the most important judgement issue is the case of the investor owning between 20 and 50 percent of the voting stock, and the exceptions from the equity method to use the fair value method. Belkaoui displays the five examples in FASB Interpretation No. 35 as amending APB No. 18 with little comment on the implementation issues related to it. These conditions leave a dangerous window of opportunity, especially in corporations with few investors, which is the real condition of hundreds of thousands of companies. I call these the theatrical conditions because as a result of these exceptions, an investor that significantly influences a company in which it has invested could collude with that company's management to file a bogus complaint against the investee with a wink and a nod. They could also seemingly fail to get information from the investee. In these cases, it may be easy to fool the regulators into believing that significant influence is not present, and that the investor that owns 20 to 50 percent of the company should be allowed to account for its investment using the fair value method, and gain whatever advantages it has over the equity method for the investing company. However, while he does not say so directly, Belkaoui does present the calculations and journal entries for each of the two methods for comparison, and thus careful readers can conclude for themselves whether one method or the other might be too advantageous for management and investors who are bent on earnings manipulation.

In contrast, no such brevity or subtlety is contained in chapter seven, "Segmental Reporting," which uses mostly paragraphed prose to go into depth to introduce and qualitatively evaluate segmental reporting, to describe U.S. requirements, and to compare them with international standards, seemingly departing from his apparent purpose of a brief explanation of current practice. He also includes some comments on the predictive ability of segmental reporting, which is a topic that is usually covered in courses on financial statement analysis, and is a perspective that is not found in the other chapters. He follows this by considering users and market perceptions and an even more theoretical topic, the merits of push-down and carve-out accounting. This is followed by a large section of notes and selected readings. Why Belkaoui expands his discussion at length in this chapter compared to his primary focus on the journal entries, calculations, and tables that comprise the other seven chapters of the book, is not readily apparent. Perhaps this is a new topic of relative concern to accounting professors, and thus he is concerned more with definitional and "schools-of- thought" matters.

Given the seemingly gratuitous use of the word "critical" in the title, it would seem that this book would be heavily laden with Belkaoui's incisive philosophical analysis. However, in the context of this book, "critical" means essential or important. Thus, with a few exceptions, each page and chapter contains the briefest of textual reading necessary for students to learn the concepts, and by being so brief, the book allows students to see how all the concepts and procedures relate to one another.

At $65, this book is relatively pricey as a second textbook for students who are already paying for a substantial text like *Intermediate Accounting*. However, the additional insight into problems that many of our students seem not to be understanding makes this book a great bargain for many students. We need place this into the perspective that many students now are eagerly paying more than $1,000 on CPA preparation courses to learn concepts that would be better taught the first time with this book.

The accuracy and sheer portability of this thin hardcover book with mostly large, easy-to-read print is perhaps most valuable for the practitioner who wants refreshing on critical journal entries. For the student, the advantage of this book is Belkaoui's clear and precise writing and his listing only what is essential so that they can see all the journal entries in a long and complex series of multiple steps at one time. For the educator, the book's value lies in Belkaoui's teaching experience in choosing what material on a particular topic, such as leases, is absolutely essential to teach students, greatly improving and simplifying lecturing to students. For these individuals with these needs, I would recommend this valuable book.

www.ingramcontent.com/pod-product-compliance
Ingram Content Group UK Ltd.
Pitfield, Milton Keynes, MK11 3LW, UK
UKHW020250290926
15470UKWH00002B/837

9 780762 3052